U.S.S.R.

SAKHALIN

50°

HEILUNGK

Harbin

KIRI

Vladivostok

40°

CHAHAR

JEHOL

LIAON

Mukden

Kalgan

Peking
(Peiping)

Tientsin

Dairen

SHANSI

HOPEH

Seoul

KOREA

Tokyo

Pusan

JAPAN

SHANTUNG

Tsingtao

30°

HONAN

KIANG

Nanking

Shanghai

HUPEH   ANHWEI

Hankow

CHEKIANG

Liu-chiu Is.

Okinawa

HUNAN

KIANGSI

FUKIEN

Foochow

Taipei

NGSI

Amoy

FORMOSA
(Taiwan)

20°

Canton

KWANGTUNG

Hong Kong
(Br.)

HAINAN

LUZON

CHINA
AND ADJACENT AREAS

Scale of Miles

0   100   200   300   400   500

The Communist Conquest of China

A HISTORY OF THE CIVIL WAR

1945-1949

The Communist Conquest
of China

A HISTORY OF THE CIVIL WAR
1945–1949

BY

Lionel Max Chassin

Translated from the French by
Timothy Osato *and* Louis Gelas

HARVARD UNIVERSITY PRESS
Cambridge, Massachusetts
1965

End-paper map by A. H. Robinson from
The United States and China by John K. Fairbank
Harvard University Press, 1948
Other maps by T. Osato and L. Gelas

Library of Congress Catalog Card Number 65–22043

Printed in the United States of America

TRANSLATORS' NOTE AND
INTRODUCTION

THIS work, which originally appeared under the title *La Conquête de la Chine par Mao Tse-tung*, was first published in France in 1952. Much has been done, both before and since that time, in the study of Chinese communism; but to our knowledge there is little available, in English, to meet the need for a concise history of the climactic phase of the long Civil War through which communism came to sovereign power in China. This work, in our view, helps to meet this need. If it seems at times to stress military factors, there is some justification for this emphasis in the fact that, for China, communism did indeed, as Mao Tse-tung prescribed, come from "the barrel of a gun."

General Chassin, whose poor health precludes the possibility of a preface to this belated English translation of his work, possesses unusual qualifications for the task he completed more than a decade ago. The author, now a retired General of the French Air Force, did most of the research for this book while he was serving, from 1946 to 1949, as Vice Chief of Staff for National Defense. This position gave him ready access to the most authoritative French sources of information on developments in China, notably the reports of the Deuxième Bureau. From this fact alone, the author's account and interpretation of the Communist conquest of China should prove to be of some interest to American readers.

The absence of a bibliography, and of notes regarding the French sources of this work, is best explained by General Chassin in a statement[1] written expressly for this American edition of his work:

> Although I never personally served in China during the Civil War of 1945–1949, I was, from 1946 to 1949, Vice Chief of the General Staff for National Defense, and as a member of the highest military body in France and an adviser to the Premier on defense matters, I had access to all National Defense documents. My book, *The Conquest of China by Mao Tse-tung,* is based on the intelligence reports, messages, and telegrams sent by the mission of the French Second Bureau (Intelligence), from China, to the General Staff for National Defense.
>
> These documents, which were extremely copious, were supplemented by personal letters and interviews with officers who had served in the Far East and whom I interrogated, when they passed through Paris, in order to gain a more vivid appreciation of the kind of war that was being waged in China. I might add that when I took command of French Air Forces in the Far East in 1951, I encountered in Tonkin and Cochin China several officers who had served in China during the Civil War, and to whom I showed my work. My thanks go, above all, to Captain Léouzon, who had retained a certain number of papers he had brought back from Chungking, and who was kind enough to review my work in its entirety.
>
> Such are the original sources of my book. Naturally, I also made use of all the (relevant) literature that had been published as of that time, while striving to avoid those sources which might have been tainted by the erroneous political opinions of their authors. Was this not, unfortunately, the case with a large number of works written by Anglo-Saxon authors?

[1] Bien que je n'aie jamais servi personnellement en Chine pendant la guerre civile de 1945 à 1949, j'ai été de 1946 à 1949 Sous-chef d'Etat-Major de la Défense Nationale et en tant que membre de la plus haute organisation militaire en France et conseiller du Premier Ministre en matière de défense,

If some of the author's political judgments seem somewhat contentious to American specialists in Chinese communism, these authorities at least have fair warning!

As to the other sources of this work—notably the State Department's White Paper on China and the words of Mao Tse-tung—the translators have attempted to locate and quote their most authoritative English-language versions, and to identify these in notes for which we, rather than the author, bear the responsibility. We have also sought to clarify, in other translators' notes, matters which may have appeared more self-explanatory to the author than they might to the nonspecialized reader.

A few words must be said regarding the transliteration problems posed in a work of this kind. As the author himself observes, "it is extremely difficult to transcribe Chinese characters into a European language," and "French interpretations of Chinese names are often fanciful indeed." We have

---

j'avais accès à tous les documents de la Défense Nationale. Mon livre: "La Conquête de la Chine par Mao Tse-tung" est basé sur les rapports d' "intelligence," les messages et les télégrammes expédiés de Chine par la mission française du Deuxième Bureau à l'Etat-Major de la Défense Nationale.

L'ensemble de ces papiers, extrêmement copieux, a été complété par des lettres personnelles et des interviews d'officiers servant en Extrême-Orient que j'interrogeais lors de leur passage à Paris — ceci pour me faire une idée plus vivante de la sorte de guerre qui se livrait là-bas. J'ajoute que lorsque j'ai pris en 1951 le Commandement des Forces Aériennes Françaises en Extrême-Orient, j'ai retrouvé au Tonkin et en Cochinchine plusieurs officiers qui avaient servi en Chine durant la guerre civile et auxquels j'ai montré mon travail. Mes remerciements vont surtout au Capitaine Léouzon, qui avait gardé par devers lui un certain nombre de papiers qu'il avait ramené de Chungking, et qui a bien voulu relire entièrement mon travail.

Telles sont les sources originales de mon livre. Naturellement, je me suis servi de toute la littérature qui avait été publiée à cette époque, en tâchant d'éviter des sources que risquaient d'entacher d'erreur les opinions politiques de leurs auteurs. C'était malheureusement le cas pour un grand nombre d'ouvrages anglo-saxons?

L. M. Chassin
General, French Air Force (Retired)
Paris, 22 June 1964

attempted to follow the Wade-Giles system of transliteration in the rendering of Chinese personal names, and that of the Chinese Postal Guide, as exemplified by such sources as *The (London) Times Atlas of the World* and the National Geographic Society's *Index to Map of China* (1945), for the rendering of place names. In a few cases, such as that of "Mukden" (rather than "Shenyang") or "Port Arthur" (rather than "Lushun"), we have departed from this rule in what we regard as the interests of the general reader.

For the sake of simplicity, consistency, and current usage, we have used the name "Peking" rather than "Peiping" throughout this translation, despite the substantial political and historical objections which may, in full justice, be raised against this practice. No disrespect toward the Republic of China, or for knowledgeable purists, is intended.

In translating General Chassin's book, we have chosen to attempt fidelity to the author's meaning and, on occasion, we may have taken questionable liberties with a literal interpretation of his words. We can only submit that the special kind of war described in this history may well be heavy with meaning, not only for the past and present, but for the future.

T.O.
L.G.

Contents

PART THREE
1947: The Communists Restore the Situation and Take the Offensive

PART FOUR
1948: The Decisive Year

PART FIVE
1949: The End of the Conquest

CONCLUSION

TABLE

MAPS

In 1949 there occurred, in full view of our somewhat unperceiving eyes, an event of extraordinary importance: China, a country of almost five hundred million people, and of immense agricultural and mineral resources, passed from the camp of the "Western" powers to that of the U.S.S.R. With this event came a shift, singularly beneficial to the Soviet camp, in the global balance of power. What is strange about this catastrophe is that, as late as 1945, it seemed to be completely unforeseeable. Yet, in only four years' time, the almost unknown leader of a weak and poorly armed political minority vanquished, without benefit of outside aid, one of the world's "Big Five," a champion who for eight long years had led China's resistance against the powerful Empire of the Rising Sun.

The great majority of Europeans still fail to comprehend the incalculable but patently profound consequences of this event. What is more, its genesis—the Civil War of 1945–1949—remains largely unknown to them. To study this fateful conflict in all its fullness, it is appropriate to resort to the historical method, and to consider first of all, if only briefly, the setting of the Civil War, both in time and place.

L. M. C.

Introduction

CHAPTER I

China: A Brief Description

Before undertaking a history of the Communist conquest of China, a few words must be devoted to a description of the ancient arena in which it unfolded, this land of the vanished "Celestial Empire," the "Middle Kingdom" of past millenia.

By virtue of its vast area and population, China is a veritable continent. Its officially claimed area of more than four million square miles equals that of all Europe, and its 483,000,000 people[1] embody one fifth of the total population of the globe. From the fact that one of every five persons on earth is Chinese, one may realize the considerable importance this country can have for the future of the human race.

In geographical terms China extends from the eighteenth to the fifty-fourth parallel North, or from the latitude of Labrador to that of Mexico.[2] In longitude it stretches from 74° E to 135° E—the meridians of Afghanistan and Vladivostok, or Bombay and Kyoto. Since 1949 the country has been divided into six Great Administrative Areas:[3]

(1) *North China*, incorporating five provinces: Hopeh, Shansi, Chahar, Suiyuan, and Pingyuan, a newly created

---

[1] Population in 1952, according to the Chinese daily *Chieh Fang Jih Pao* (*Liberation*) of Shanghai.

[2] Or, if one prefers, from the mouth of the Elbe to that of the Senegal.

[3] The Communist regime has made several changes in these since 1952. *Tr.*

province of the People's Government carved from the counties of South Hopeh, West Shantung, and North Honan;

(2) *Northeast China*, or Manchuria, divided into six provinces:[4] Liaotung, Liaosi, Kirin, Heilungkiang, Sungkiang, and Jehol;

(3) *East China*, with six provinces: Shantung, Kiangsu, Anhwei, Chekiang Fukien, and, theoretically, Taiwan;

(4) *South-Central China*, with six provinces: Honan, Hupeh, Kiangsi, Kwangtung, and Kwangsi;

(5) *Northwest China*, with five provinces: Shensi, Kansu, Ningsia, Sinkiang, and Tsinghai; and lastly,

(6) *Southwest China*, with four provinces: Szechwan, Sikang, Kweichow, and Yunnan, plus the "autonomous" region of Tibet.

Exclusive of the near-barren borderlands—Tibet, Turkestan, and Mongolia—and of Manchuria, a vast and densely populated sunken plain stretched out between two north-south mountain ranges, China Proper, or the China of the eighteen provinces, is divided into two distinct zones which differ greatly in relief, climate, vegetation, and even in people: North China and South China, which are separated by the wide barrier of the Chin Ling mountains, eight thousand feet high.

In the western part of North China stand the old and coal-rich plateaus of Kansu and Shansi; to the east lie the great alluvial plains of the Hwang Ho, and the mountainous peninsula of Shantung. The climate is harsh, with freezing winters, burning summers, and rain that comes only with the summer monsoon. North China is the land of loess, that famous, fertile "yellow earth," four feet to six hundred feet deep, in which the peasants burrow their cave-like homes. It is also the basin of the Hwang Ho, the Yellow River of terrible floods, which

[4] In place of nine provinces in 1945.

has changed its 2,700-mile course five times in recorded history, and flows within dikes some twenty feet above the plain, past the distant and fearful towns and villages.

Unlike North China, South China is essentially mountainous in topography; its climate, vegetation, and agriculture are of the tropical type; and its great river, the Yangtze, in contrast to its scourge-like northern brother, is a source of life and a central artery of the surrounding region. The "Long River" begins its 3,400-mile course high in the mountains of Tibet, over fifteen thousand feet above sea level. At first it tumbles tumultuously to the south, through the deep gorges of the Szechwanese Alps; then it turns to the north and, reaching the plain, forms a series of basins as richly fertile as they are heavily populated. The first of these, the Red Basin of Szechwan, with its cities of Chengtu and Chungking, is completely surrounded by mountains, and reserves for itself its riches of rice, tobacco, cereals, vegetables, and important mineral resources. Here the population reaches a density of 474 inhabitants per square mile. After traversing the remaining mountainous regions in a series of rapids as redoubtable as they are picturesque, the Yangtze, which at Ichang is now no more than three hundred feet above sea level, slowly flows eleven hundred miles across fertile, prosperous, and well-populated plains, and empties into the sea near Shanghai in a marshy delta where the population reaches densities of up to 3,100 people per square mile. Apart from the valleys of the Yangtze and the Si, and the mountainous region to the east of Kweichow, South China is a scenic land of hills no higher than 2,700 feet, where the rains are regular and plentiful, and the vegetation is very beautiful. The rugged, indented coast shelters numerous ports and harbors, from Shanghai southward through Ningpo, Foochow, and Amoy to Canton and Hong Kong. Off the coast of Fukien lies the fertile and thickly populated island of Formosa, highly developed by the Japanese; in stark contrast is the still savage island of Hainan, which drops away, like a tear, from the coast of Kwangtung.

China's economy is fundamentally agricultural, with rice as the basic crop. For centuries it has been the land of tea and silk; and it is gradually becoming a land of cotton and soybeans as well. From the industrial viewpoint its resources, still unexploited, are immense: coal reserves estimated at 240 billion tons in Shansi, Shensi, and in Manchuria; oil in Sinkiang; iron ore in Manchuria; tin, copper, lead, zinc, manganese, mercury, antimony, bauxite, and very large deposits of tungsten —all these assure an astonishing future, once the country is industrialized and the necessary communications system is constructed. We now know, from the example of Russia, that it takes only a score of years, and a will of iron, to transform an agricultural country into a great industrial power; and China will be aided in this task by the nature of a people who are intelligent, adroit, patient, and hard-working, and whose talents for commerce are superior to those of any other race.

In this history of the Communist conquest of China—an upheaval of as yet little-appreciated importance to the whole world—is reflected a profound change in China itself. Here can be seen a transformation in philosophy and in way of life, through which "classical" China, frozen in scornful and sterile immobilism, gradually rouses itself to become a great power. And this new power will henceforth permit an eager China to take a leading role not only in Asia, but in the entire world.

ORTHOGRAPHY AND NAMES

It is extremely difficult to transcribe Chinese characters into a European language. Since French interpretations of Chinese names are often highly fanciful, the English orthography officially adopted by the Chinese Postal Guide, and used by the Chinese for their Romanized maps, has been followed in the rendering of place names in this work.

As regards the meanings of place names, it is useful to know a few general terms concerning:

(1) Direction: North, *Peh*; South, *Nan*; East, *Tung*; West, *Si*;

(2) Relief: mountain, *Shan*; range, *Ling*; pass, *Shen*; sea, *Hai*; lake, *Hu*; river, *Kiang* or *Ho*; stream, *Chwan*; mouth, *Kow*;

(3) Colors: black, *Hei*; white, *Pai*; red, *Hung*; yellow, *Hwang*;

(4) Numbers: one, *E*; two, *Erh*; three, *San*; four, *Sze*; five, *Wu*;

(5) Positions: high, *Shang*; low, *Hsia*; center, *Chung*;

(6) Finally, administrative subdivisions: prefecture, *Fu*; sub-prefecture, *Chow*; county, *Hsien*. Knowing these, one can comprehend the meaning of the names of the principal Chinese provinces, rivers, or towns. For example, Hopeh means "north of the river"; Shantung means "east of the mountains," and Shansi, "west of the mountains"; Honan means "south of the river," and so on.

As for other proper names, it is well to know that for thousands of years there have been only one hundred family names in China, all of them monosyllabic, such as Chiang, Li, Wang, Sun, Chang, Mao, Lo, Hu. These theoretically represent the hundred legendary families that originally peopled China; until the Revolution of 1911, it was unlawful to assume any other family name. Two persons bearing the same family name were likewise forbidden to marry each other. Given names, in China, come after the family name, and usually consist of two characters with a meaning intended to be descriptive of the particular individual: "Kai-shek," for example, means "hard rock," or "firm as a rock." Other given names have such meanings as "little dog," "red flower," "little cucumber," "tall building," "precious stone." Christian names also are found among certain families: Eugene Chen, for example. In the past the Chinese would change their given names several times during their lives, childhood names being succeeded by marriage names, graduation names, and so on. The result was enormous confusion in proper identification. The People's Republic has henceforth forbidden these changes in given names.

CHAPTER II

The First Stage: 1911-1945

FOLLOWING the Revolution of 1911, the proclamation of a republic by Sun Yat-sen, Yüan Shih-k'ai's attempt to found a new dynasty and Chang Hsün's attempt to restore the old one, China fell into an era of feudalism. During this period numerous war lords—*tüchuns* such as Chang Tso-lin in Manchuria, Yen Hsi-shan in Shansi, the "Christian General" Feng Yü-hsiang in Peking—succeeded in carving out virtually independent principalities for themselves. Meanwhile Sun Yat-sen and his party, the Kuomintang,[1] had withdrawn to Canton and knotted close ties of friendship with Soviet Russia. In 1923, Lenin had sent Joffe, one of the negotiators of the Brest-Litovsk treaty, to Canton; behind him had come Borodin, to act as a political mentor to the Kuomintang. For his part, Dr. Sun had sent to Moscow an important military mission, the head of which was a young general with the greatest of destinies: Chiang Kai-shek.

Born on 31 October 1887 at Fenghwa, in the province of Chekiang, Chiang Kai-shek was one of the five children of a merchant of modest means. Having lost his father at a very early age, he was brought up, in austere circumstances and Buddhist discipline, by his mother. In 1906 he stood at

[1] Hereafter abbreviated, on occasion, as KMT. *Tr.*

the top of the first class to enter the new Imperial Military Academy at Paoting, and was later sent to Japan to complete his military studies. While in Japan he served three years with a Japanese artillery unit, the 13th or "Takada" Regiment. Returning to Shanghai in 1911, he left the army, joined the Kuomintang, became one of the leading disciples of Sun Yat-sen, and acquired—by means which appear to have been very dubious—a considerable fortune. After an unhappy first marriage which ended in divorce, he resumed his military career in 1923, at the time of his departure for Moscow. He came back in the following year, bringing with him, under the pseudonym of "Galen," the famous Bolshevik general, Vassily Blücher. Together with this Russian colleague, Chiang organized the army of the Kuomintang. In 1926, a year after the death of Sun Yat-sen, Chiang was named Generalissimo,[2] and shortly thereafter commenced, in pursuit of national unification, a victorious campaign against the armies of the *tüchuns*. In 1927 he seized Nanking, and followed this conquest by marrying Soong Mei-ling. With this marriage, Chiang was not only led to become a Protestant by his bride; he also became the brother-in-law of Sun Yat-sen's widow, and of T. V. Soong and H. H. Kung, the famous Chinese financiers.

Suddenly there was a reversal in Chiang's relations with the Reds: now feeling himself to be strong enough to do without them, he abruptly broke off the Communist connection. By his order the Communists were excluded from all the higher posts in the Kuomintang. Borodin and Blücher fled back to Moscow; in all the cities where the Communists had begun to form autonomous groups, they were disarmed. Hesitating to unleash civil war, Ch'en Tu-hsiu, at this time the head of

---

[2] A purely unofficial title, probably reflecting Chiang's designation as "Commander in Chief of the Revolutionary Armies" in 1926, shortly before the Northern Expedition. As hereafter used, "Generalissimo" invariably refers to Chiang Kai-shek. *Tr.*

the Chinese Communist Party,[3] submitted. He was replaced by such extremists as Li Li-san, who declared China to be in a state of "permanent revolution" and tried, without success, to foment mass uprisings in the large cities. At Canton the Red revolt of December 1927 was drowned in a bath of blood.

Meanwhile, as Chiang moved north and made himself the master of Peking,[4] a certain number of Communist leaders who had escaped the repression resorted to guerrilla warfare in the mountainous regions, where regular troops could be easily resisted. This was the case with two leaders who were to become famous—Chu Teh and Mao Tse-tung.

General Chu Teh, whose name means "Red Virtue," was born in 1886 at Ilung, in Szechwan province. His family were landlords, and quite well off. A graduate of the Yunnan Military Academy, where he studied under European instructors, Chu distinguished himself as a battalion commander in 1912; as early as 1916 he was promoted to brigadier general, then made Chief of Public Security of Kunming, and then Commissioner of Finance for Yunnan. He was now immensely wealthy; he possessed nine concubines and a sumptuous palace, in which he devoted himself to opium smoking and a life of debauchery. Suddenly, in 1922, he became a convert to Communism. Abandoning all his riches, he took the "cold-turkey" cure for his opium habit by signing on as a sailor with an English river boat on the Shanghai-Hankow run. He soon made contact with the Kuomintang revolutionaries, who looked upon him with suspicion. In 1923 he went to Germany and then to Paris, where he founded some Chinese Communist cells; then he went to Moscow, where he studied Marxist doctrine. Returning to China, he became one of the

---

[3] Hereafter abbreviated, on occasion, as CCP. *Tr.*
[4] It was at this time, the spring of 1928, that the Nationalists renamed the city Peiping, or "Northern Peace." *Tr.*

Kuomintang's most highly regarded military leaders. But in 1927, when Chiang Kai-shek declared war against the Communists, Chu Teh refused to fight the Reds, and left Nanchang to join the rebels. With a band made up of workers, peasants, deserters, and students, he started in to wage guerrilla warfare in the Hunan-Kiangsi-Kwangtung border area.

In 1928 Chu Teh joined forces with Mao Tse-tung. Mao, a cultivated and ironical young man, a country schoolteacher turned politician, had at first centered his political activity at Changsha; then he too had been forced to seek refuge in the mountains which border Kiangsi. The two leaders set up their command post in the Chingkanshan mountains, where they created a small Communist state, Mao occupying himself with the political direction of the movement while Chu Teh became commander in chief of the army. By 1933 they had succeeded in forming four army corps, and had amassed some fifty thousand rifles and several hundred machine guns. For his part, Chiang Kai-shek had called upon a German military mission to fashion his army along modern European lines. Successively, Colonel Bauer, then Colonel Kriebel, General Wetzell, General von Seekt—the former Chief of Staff of the Reichswehr—and finally, General von Falkenhausen, formed and trained Chiang's cadres until Hitler, under the pressure of Japanese protests, recalled Falkenhausen.

In September 1933 Chiang launched a great "extermination campaign" against Mao and Chu. Despite Chiang's commitment of hundreds of thousands of trained troops, supported by artillery, tanks, and aircraft, the Nationalists were held at bay for more than two years; then, finally, the Communists were forced to abandon Kiangsi and set out upon their "long march." Taking everything with them—women, children, and baggage—the Communists marched more than six thousand miles, through Kwangtung, through Kwangsi, through Yunnan and Szechwan, fighting all the way, until finally, in October 1935, they reached the dusty plains of North Shensi. Here they established a "Soviet base," with Yenan as its capital. Of the 300,000 people who had left Kiangsi, no more than forty thousand reached Shensi.

Chiang tried to oust these remnants from their ultimate haven, because he understood very well the danger of leaving his adversaries free to establish direct links with Mongolia and the U.S.S.R. But in December 1935, during a trip to the Northwest which took him to Sian, he fell into the hands of Chang Tso-lin's son, the "Young Marshal" Chang Hsüeh-liang, who had decided to revolt against the Generalissimo. What really lay at the bottom of this incident has remained a mystery, because at the end of eight days of talk Chiang was released by his mortal enemies—and at the instigation, according to reliable evidence, of Mao Tse-tung himself! The precise conditions of this extraordinary liberation are unknown. It should be recalled, however, that the Chinese do not think like Europeans: during the campaigns of 1945, for example, they never failed, despite the formal orders of their American instructors, to leave a way of "honorable retreat" open to encircled Japanese troops. It has been said that the Chinese Communists, obedient to Moscow's directives in this matter, were satisfied with extracting Chiang's promise to adopt a clearly anti-Japanese policy and join with them in a struggle for the liberation of China.

It is certain that Chiang at that time considered his fight against communism to be more important than a struggle against the Japanese invader. Profoundly imbued as he was with the old principles of Chinese civilization, and with those of the Christian faith as well, Chiang's war upon the movement led by Mao and Chu Teh had been a virtual war of religion. But after the Sian "incident," Chiang, who did not abandon his desire to crush his Communist adversaries, nevertheless gave first priority to the struggle against the invader.

As early as 1931 the Japanese had commenced to carry out their plan for continental conquest. During the night of 18–19 September, following the Mukden incident (in which a Japanese officer, Captain Nakamura, who had conducted a "military reconnaissance" while in mufti, was arrested and executed by the Chinese), they had invaded Manchuria. Shortly thereafter, in February 1932, they had organized their conquest as a satellite state called "Manchukuo." In the spring of 1933 Japan seized Jehol, and the Tangku Truce gave her control of Liaoning, Kirin, and Heilungkiang, which were incorporated into Manchukuo. Moreover, the terms of this truce also compelled the Chinese to withdraw their troops from the entire region between the Great Wall and the outskirts of Peking. In 1935 Japan obtained Chinese demilitarization of eastern Hopeh and all of Chahar, Shansi, Shantung, and Suiyuan; an "autonomous regime" was sponsored by the Japanese in Chahar and Hopeh. Not feeling strong enough to resist, Chiang Kai-shek submitted to all these encroachments, despite the violent protests of enlightened opinion in China.

But to the aggressors themselves, their success seemed insufficient. On the night of 7 July 1937, an incident[5] took place at the Marco Polo Bridge, on the outskirts of Peking, which gave them the occasion to present new demands. This time Chiang Kai-shek refused to submit. And so began a war which was to last eight years and end in Japan's defeat.

In a Kuomintang-Kungch'antang[6] agreement signed on 22 September 1937, the warring brothers united in a common front against Japan.. The Nationalists officially recognized the

[5] Following the disappearance, during maneuvers, of a Japanese soldier, Chinese authorities refused to permit Japanese officers to make a search inside the town of Wanping.

[6] "Kungch'antang" is Chinese for "Communist Party." *Tr.*

"Shensi-Kansu-Ningsia Border Region." Chu Teh's Eighth Route Army, three divisions strong, was also recognized by the Nationalists and theoretically integrated into the 18th Group Army under Marshal Yen Hsi-shan, the "model governor" of Shansi. A representative from Red Army headquarters at Yenan took a seat in Chiang Kai-shek's Military Council[7] and, beginning in the summer of 1938, Communists also sat in the "People's Political Council." As early as 1937 a second Communist field army, the New Fourth Army, was formed, with the Kuomintang's assent, to operate to the north of the Yangtze.

The war against Japan gave the Communists the opportunity to expand their influence throughout all of Northeast China. As the government's troops retreated, Communist guerrillas would infiltrate behind the lines of the advancing Japanese, organize resistance, and take over the administration of these "liberated" areas. Chiang Kai-shek soon perceived that he had put too powerful a weapon into the hands of his enemies. He thus began a close blockade of the Communist zone in Shensi and Kansu, which he ringed with a fortified line of more than ten thousand blockhouses and pillboxes manned by several hundred thousand troops. By such means the area of the Red "Border Region" was reduced to about ninety thousand square miles.

But all this effort was in vain: little by little, and despite the presence of the Japanese, the Communists came to dominate all of Northeast China. What is more, Mao Tse-tung, profiting from circumstances, broke his promises and slipped his New Fourth Army to the south of the Yangtze. Now for Chiang to permit a Communist intrusion into South China

[7] Chou En-lai represented the Yenan regime in the Political Department of the National Military Council, of which Chiang was the chairman, from 1937 until his walkout from that body in 1940. *Tr.*

was absolutely out of the question. On 18 January 1941 he ordered the arrest of the offending Red commander, General Yeh T'ing, and announced the dissolution of the New Fourth Army—a dissolution which, unlike the arrest, was never brought about. In the face of invasion, civil war broke out anew. As for the Japanese, they were always careful to refrain from a westward attack across the Yellow River against Yenan —a possibility which, in their view, would only play Chiang's game against the Reds.

To the Chinese people, deeply anti-Japanese as they were, Chiang's policies at this time were no more comprehensible than they were to the West. Mao Tse-tung became increasingly popular in Central China. Here, his disciples, following the classic Communist tactics of the "first phase," brought with them no doctrines of total collectivization, but an "agrarian democracy" in which the peasant owned his land and collective efforts were limited to such major tasks as the harvest.

Mao Tse-tung's principles were set forth in a book, *On the New Democracy*, for which he had asked, as an obedient Stalinist, the imprimatur of Moscow, and which he aimed at Western opinion in particular. In this work he declared that China was not yet ripe for socialism, but only for a "democratic revolution." He observed that such a revolution had been brought about in Europe by the bourgeoisie, for ends which were strictly capitalistic. But because of China's backwardness, and because of her Communist Party, it would be possible to avoid classical capitalism and create a "new capitalism" which would function in the interests of all the people. For the same reasons, Chinese democracy would be of neither the bourgeois nor the Russian type, but a "new democracy" characterized by the coalition of all revolutionary classes:

16

peasants, workers, the petty bourgeoisie, and even those capitalists who showed themselves to be antifeudal and patriotic.

Faithful to these theories, the Communists contented themselves with only one third of the key political posts in the zones under their own occupation, leaving the other two thirds to non-Communists. They plied the people with skillful and appropriate propaganda, cleverly blending free theatrical shows with the presentations of itinerant political agitators. They assigned control teams to take over immediately in the administration of newly occupied areas, and these Red officials were more honest than their Kuomintang predecessors. They carried on an energetic resistance against the Japanese, and their troops were under iron discipline. Incredibly, they even succeeded in restoring respectability to the soldier's calling, so strongly discredited in the eyes of the populace. In so highly civilized a country as China, soldiers were looked upon as a plague, or as obnoxious parasites at best. In the words of an old proverb:

> *Hao tieh pu ta ting*
> *Hao jen pu tang ping*

or:

> "Good iron is not used to make a nail,
> Nor a good man to make a soldier."

Meanwhile the war had spread throughout the entire world, and after December 1941 China no longer stood alone. But General Joe Stilwell, America's top military man in China, rapidly came to a realization of the unbelievable situation that prevailed there: the best Nationalist troops, with the most modern matériel, were occupied in mounting guard on Yenan, while the Japanese gradually overran the whole country. To him, this state of affairs appeared inadmissible. But the Generalissimo met Stilwell's objections with strategic conceptions of astounding remoteness:

For me the big problem is not Japan, but the unification of my country. I am sure that you Americans are going to beat the Japanese some day, with or without the help of the troops I am holding back for use against the Communists in the Northwest. On the other hand, if I let Mao Tse-tung push his propaganda across all of Free China, we run the risk—and so do you Americans —of winning for nothing. I say this because behind Mao there is the religion of Communism—and in consequence, Russia.[8]

At that time, this plain language could come only as a mystery to the Americans; and it was American refusal to recognize reality that was to lead to Stilwell's departure in 1944. However, his replacement, General Wedemeyer, did succeed in persuading Chiang to shift some of the troops from his *cordon sanitaire* against the Reds to Kwangsi, in order to meet the Japanese attack on Kweiyang.

At the beginning of 1944 President Roosevelt had sent Vice President Henry Wallace to China "to see what could be done to increase the Chinese war effort against Japan." Wallace concluded that a solution would have to be based upon achievement of a real agreement between the Communists and the Nationalists. Following this advice, the President in September 1944 dispatched to Chungking his personal friend, General Patrick Hurley, to act as mediator between the two adversaries. Shortly after his arrival, Hurley also replaced Clarence Gauss as American Ambassador to China.

Hurley, like Roosevelt, was a devoted champion of democracy. At the time of his arrival in China, he believed that it would be possible to form a coalition government and bestow

[8] The source of this account is a highly placed Nationalist general officer whose identity the author cannot disclose. *Tr.*

upon the Communist Party a legal basis for its existence. In November 1944 he personally drew up the draft of a five-point agreement, to which he obtained the signature of Mao Tse-tung. He flattered himself that he would get Chiang Kai-shek to sign it, too; but he was quickly disabused of this notion by the snail-like pace of Chinese-style negotiations, and by counterproposals, lies, and broken promises. Moreover, he soon came to share the ideas of Chiang Kai-shek, who convinced him of the noxious and intrinsic peril that the Chinese Communist Party posed for the future of Western civilization and the interests of American democracy. Hurley also discovered that many American diplomats, amazed by the efficiency of the Communists and their ability to gain popular support, were secretly favorable to Yenan. This is what brought him to resign, on 26 November 1945, and to quit China with such a slamming of doors behind him.

Be that as it may, by the time of the Japanese surrender the Communists had gained control of a territory of almost 400,000 square miles, inhabited by one hundred million people, and divided into sixteen "semi-independent" anti-Japanese base areas. Their regular armies had grown to a strength of 900,000 men, and their people's militia now numbered about two million men. The Communists hoped to retain a certain amount of autonomy within newly liberated China, keeping their dominant position in some of the provinces, leaving the others to the Nationalists, and relying upon peaceful propaganda as the means to attain their final goal.

For their part, the Nationalists were set in their determination to wipe out the *imperium in imperio* Mao had established in the heart of China, a task in which they could profit from the modern matériel and military training they had acquired during the war against Japan. Before undertaking this operation, Chiang Kai-shek made sure of Moscow's neutrality. On

14 August 1945 he concluded an accord with the U.S.S.R. in which he agreed to recognition of the independence of Outer Mongolia, to the establishment of a joint Sino-Russian base at Port Arthur and of a free port at Dairen, and to a thirty-year concession for joint exploitation of the Manchurian railroads. In return the Soviet Union promised to give its support to the Nationalist government, to refrain from intervention in China's internal affairs, and to respect Chinese sovereignty in Manchuria. Having thus secured the rear, Chiang now prepared for war.

✧ PART ONE ✧

1945

THE ADVERSARIES

MOVE INTO POSITION

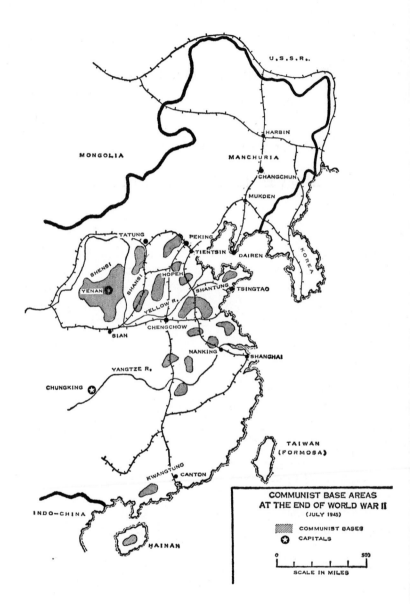

COMMUNIST BASE AREAS
AT THE END OF WORLD WAR II
(JULY 1945)

▨ COMMUNIST BASES
✪ CAPITALS

0   500

SCALE IN MILES

CHAPTER III

The Two Camps on the Eve of Civil War

Lᴋᴇ all modern wars the Chinese Civil War was, within China's means, a total war, in which the military factor was only one of several determinants. To draw a true picture of the opposing forces it is therefore necessary to analyze not only the military factor, but political, social, and economic factors as well.

THE POLITICAL SITUATION: THE NATIONALISTS

With the surrender of Japan, China realized all her national aspirations in the field of foreign relations. The unequal treaties had been abolished; except for Hong Kong, all foreign concessions—those thorns embedded in China's living flesh —had been returned to her. Foreigners no longer enjoyed the right of extraterritoriality, which had so greatly humiliated Chinese self-respect. China was about to recover her lost lands: Formosa, occupied and exploited by Japan since 1895, and Manchuria, the richest region in the Far East. Her international position had never been so favorable: China had become one of the Big Four, before even France gained admittance to this holy of holies; and she held a position of authority in the United Nations, especially in the Security Council. With the obliteration of Japan, China had become the great Asian nation of the world, her prestige enhanced by her long resistance against the common foe. Japan having been crushed, China had no more enemies. She had the support, both moral and material, of the United States. With Great Britain, there were no problems other than Hong Kong, and each side strove to avoid aggravation of this issue. Chinese troops occupied Indo-China north of the sixteenth parallel, and the inevitable incidents with the French were settled without any serious repercussions. Only the Soviet Union could have constituted a threat to China. But in August of 1945 the U.S.S.R. had signed in Moscow a treaty by which it pledged itself to respect the territorial integrity of China, to recognize the Nationalists as the only legitimate government of China, and to withhold its support from the Chinese Communists. In return the U.S.S.R. had obtained the right to establish a naval base at Port Arthur, joint administration with the Chinese of the port of Dairen, and certain advantages in Manchuria. In signing this accord China's hand had, of course, been somewhat forced by the United States, at a time when the Americans believed in the advantages of a Russian intervention in the war against Japan. But if Russia were to respect the terms of the treaty, the few concessions agreed to by China would be amply compensated. Deservedly or not, the credit to be gained from all these achievements accrued, within China as well as abroad, to the Nationalist government and to its leader, Generalissimo Chiang Kai-shek, who had been variously depicted by wartime Allied propaganda as a sort of Chinese Napoleon or Cincinnatus.

Unfortunately, the internal situation of the country was far less favorable than its world position. China's push toward progress, started in 1930, had been halted by the war against Japan; even worse, China seemed incapable of resuming its forward movement. She had known no peace for thirty years, and now she was exhausted. She needed tranquility in order to rebuild; but civil war was at the door. She needed far-reaching reforms; but the Kuomintang, in former times her engine of progress, showed itself to be almost completely worn out.

In his political testament Sun Yat-sen had entrusted the tutelage of China to the Kuomintang, until the day when the political maturity of the country would permit the functioning of democratic institutions. This day had seemed in sight, and then came Japanese aggression to delay the transition to democracy. After the first access of popular enthusiasm died down, and as soon as the failings of the Kuomintang were revealed by the tests of war, numerous critics arose to contest the validity of the Kuomintang's tutelage and its capacity to exercise sole leadership of the embattled nation. Lacking an organized liberal party,[1] these critics were isolated and powerless; since they lent some weight to the Communist viewpoint, they were also ruthlessly suppressed within the Kuomintang itself. Although it had been organized along the same lines as the Russian Communist Party, the Kuomintang had lost the monolithic aspect of its model; it had a right wing, a center, and a left wing—or, rather, a certain number of cliques which more or less represented these tendencies. To the right there was the CC clique, so named because of its leaders, the brothers Ch'en Li-fu and Ch'en Kuo-fu, conservatives for whom the salvation of China lay in a return to the sound traditions and paternalistic philosophy of Confucius. In the center, the clique of the generals, named after the Chinese

---

[1] The Democratic League, which attempted to create an opposition party, was dissolved as pro-Communist in 1948, without ever exerting any real influence.

St. Cyr,[2] Whampoa, constituted a sort of Mafia, grouping certain graduates of this institution who had few political views other than loyalty to Chiang Kai-shek. There was also the clique of "the two Kwangs," so called for the southern provinces of Kwangtung and Kwangsi, led by the ex-war lords Li Tsung-jen and Pai Ch'ung-hsi. To the left was the "Political Science Group" of bankers, administrators, and technicians, who, liberal by education, favored a transfer of power from the hands of the military to their own. Lastly, certain other groups, of varying importance and distinctness of definition, oscillated opportunistically from one side to the other. All these cliques were jealous of one another and undermined each other, overtly as well as covertly. The Kuomintang was not, however, the only influential political element on the Nationalist side. Traces of pure feudalism had not completely disappeared with the unification of China in 1927. Several war lords retained an attitude of independence toward the central government, and ruled as virtually absolute sovereigns of their own domains. Such were Yen Hsi-shan, the famous marshal of the "model province" of Shansi; the Moslem generals of the Northwest, Ma Pu-fang in Tsinghai and Ma Hung-k'uei in Ningsia; Teng Hsi-hou in Szechwan, and so on. There was also "The Family," the Soongs: T. V. Soong; his brother-in-law, H. H. Kung; and the three Soong sisters. Ch'ing-ling, Sun Yat-sen's widow, had withdrawn into self-imposed isolation since 1927, deeming that her brother-in-law Chiang had betrayed the revolutionary ideal of her husband, and devoted herself to charity. But all the rest of the family constituted a new sort of ruling dynasty, thanks to its supporters and to its fabulous wealth; and when public opinion forced T. V. Soong's withdrawal, it was Kung who would take his place, and vice versa. What cement held all these clans and cliques

[2] The French equivalent of West Point. *Tr.*

together? For one thing, their common enemy—communism; for another, Chiang Kai-shek.

The Generalissimo had aged since 1927, and the exercise of power had hardened him. He had always had an almost inhumanly iron will, which held him to his course when everyone else yielded to contrary evidence and to the crushing onslaught of events; he had a limitless self-confidence, warranted by his rapid ascent to power and the perpetual approbation of his entourage; he had a blind, pure faith in the sacred character of his mission. His sly peasant cunning lacked, however, any breadth of view, and he had the shortcoming of all dictators: nepotism, and a weakness for the comrades of his early days. With these qualities and these faults, his moral authority today remains unchallenged in Nationalist China; everyone knows that when he dies the Nationalist camp will immediately fall into chaos. He is irreplaceable, though his power is far from absolute. Given the structure of his government, Chiang could enjoy neither the advantages of a democratic regime nor those of a dictatorship. He kept on top of the system by playing one group off against the other, and wasted all his energy in that sterile game, accomplishing nothing positive except in the international field, where his crafty Chinese mentality worked wonders.[3]

From top to bottom of the administrative hierarchy, the picture was the same, but complicated by local problems.

[3] On this point, the evidence of General Stilwell, taken from his book *The Stilwell Papers* (New York: William Sloane Associates, Copyright, 1948, by Winifred A. Stilwell), pp. 315–316, is of interest:

I never heard Chiang K'ai-shek say a single thing that indicated gratitude to the President or to our country for the help we were extending to him. Invariably, when anything was promised, he would want more. Invariably, he would complain about the small amount of material that was being furnished. He would make comparisons between the huge amounts of Lend-Lease supplies going to Great Britain and Russia with the meager trickle going to China. He would complain that the Chinese had been

And a fact of primary importance must be noted: in the countryside, authority and wealth were merged in the local cell of the Kuomintang, which alone held power.

The great question at the end of 1945 was that of political reform. Everyone knew its urgency, but the Kuomintang was scarcely inclined to undertake reform. The Sino-Japanese War had furnished justification for the continued tutelage of China by the Kuomintang; now, with the war's end, the Communist danger became the excuse to strengthen the party's control. In fact, what the Kuomintang feared most, and rightly so, was the verdict of a genuine popular consultation. The party was worn out; it had renewed neither its men nor its ideas. Corruption and nepotism ruled shamelessly—corruption as the almost necessary result of inflation and the ridiculously low salaries of officials; nepotism as the legacy of ancient traditions which had survived the upheavals of revolution. Hon-

---

fighting for six or seven years and yet we gave them practically nothing. It would of course have been undiplomatic to go into the nature of the military effort Chiang K'ai-shek had made since 1938. It was practically zero.

Whether or not he was grateful was a small matter. The regrettable part of it was that there was no quid pro quo. We did what we could, furnished what was available, without being allowed to first ask what he would do, etc. The result was that we were continuously on the defensive and he could obstruct and delay any of our plans without being penalized.

[I have] faith in Chinese soldiers and Chinese people: fundamentally great, democratic, misgoverned. No bars of caste or religion. . . . Honest, frugal, industrious, cheerful, independent, tolerant, friendly, courteous.

I judge Kuomintang and Kungchantang [Communist party] by what I saw:

[KMT] Corruption, neglect, chaos, economy, taxes, words and deeds. Hoarding, black market, trading with enemy.

Communist program . . . reduce taxes, rents, interest. Raise production, and standard of living. Participate in government. Practice what they preach.

Obviously, General Stilwell saw only the early stages of communism in China.

est people were powerless. The government had so often denounced these evils, and so often promised to eradicate them, with so few results, that it seemed all hope was lost.

THE COMMUNISTS

In contrast to the Nationalists, the war against Japan yielded no diplomatic advantages to the Yenan government, which came out of the war as it had gone in—an armed political party. No government recognized it. In 1945, thanks to Ambassador Hurley's insistence, the Communists were granted representation in the Chinese delegation to the San Francisco Conference of the United Nations, but not, obviously, representation as a sovereign state. In this regard, it is curious to note that the CCP never sought formal recognition of its rights until its final victory, perhaps because such a move would have alienated the sympathies of the Chinese people, reluctant as they were to admit the *de facto* existence of two sovereign Chinese governments. The Chinese Communists shared the ideology of the U.S.S.R.; but this tie did not prevent the Russians from abandoning their Chinese comrades to their difficult fate in 1927, or from reserving their material aid for the Nationalists only in 1938, or from signing an agreement with the Nationalists in 1945. Strangely, this attitude failed to shake the Marxist faith of the Chinese Communist Party which, without rancor, continued in its adherence to the Stalinist line.

Although the CCP was more united than the KMT, certain cliques were nonetheless discernible in 1945, at a time when a Communist victory was still far from certain.

The first of these was made up of the sincere partisans of Mao Tse-tung: Liu Shao-ch'i, his old comrade from Hunan, who had the title of Minister of Organization, and his deputy, Jen Pi-shih, the Vice Minister; Lu Ting-i, the Minister of Propaganda; Li Fu-ch'un, Minister of Finance; and lastly, among the members of the Central Committee, T'an Cheng, Ch'en Yün, Kao Kang, Wu Yü-chang, Hsieh Chüeh-tsai, and Tung Pi-wu. Among the military chiefs this group numbered P'eng Te-huai, deputy commander of the Red armies; Hsiao K'e; T'eng Tai-yüan; Ch'en Keng; and Lin Tsu-han, who held the important post of Chairman of the Shensi-Kansu-Ningsia Border Region Government.

Opposing this clique was a group of Communists who in 1945 still set themselves against Mao Tse-tung. Their leader was Li Li-san, the former leader of the CCP who, ousted by Mao and his supporters, had returned from a subsequent sojourn in Moscow with all the prestige of one who had resided within those sacred precincts. Around him were grouped Ch'en Shao-yü, Chang Wen-t'ien and, above all, the two great military leaders: Lin Piao, "The Invincible," commander of the Army of Manchuria; and Ch'en I, commander of the New Fourth Army, which held the provinces of Shantung and Kiangsu.

Between these two groups stood the "Opportunists," who waited to see how things would turn out and who gathered around K'ang Sheng, a crafty and brutal ex-pupil of Moscow's OGPU who as chief of Social Affairs controlled the secret police; Chou En-lai, the diplomatist of the party; and Yeh Chien-ying. General Chu Teh, the chief of the Red Army, and Liu Po-ch'eng, the "One-Eyed General" commanding the Army of the Central Plains, maintained a strict neutrality. In general, the "Hunan Clique" controlled the party, while the "Szechwan Clique" controlled the army.

These internal disputes were of little importance, however, and the government of the Red zone clearly profited from the advantages of dictatorship. The CCP enforced its authority without having to take into consideration either cliques or an opposition. Yet it always attached great importance to public opinion, and did not hesitate to make timely concessions. Even though the Communist government was no more the product of popular elections than was that of the Nationalists, it succeeded in avoiding the stigma of dictatorship. At village and district levels the Communists set up administrations which were, to a certain extent, democratic. In the local soviets the CCP made sure that the proportion of Communist members was no more than one third, the other two thirds being reserved for the regularly elected representatives of the people. In these assemblies criticism was not only permitted but encouraged. The Communists therefore represented progress to the majority of peasants, who had hitherto known only oppression or, at best, governmental neglect, and who did not dream of questioning the abstract and long-range implications of communism. On the other hand, those who opposed communism on principle, and those who deviated from the party line, were denied any means of spreading their views. The party "forgave" errors made in good faith; to correct and prevent such errors, it had established "political study centers" which all party members, whatever their positions in the hierarchy, were compelled to attend. For those who did not submit to persuasion, there were "rectification camps." Moreover, the traditional character of the Chinese, inclined as he is to accept circumstances over which he has no control, made him a docile instrument. In the Red zone, opposition was a negligible, if not nonexistent factor.

The party alone had a decisive voice in the highest circles of power. At the summit, Mao Tse-tung showed himself, more and more, to be a statesman of the first order. When the Marxist jargon is cleared away, his speeches reveal a wide breadth of view and a profound realism; his words seem to translate themselves into concrete acts; and Mao has the gift of sound judgment of men and situations. He is far more than the poet so often depicted in France. It should be noted that Mao, though he has carefully read all the Marxist, Leninist, and Stalinist literature, is nonetheless a self-made man; and, also, that he is the only party leader never to have traveled outside China.[4]

Around Mao Tse-tung were Chu Teh, Chou En-lai, and Lo Fu, his close associates. Beneath them, the structure of the CCP, organized along classical Communist lines, remained changeless: between the central committee and the village soviet was the usual chain of command, with its responsible officials, its political commissars, and its unceasing mutual surveillance. There is no need to expand upon the discipline of this party. Decisions made at the top of the hierarchy were implemented right through to the bottom, and the political commissars corrected, sooner or later, whatever mistakes were made. The tremendous superiority of the CCP, it must be emphasized, lay in the absence of corruption among the officials placed over the people at this time. On this point, the testimony of all witnesses is unanimous. Party discipline suppressed with impartiality the personal intrigues which otherwise would certainly have manifested themselves on the battlefield. In brief, facing a worn-out party rotted by corruption and intrigue, there was a young party, ardent, disciplined, full of faith—and clever enough to conceal the long-range goal toward which, with carefully graduated steps, they led the Chinese people.

---

[4] As the author later points out in Chapter XVIII, Mao did travel to Moscow in December 1949, to conclude the Sino-Soviet treaty of 1950. *Tr.*

THE SOCIAL SITUATION: THE NATIONALISTS

Broadly speaking, the history of China can be summarized as follows: the reigning dynasty becomes rotten with corruption; the people revolt; a successful chieftain seats himself upon the throne and founds his own dynasty. The first sovereigns of this new dynasty rule the country well; but their successors become progressively weaker, and the cycle begins all over again. The most astonishing feature of this history is that, despite the often violent convulsions characterizing the transition from one cycle to another, the social structure of China remains untouched. It is as if this structure had found, after centuries, its most satisfactory form and its final equilibrium. Now, unlike its predecessors, the upheaval of the twentieth century entailed a profound transformation of the social order in China. Three new factors appeared in the nineteenth century: the end of China's isolation; the growth of its population; and the industrialization of the Western world. In the face of such an assault, the millenial traditions which had for so long maintained the framework of Chinese society were suddenly swept away.

It should not be forgotten that the Revolution of 1911 was, above all, a nationalistic uprising against the Manchus. Its objective, the unification of China, was achieved by the Koumintang in 1927, if one excepts the Communist rebellion. But though the Kuomintang had made real progress in the political field during the decade that preceded the Sino-Japanese War, little if anything had been accomplished in the field of social reform. Superficially, Chinese society in 1945 did not differ essentially from the appearance it had presented for the past twenty centuries. To realize this, one had only to take a short walk in the streets of any Nationalist-held town, where daily life appeared to go on at its traditionally slow pace.

Yet, beneath the surface, there seethed the dangerous phenomenon of a profound social unrest. To this unrest contributed not only the three new factors brought into play by the nineteenth century, but the unprecedented fact that, unlike all previous dynastic changes, the upheaval of 1911 had failed to produce the traditional improvement in public administration.

Eighty per cent of China's population were peasants, of whom only twenty per cent were landowners. Landless peasants hired themselves out as agricultural laborers, or rented small plots of land at exorbitant rates. Because landowners also represented the local political authority, it was easy for them to escape taxes, compulsory labor duties, and military conscription, the burdens of which thus fell even more heavily upon the peasantry. When it came time for the peasant to sell his crop, prices invariably fell. Because of the poor transportation network there was no nation-wide market in China, which might have played a regulatory role, and there were incredible fluctuations in farm prices from one week to another and between one district and another. Hunan province could die of starvation while Szechwan wallowed in a superabundant crop. As a consequence, the market was at the mercy of wealthy manipulators. When the peasant wanted to buy seed, prices suddenly went up; the peasants were thus permanently in debt, with no possibility of recovery. This in turn bred banditry, still a seasonal occupation in certain parts of China. Before the opening of China to foreign commerce, the peasant could work as an artisan during the off-season, earning enough to make ends meet; but with the influx of cheap manufactured goods from abroad, this source of income rapidly disappeared. In short, it was the peasantry, more than any other class of Chinese society, who always paid the costs of war and of the chronic disorder of the country.

34

The great majority of the Chinese population being peasants, and the economy of China predominantly agrarian as it was, the pattern of land tenure urgently required a radical reform. It is true that the Kuomintang had enacted a law limiting land rents to reasonable levels, but since the party contained precisely those elements with the greatest interest in maintaining the status quo of a country whose 450 million inhabitants led the harshest of struggles for existence, it is easy to understand why this law was never enforced.

The Chinese proletariat did not yet constitute an important part of the population. Concentrated in a few industrial centers, such as Canton, Shanghai, Tientsin, and Hankow, it was easy to keep under surveillance and was always under a tight rein. Its misery was no less acute than that of the peasants. The worker, buffeted by inflation and foreign competition, was also ruthlessly exploited, despite the Nationalist social legislation which—like agrarian reform—remained always a dead letter. Sporadic riots and looting of rice shops reflected the unrest of the workers. The only measure taken to remedy this situation was to pay a portion of wages in kind, a measure extended also to the swollen ranks of the bureaucracy, inevitable victims of inflation.

Students, traditionally involved in the political life of the country, vested with the privilege of voicing their sometimes abusive opinions, in consequence made up a social category that was particularly feared by the government. Most of them being poor, the Spartan existence of the students was subsidized by the government, and they enjoyed exemption from conscription. Despite these relative advantages, their sympathies did not lie with the Nationalist government; their juvenile intolerance, inflamed by reading and propaganda, made them bitterly resent the immutability of a social order in which they had no real place. Yet technicians were numerous in China and, had they been properly utilized, their numbers would have sufficed to bring progress to the country. Unfortunately, the student without personal connections was in most cases without chance of a suitable job. As examples, there was the case of a statistician who, after eight years' study in France, could find no employment upon his return to China except as a grade school teacher; and the Belgian-trained chemical engineer who could find in Chungking no other way to make a living than to concoct artificial *apéritifs*.

In stark contrast to all this misery, often made even more tragic by famine, flood, and war, a small minority of the regime's new rich happily accommodated themselves to the situation, becoming major stockholders in American firms, and selling, on the black market, U. S. goods and drugs sent to China under Lend-Lease.

In the social field, the Kuomintang must be given credit for advances in public education. A similar effort was made to improve sanitary conditions, which had remained the same since the days of Confucius. This effort achieved only a partial success. Although large epidemics were held in check, infant mortality remained as high as ever, and notions of personal hygiene had reached only a small minority of the bourgeoisie. Opium, the scourge of China and a major target of the Communists, was effectively controlled by the Nationalists, but it should be noted that tobacco had everywhere replaced opium, with Mao Tse-tung himself chain-smoking some sixty cigarettes per day.

To conclude this brief sketch, the fact must be emphasized that Chinese society, unlike that of the Hindus, has never known a hereditary caste system. With luck, a coolie could become a mandarin. This is a very important fact, for the existence of a caste system has always been a considerable obstacle to profound social change.

THE SOCIAL SITUATION: THE COMMUNISTS

The great fault of Chiang Kai-shek, then, was his failure in ✗
the field of social reform; and it was precisely here that the
Communist Party put its emphasis, focusing its principal effort upon the number-one social problem, agrarian reform. To
solve this problem, the party pushed programs for the redistribution of land, improvement of productivity, elimination of
corruption, and equitable distribution of the tax burden.

When the local soviets were first established by the Communists, the landowner was expropriated, even massacred, and
his lands redistributed; but soon, as the result of Mao's influence, expropriations were halted in order to retain control
of rents. In 1946 the Communists revived their program of
land redistribution, but this time there was no liquidation of
landowners, who were permitted to retain the maximum legal
holding, fixed at about 1.5 acres per person, with local varia-
tions according to the quality of the land and the density of
the population. The distribution of plots was determined by
the local soviets. With 1.5 acres per person there would no
longer be "feasts for the few and famine for all the rest." Since
about three quarters of an acre is estimated to be the area
needed in China to feed one person, one wonders about the
long-range effects of this radical reform upon the birth rate
in a country already overpopulated, and the effects upon agriculture, where the modern trend has been toward the large
holdings which alone permit the efficiency of mechanization.

Be this as it may, the Communist program apparently
gained the approval of the majority of the peasantry. Moreover, the Communists implemented this program in appro-
priately gradual steps. In areas long dominated by the Communists, where land redistribution had already been accomplished, they sought to improve redistribution and increase

crop yields. In areas occupied during the war, they concentrated on land redistribution alone. In areas only recently conquered, they limited their reforms to reduction of rents and taxes. A good example of the flexibility of Communist policy in this field occurred in the spring of 1948 when, the majority of the population of Honan province proving to be opposed to land redistribution, the Communists deemed it necessary to delay this move "until the time when political education would permit the application of this reform."

The improvement of productivity offered a practically untouched field to the reformer. Since time immemorial the Chinese peasant has cultivated his land according to precepts adhered to by reason of their very antiquity.[5] In China such modern techniques as seed selection were completely unknown, and entire regions were permitted to lie fallow because no one had even heard of such a thing as dry farming. It was in just such a region that the Communists established themselves in 1935. Popularizing the new methods worked out by their experimental farms, the Communists obtained results that not only permitted them to survive the Nationalist blockade, but provided a surplus which could be traded, in the black markets of the Nationalist zone, for the manufactured products that they lacked.

Since there were no major industries located in the Communist zone, there were very few industrial workers, and Communist social reforms involving labor remained perforce only promises as of 1945. The Communists had, however, developed small industries and artisanry; and their concern for the worker's lot was tempered by their realization of the need to produce enough to make themselves independent of imported

[5] The peasant is sometimes right. Take, for example, the case of the missionary in Chahar who, in attempting to demonstrate the merits of deep plowing to peasants who seemed content with merely scratching the land, lost all his topsoil to the spring winds blowing in from Mongolia.

manufactured goods. For this reason the CCP kept a close watch on the maintenance of satisfactory labor-management relations.

In the field of education the success of the Kuomintang was limited by lack of schools. Many children went without schooling, and nothing had been done for adult illiterates. The Communists attempted to fill this void by a method as simple as it was effective. In each village, in each military unit, in each party group, those who knew one thousand characters of the Chinese language were to teach them to those who knew only five hundred. These, in their turn, became the instructors of the illiterate. Hygiene was popularized in the same way: instructors trained in higher schools of the party trained other instructors, who in turn fanned out to teach at lower echelons.

In summary, the Communist Party in social matters had succeeded in persuading the people that their methods brought undeniable progress. It understood very well indeed that without popular support it would be impossible to carry on the military struggle against the Kuomintang.

THE ECONOMIC SITUATION: THE NATIONALISTS

Contrary to appearances, the economic situation of China at the end of World War II offered good reason to hope for a rapid recovery. Its compartmentalized agrarian economy had not suffered, except in the areas directly exposed to the combat operations of 1943–1944. Its industrial production, except for textiles and mining, had increased under Japanese exploitation. The rail system, and inland and coastal navigation, had suffered some damage, but not to any grave extent. The important problem was thus not so much reconstruction as revival of the flow of exchange and distribution.

Inflation was the second major problem. Deprived of its principal sources of revenue by the Japanese occupation, the Nationalist government had been forced to resort to the printing press in order to finance its war effort. The American loan of $500 million in 1943 had failed to check the fall of the Chinese currency; from one American dollar for two Chinese dollars (*fapi*) in 1937, the rate of exchange had reached 1,200 *fapis* per dollar by 1945.

With victory in World War II, the Nationalist government now had the means to solve both of these problems. It was in the process of recovering practically all the resources it had possessed before the war. Particularly important was the fact that, controlling as it did all the ports except Dairen and Chefoo, it could count on the customs duties which, for all the various Chinese governments of the previous three decades, had constituted the greatest and most stable source of income. Moreover, among its assets was a credit of 900 million U. S. dollars, the largest amount ever possessed by any Chinese government. It also had $800 million worth of Chinese holdings abroad. The reoccupation of Manchuria, highly developed by Japan, would give the Nationalists an industry four times greater than that of China Proper, and agricultural surpluses as well. To be sure, these expectations were soon to be nullified by the looting of Russian troops, who sent all the industrial machinery home to Russia, and permitted the local population to pillage all the rest. Nevertheless, Formosa, developed by fifty years of Japanese occupation, brought a prosperous industry (cement, aluminum, lumber, oil) and surplus food production (sugar, canned goods, and so on). The government also inherited the Japanese holdings in China which, whether directly exploited or transferred to private enterprise, assured important new sources of income. Also, it could count on Japanese reparations, to which China could lay legitimate claim for a substantial amount, and on aid from UNRRA, which was eventually to reach a total of $660 million. Finally, it was almost certain of obtaining American financial and material assistance, in the form either of loans or of surpluses sold to China at one tenth their real value.

Military expenditures constituted the immediate cause of inflation: eighty per cent of the budget was devoted, with little accountability, to the maintenance of an army as burdensome as it was inefficient. If the defeat of Japan brought urgent new tasks for the military, it also furnished an excellent opportunity to reform the army and to limit, without risk, military spending. In any case, even if this reform were not undertaken, the government's new resources should have assured so favorable a margin of income that it could easily have been able to balance its budget. That it was unsuccessful in this endeavor is clear evidence of the corruption and wastefulness of the Nationalist regime, even when the Communists' attempts to destroy the government's material advantages are taken into account.

The Nationalist economy was certainly very vulnerable. The reoccupation of southern China, a food-deficient area, and the reoccupation of large cities such as Shanghai, Tientsin, Peking, Tsingtao, and Mukden, imposed enormous supply burdens upon the government. Thus, the solution of the problem depended upon the agricultural production of the countryside and the smooth functioning of the transportation system.

THE ECONOMIC SITUATION: THE COMMUNISTS

The Communists enjoyed none of the advantages mentioned above. Their share of UNRRA aid, which in theory was to be distributed *pro rata* to the population without regard to political affiliations, never reached ten per cent of the total. They received no financial aid whatsoever from the U.S.S.R. and, lacking seaports, they were completely cut off from foreign trade. Their economy thus remained primarily agrarian. This posed a serious disadvantage in that the Reds, who held no major industrial centers and had no foreign trade except for the uncontrollable traffic which later developed between northern Manchuria and Siberia, depended on the output of their artisans and trade with the Nationalist zone for the minimum of manufactured goods necessary to them. Fortunately for them, their needs were limited, and they had developed small industries as much as possible. Also, it was easy to carry on trade with the Nationalist zone, since the Nationalist government needed the agricultural production of the Red zone to feed its food-deficient regions and its great commercial centers. This trade was strictly controlled by the CCP, which saw to it that demand in the Communist zone did not get out of hand and that imported products were distributed through cooperatives kept under their close surveillance. This system conferred an enormous advantage upon the Communists. The Communist-held regions, thanks to their uniformly primitive state of economic development, were interchangeable. Thus, the Communists could sacrifice a region without decisive loss; their economy was effectively protected against military setbacks.

The inflation of Nationalist currency had, of course, repercussions in the Communist zone, but the Communists were cushioned against its effects by the economic compartmentalization of their zone, in which each region had its own bank of issue, as well as by the effectiveness of their ever-present controls. There was practically no black market and, like it or not, neither producers nor retailers could possibly evade the price ceilings fixed by the party.

The administration, and above all the Red Army, which required continuous expansion, necessarily absorbed a major portion of the Communists' revenues. As the party did not want to lose the good will of the population, it was reluctant to raise taxes. Thus, except for inflation, the only solution was to make the administration and the army not only productive, but self-supporting. This was the solution adopted, and the efforts undertaken as early as 1934–1935 succeeded in bringing partial relief to the Communist budget. Each official, with Mao Tse-tung himself in the lead, was required to work his small plot;[6] each army unit, when not engaged in combat, tilled the land assigned to it, or lent a hand to the peasants. School children also were brought into this program. The organization of the Communist armed forces, with a nucleus of regular troops supplemented by local units of militia mobilized for particular operations, permitted the release of large numbers of troops at sowing and harvest time.

THE MILITARY SITUATION: THE NATIONALIST CAMP

Without any doubt, the best appraisal that can be found of the quality of the Chinese Nationalist Army in 1944 comes from General Stilwell:

In 1944, on paper, the Chinese Army consisted of 324 divisions, 60-odd brigades and 89 so-called guerrilla units of about 2,000 men each. This looks formidable on paper, till you go into it closely. Then you find:
1. That the average strength per division instead of 10,000 is not more than 5,000.
2. That the troops are unpaid, unfed, shot with sickness and malnutrition.
3. That equipment is old, inadequate, and unserviceable.

[6] Mao, of course, grew tobacco; Chu Teh grew lettuce.

43

4. That training is nonexistent.

5. That the officers are jobholders.

6. That there is no artillery, transport, medical service, etc., etc.

7. That conscription is so-and-so.

8. That business is the principal occupation. How else live?

How would you start to make such an army effective?[7]

At the end of 1945, a serious effort had nonetheless been made. The strength of the army was raised to about 2,500,000 regulars, formed into 278 brigades which were reorganized beginning early in 1946.[8] The elite of this army consisted of thirty-nine divisions which had been trained and equipped by the Americans; although some of these had not yet received all of their equipment at the time of Japan's surrender, the Americans left enough matériel in China to fully equip these divisions. Among these thirty-nine divisions, those of

---

[7] *The Stilwell Papers*, pp. 316–317. *Tr.*

[8] During this period of reorganization—as well as before and after it—the terms "brigade" and "division" appear to have been loosely synonymous, since both referred to a formation of about 10,000 men supported by one battalion of organic light artillery (usually 75 mm. pack howitzers). When the infantry firepower of a brigade attained the planned levels prescribed by U.S. military advisors—or when an "army" was reorganized and trimmed down to such a level—the term "division" would be applied to a force of this strength and firepower. In general, a Chinese Nationalist infantry division of the Civil War period had about two thirds the personnel strength, and less than one third the artillery, of a World War II-type U.S. infantry division. A Chinese Nationalist "army," with three divisions, was therefore the rough equivalent of a small U.S. corps in strength, and of a U.S. division in artillery firepower. A Nationalist "group army," consisting of a variable number of armies, had the approximate strength of a large U. S. corps or, in the case of a large group army, of a U.S. field army. For more detailed discussions of Nationalist organization and reorganization, see Charles F. Romanus and Riley Sutherland, *United States Army in World War II, China-Burma-India Theater, Time Runs Out in CBI* (Washington, D.C.: Office of the Chief of Military History, Department of the Army, 1959), pp. 232–233, 382; see also the Chinese Ministry of Information, *The China Handbook, 1937–1945* (New York: The Macmillan Company, 1947), p. 286, and The China Handbook Editorial Board, *The China Handbook, 1950* (New York: The Rockport Press, Inc., 1950), pp. 187–188. *Tr.*

the New First and New Sixth armies[9] had fought with distinction in Burma; and "Youth Divisions," originally made up of student volunteers, could also be counted among the army's elite units.

But the bulk of the Nationalist Army had not been affected by the work of reorganization undertaken by the Americans during the war. It was made up of units of mediocre quality, which were deeply rooted in obsolete military traditions; the worst were the troops of Wang Ching-wei's puppet government, who were taken into the Nationalist Army after the defeat of Japan. To these units, directly subordinate to Nationalist command, could be added local troops in the pay of the war lords, as well as a large but indeterminable number of miscellaneous militiamen (1,500,000, at least). All of these units, with the exception of one armored and several cavalry brigades, were infantry brigades. Each brigade consisted, at least theoretically, of three infantry regiments and one or two battalions of artillery. Their light weapons were in general abundant, though sometimes mixed in origin; a third were of American make, a third were of Japanese origin, and the rest came from Chinese and various other sources. The state of discipline was extremely uneven, being very poor in most of the armies, and barely acceptable in the armies of the central government. Although the quality of junior commanders was generally satisfactory, command at the higher levels was deplorable. Good Nationalist generals, such as Fu Tso-yi, Pai Ch'ung-hsi, and Chiu Ching-chuan, were very few. Finally, the technical services were practically nonexistent. Generals never gave due consideration to the importance of regular re-

---

[9] The designation, "new" army, referred to Chinese forces (the "X-Force") originally organized and trained in India by General Joseph Stilwell, who led them in the invasion of Burma in 1944. See F. F. Liu, *A Military History of Modern China, 1924–1949* (Princeton University Press, 1956), p. 215. *Tr.*

supply of weapons, rations, or ammunition. The medical service was wholly inadequate. The soldiers—ill-fed, ill-paid, short of ammunition—thought mostly about looting. Although those Nationalist field armies that had been trained by the Americans were of comparatively good quality, thanks to the relative regularity of their supply and pay, most of the Nationalist forces bore a far greater resemblance to the Chinese hordes of the past than to modern armies.

Consequently, morale was low. Undernourished conscripts, forcibly drafted by the uncontrolled authority of village bosses, arrived in training camps, often completely exhausted, only to find a more deplorable and harsher life. Yet, when well trained, well fed and well led, the Chinese peasant, extremely enduring and patient, intelligent, and not without courage, can become an excellent soldier—provided he has faith in a cause. The Communists undertook to prove this point; but Nationalist officers never proved themselves to be capable of infusing their men with faith in the cause for which they fought. These officers, themselves extremely poor because of miserable pay, afflicted by a fearful feeling of inferiority toward their adversaries, often indulged in corruption and ended, finally, in treason.

The Navy

The Nationalist Navy, though relatively small, enjoyed total superiority over the Communists, who had no naval forces at all. It consisted of a small core of warships, the largest of which was the ex-British cruiser *Aurora*, rechristened *Chungking*, and a large number of gunboats. To these there were soon added 131 landing craft (LCT, LSM, LCI, LST, and so forth) turned over to China by the United States shortly after V-J Day. Also, the Americans rapidly established a naval training center at Tsingtao, where a total of three hundred officers and ten thousand enlisted men of the Nationalist Navy were trained in modern methods.

The major missions the Nationalist Navy should have accomplished were interdiction of arms-smuggling by junks on the big rivers (especially the Yangtze), and attack of enemy forces moving close to the coasts (for example, along the Liaoning corridor). The Chinese Navy was incapable of accomplishing either of these tasks. Its morale was low and its officers, among whom corruption was rife, often found it more profitable to protect smuggling than to stop it.

The Air Force

It was in 1929, at the time the Central Military Academy was founded at Nanking, that the Chinese bethought themselves of the need for an air force. Two years later, in 1931, a Central Aviation School was established at Hangchow, near Shanghai, under the auspices of a private American mission supported by T. V. Soong. While this school vegetated for lack of means, all the war lords decided to create their own private air forces. Thus, in Yunnan and Szechwan, in Kwangtung, Kwangsi, and Manchuria, a hodgepodge of aviation units appeared, each with assorted types of aircraft lacking in spare parts as well as in standardization. Actually, there was no Chinese Air Force. Fortunately, toward the end of 1936 a retired American colonel, Claire Chennault, was able to hire out to China some Northrop, Douglas, and Martin aircraft, and about one hundred trained American pilots, who fought heroically at the outbreak of the war against Japan. The Russians also contributed to the struggle by sending a mission with some IL–15 and IL–16 fighters. In 1938 even an international squadron was organized in China.

During the war (November 1943) the "Flying Tigers" became an official Sino-American force, designated the "Chinese-

American Composite Wing" and equipped with P-40 fighters, B-25 light bombers, and C-47 transports.

This force achieved some remarkable successes, shooting down six hundred Japanese fighters and sinking seven thousand boats along the coasts. Little by little the Chinese Air Force became independent, thanks to pilots and mechanics trained in the United States, and to the eight schools[10] set up in China. Organized with five fighter groups (one with P-40's and four with P-51's), two medium bombardment groups (B-25), one heavy bombardment group (B-24), one reconnaissance squadron (P-38), and two transport groups (C-47), this air force had a grand total of 500 aircraft—including 200 fighters, 60 medium bombers, 30 heavy bombers, 15 reconnaissance and 120 transport planes. At war's end the supply of spare parts for these aircraft, left in place by the departing Fourteenth U.S. Air Force, was theoretically sufficient. But soon the Nationalists' lack of organization, of skill, and of honesty diminished the number of operationally ready aircraft on line, despite the efforts of the Air Advisory Division of the Joint U.S. Military Advisory Group. The same was true of the infrastructure—airfields and radio installations—which, left in place by the Americans, would have been more than adequate had they been properly maintained. The Nationalist Air Force should have played a considerable role in the civil war against the Communists. But its poor organization, its poor doctrine, its poor leadership, the dissimilar training and poor morale of its key personnel, made its services far fewer than those which could normally have been expected of such a force. It was only in transport operations that it gained some

[10] These schools were the following: General Staff School at Nanking; Air Academy at Hangchow; Logistics School at Nanking; Meteorology School at Shanghai; a school for mechanics and radiomen at Chengtu; Antiaircraft Defense School at Peking; Medical Service School at Hankow; and a recruit training center at Chungking.

measure of success by supplying encircled garrisons until the arrival of relieving forces.

THE COMMUNIST ARMIES

On paper the regular Communist forces appeared to be very much inferior to the Nationalist armies. To be sure, they had grown very rapidly, increasing from 10,000 men in 1928 to 300,000 in 1945; but only half of these men had firearms, and the weapons of those who had them were of largely obsolete and widely assorted varieties.

These forces were at first organized in regiments of one thousand men; but eventually the "column," with an average strength of ten thousand men, became the standard tactical organization. The column comprised two light divisions, each division consisting of three or four regiments of fifteen hundred men each. Equipment was obtained, very soon after V-J Day, by the disarming of Japanese units in Manchuria as well as in China; but it was American matériel, captured from the Nationalists, which was to provide the great bulk of Communist equipment. As for Russian matériel, it was almost never seen in the hands of Chinese Communists. They went into the Civil War with fewer than six hundred pieces of artillery, and with no tanks at all. Ammunition was procured from the primitive arsenals which the Communists were to perfect gradually during the war, or captured from the enemy, or purchased from smugglers. The real strength of the Communist armies was to be found not in material factors, but in their morale, their discipline, and their leadership. Thanks to their program of daily "indoctrination," the Communists succeeded in infusing their troops with a faith which was to sustain unhesitating willingness to fight to the death for the triumph of their cause. They were thus to succeed in making the Chinese soldier an upright and disciplined fighting man, who was to obtain the help and friendship of the people because, for the first time in centuries, he would pay for what he took and would never pillage the peasantry.

Communist officers, trained at the Yenan military academy in an atmosphere of austerity and enthusiasm, were to enjoy the advantage of being led by intelligent and audacious chiefs whose aggressive spirit was to provide a striking contrast to the conservatism and defensive spirit of Chiang Kai-shek's commanders.

Finally, the Red Army was to find, in the joint leadership of Chu Teh and Mao Tse-tung, a high command of extraordinary quality.

As early as 1936, Mao, in his book *The Strategy of Revolutionary War in China*[11] had prescribed with remarkable clarity the strategy and tactics the Red Army was to employ until the time of its success in attaining equality of force with the enemy:

A vast semi-colonial country that is unevenly developed politically and economically and that has gone through a great revolution; a powerful enemy; a weak and small Red Army; and the agrarian revolution—these are the four principal characteristics of China's revolutionary war. They determine the guiding line for China's revolutionary war and its strategic and tactical principles. The first and fourth characteristics determine the possibility of the Chinese Red Army growing and defeating its enemy. The second and third characteristics determine the impossibility of the Chinese Red Army growing speedily or defeating its enemy quickly, or in other words, they determine the protracted nature of the war and, if things go wrong, the possibility of the war ending in failure.

These are the two aspects of China's revolutionary war. They exist simultaneously, that is, there are favorable as well as difficult

[11] Usually known in this country by the title *Strategic Problems of China's Revolutionary War. Tr.*

conditions. This is the fundamental law of China's revolutionary war, from which many other laws are derived. The history of ten years of our war has proved the validity of this law. He who has eyes but does not see these laws of a fundamental nature cannot direct China's revolutionary war, cannot lead the Red Army to win victories.

It is quite clear that, in order to determine correctly our strategic direction, it is necessary to solve correctly all problems of principle, as for instance: *against* adventurism during offensive operations, *against* conservatism while on the defensive, and *against* flight-ism when shifting our forces; *against* guerrilla-ism in the Red Army, yet *for* its guerrilla character; *against* protracted campaigns and a strategy of quick decision, and *for* a strategy of protracted war and campaigns of quick decision; *against* fixed operational fronts and positional warfare, and *for* fluid operational fronts and mobile warfare; *against* the mere routing of the enemy, and *for* a war of annihilation; *against* the principle of striking with both fists, and *for* the principle of striking with one fist; *against* a large rear area and *for* a small rear area; *against* absolute centralized command and *for* a relatively centralized command; *against* the purely military viewpoint and the idea of roving insurgents, but *for* the view that the Red Army is a propagandist and organizer of the Chinese revolution; *against* banditry and *for* strict political discipline; *against* warlordism and *for* a democratic way of life within limits and authoritative military discipline; *against* an incorrect sectarian cadres policy and *for* a correct cadres policy; *against* isolationism and *for* the winning over of all possible allies; and finally, *against* keeping the Red Army at its old stage and *for* striving to bring it to a new stage.[12]

Such a doctrine, perfectly executed due to unity of command and complete agreement among all the army leaders, was to prove itself extremely effective. Yet the final victory to which it led was far from easy to foresee.

[12] The English translation is from *Mao Tse-tung: Selected Works*, vol. I: *1926–1936* (New York: International Publishers, 1954), pp. 197–198. Quoted by permission of International Publishers. *Tr.*

In addition to its regular units, the Red Army was composed of two other kinds of forces. The *ming ping*, or militia, were charged with local defense and support of the regular forces. Formed mainly from peasant volunteers, they were poorly armed but capable of reinforcing the regulars when needed. These men made their own primitive weapons— medieval scythes and bills, hand grenades stuffed with nails, wooden cannon firing stones or shrapnel balls, old muskets dating back to the T'ai-p'ing Rebellion. At the end of 1945 these militiamen numbered about 700,000. Lastly, the Red forces included innumerable guerrilla groups, based in the mountainous wilds of Shantung and South China, on Hainan, in Kwangtung, Kwangsi, even in Fukien. These groups attacked local Nationalist forces, cut communications, and devoted themselves to intensive propaganda work. Chiang Kai-shek, who concentrated all his efforts upon the regular Communist forces in the north, neglected them. But when the over-all balance of opposing forces started to change, these guerrillas were to play a considerable role.

In brief, when the Civil War broke out all foreign observers predicted a quick victory for a Chiang Kai-shek, who, haloed by the nimbus of triumph over Japan, was assured of American aid as well as the neutrality of the U.S.S.R. But the factor of morale was to show itself, once again, to be decisive in war. It is not enough to have soldiers and weapons: soldiers must have the will to use their weapons, or nothing can be done. Behind matériel, there is always man. In our own times, as in the days of Marshal de Saxe, "It is deep in the human heart that one must seek the secret of victories."

CHAPTER IV

From Japan's Surrender
to the
Arrival of General Marshall

Aт the time of Japan's surrender the situation, so far as geography was concerned, favored the Communists. Red guerrillas held almost all of North China, and had reached as far south as the Yangtze. On 4 September Yenan announced: "We hold the entire region stretching from Kalgan to the mouth of the Yangtze, and from Shansi to the China Sea, except for the largest cities and some fortified points along the railroads." In September Weihaiwei and almost all of Shantung, as well as more than half of Hopeh and all of Kiangsu north of the Yangtze, fell into the hands of the Reds. Aided by the cells they had established in all the large cities, there is no doubt that the Communists could have occupied Shanghai and Wuhan, had they not feared diplomatic complications.[1] In any case, they were well poised to seize political power in North and Central China, to occupy the historic cities of Peking and Tientsin, and to be the first to enter Manchuria.

[1] They nevertheless occupied Wuhu, a large rice port on the Yangtze.

A good strategy for Chiang, whose prestige was now at its zenith, would have been to consolidate his position south of the Yangtze and then move forward cautiously, at the same time trying to regain the confidence of the peasants by implementing a program of agrarian reform. For the Generalissimo, however, any loss of face was unthinkable. Thus the mastery of North China had at all costs to be his, and the Nationalists had to be the first into Manchuria. In view of the vast distances which separated these territories from the Nationalist bases in South China, Szechwan and Yunnan, such an operation could not but be extremely difficult. But Chiang Kai-shek counted on American support, which he was indeed to obtain.

For the Communists, abandoned by Russia as they were, the problem was to take as many territorial bargaining counters as possible, in order to negotiate for a coalition government which would permit them to persist in their propaganda.

The Russians, little desirous of diplomatic complications with the United States, adhered fairly strictly to the "Big Four" agreements, and did not help the Chinese Reds significantly in their rush to occupy Manchuria. As for the Americans—misled as they were by Hurley, by the charm of Mme. Chiang, and by the craftiness of Chinese diplomats in Washington—they committed themselves completely to the military and economic support of the Nationalist government.

In China, two acts were to be played simultaneously: the negotiations at Chungking and, throughout the entire country, the race to occupy strategic points.

At Chungking the two sides reached agreement, in principle, on many points, but remained opposed on the two main questions: the army, and control of the regions liberated by the Reds. With regard to the composition of a new national army, the Reds laid claim to a proportional strength of forty-eight divisions, while the Nationalists, projecting a peacetime total strength of no more than one hundred divisions, would grant the Reds only twenty. As for the second question, the Chungking government wanted to name all the governors of provinces and the mayors of large cities, while the Reds wanted to retain their own men at the head of the regions they had occupied.

On 11 October the government published the record of its conversations with the Communists. This text reflected the same difficulties. The Communists had agreed to withdraw their troops from Kwangtung, Chekiang, southern Kiangsu, southern and central Anhwei, Hunan, Hupeh, and southern Honan, and to a gradual concentration of these forces to the north of the Lunghai railroad[2] and in northern Anhwei and Kiangsu. After prolonged discussion, they had indicated that they would be satisfied with the governorships of Shenkanning,[3] Jehol, Chahar, Hopeh, and Shantung; the vice-governorships of Shansi and Suiyuan; and the installation of Communist deputy mayors in Peking, Tientsin, and Tsingtao. Finally, they had asked for authorization to accept the surrender of Japanese troops. On these major points, agreement could not be reached. Mao Tse-tung, who had come to Chungking for the negotiations, went back to Yenan, and the Civil War was on.

As the fighting began, the Nationalist government received the support of the Japanese, and of puppet troops, who attacked the Communists in Central China. On 21 October, Mao, a better strategist than Chiang Kai-shek, announced that he was evacuating his forces from regions south of the Yangtze; in North China, he concentrated his forces and destroyed all

---

[2] This line, which runs from Tunghai westward through Suchow, Kaifeng, and Loyang to Sian, was to play a highly important role in military operations of the Civil War.

[3] The Communist Border Region, incorporating parts of Shensi, Kansu, and Ningsia. Its principal town was Yenan, Mao's capital.

the railroads in order to slow down the movements of the Nationalists.

Influenced by Ambassador Hurley, the government on 10 November presented new proposals to Mao. Regarding the political problem, it proposed that the Political Consultative Conference, the supreme legislative organ, be composed of eight Nationalists, seven Communists, thirteen members from other parties, and nine non-party members. In the military sphere, the Communists were to cease the cutting of communications and remain where they were until the government decided upon new zones to be assigned each division. The Communists refused to accept these proposals; on 25 November Chou En-lai, in his turn, left Chungking.

In the face of this complete failure, General Hurley resigned, vehemently accusing the professional diplomats, especially George Atcheson and John Service, of undermining his policies and playing the game of the Communists. The fact was that they had simply shown more discernment and foresight than Hurley had. So too had General Wedemeyer, who had written, on 20 November:

I have recommended to the Generalissimo that he should concentrate his efforts upon establishing control in north China and upon the prompt execution of political and official reforms designed to remove the practice of corruption by officials and to eliminate prohibitive taxes.[4]

He further stated:

The Generalissimo will be able to stabilize the situation in south China provided he accepts the assistance of foreign administrators and technicians and engages in political, economic and social reforms through honest, competent civilian officials.[5]

[4] U.S. Department of State, *United States Relations with China, with Special Reference to the Period 1944–1949* (U.S. Government Printing Office, 1949), p. 131. *Tr.*
[5] *Ibid. Tr.*

On the other hand, Wedemeyer did not believe that it would be possible to stabilize the situation in North China unless there was an agreement with the Communists; as for a Nationalist occupation of Manchuria, it was impossible without an agreement between Chiang, the Chinese Communists, and the U.S.S.R.[6]

But Chiang did not care to follow this wise advice, and persisted in sending his best armies into Manchuria—a strategic trap from which they were never to escape.

THE MILITARY OPERATIONS

As soon as the Japanese government announced its intention to accept a cease-fire, the Communists, on order of Chu Teh, took the offensive in all of Northeast China.

On 19 August Chiang Kai-shek, whose troops were very poorly positioned for occupation of the large cities in the north, ordered the Reds to stay put. Yenan refused to obey: "We consider," wired the members of the CCP, "that you have sent us an erroneous order: this error is very serious. We are thus obliged to inform you that we refuse to carry out this order." Chiang Kai-shek then turned to the Americans for help. By his General Order No. 1, General MacArthur directed Japanese troops to surrender only to Nationalist forces and, pending the arrival of the latter, to "maintain order" in the areas they occupied. As American planes prepared to transport Nationalist armies to the north, clashes broke out between the Japanese and the Reds, and between the Communists and the Nationalists as well. The Japanese, who in a moment of post-defeat depression had evacuated Kalgan on 20 August, now pulled themselves together and prevented the Reds from laying hold of Peking, Tientsin, and Shanghai.

[6] See *ibid*, p. 132, for this portion of Wedemeyer's report of 20 November 1945. *Tr.*

As rapidly as possible, the Nationalists sent their troops into the large cities. On 25 August the New Sixth Army, of Burma fame, entered Nanking. On 10 September the Ninety-fourth Army moved into Shanghai. A few days later the Third Army occupied Hankow. As early as 9 September, General Li established a forward echelon of Chiang Kai-shek's headquarters at Peking. On the 16th, Yenan voiced bitter complaints about attacks on its Eighth Route Army in Shantung and Shansi, where the Reds had been forced to abandon Chaocheng and Wencheng. On the 17th, the first Nationalist units entered Peking.

Meanwhile, General Wedemeyer had moved to Shanghai, whence he declared that his government would assist China "in evacuating Japanese occupation troops," whose number amounted to some two million men. Also, on 20 September Chiang requested the United States to land American troops at Shanghai, Nanking, Peking, and Tientsin, "to aid the Chinese in disarming the Japanese." The next day, ships of the British Navy and the U.S. Fifth Fleet entered the great harbor of Shanghai. The American action induced the angry Communists to withdraw their troops, little by little, from Central and North China. They hoped for better breaks from the Russians, who now occupied all of Manchuria, and they did, in fact, succeed in infiltrating the countryside and in disarming numerous groups of Japanese.

Because it throws light upon the Chinese mentality, it is interesting to note that the two sides now adopted strategic plans which were curiously reminiscent of maneuverings in the bygone days of the ancient Chou and T'ang dynasties. In China, from earliest times, kingdoms based in Shensi always attempted to apply what the classics call the "horizontal plan": the conquest of a strip of land which, following the course of the Yellow River, would extend eastward from Shensi to the sea. The states of the south, on the other hand, always sought to apply the "vertical plan," which called for the formation of a north-south bulwark capable of confining their enemies to the west. "A study of the map of North China," says C. P. Fitzgerald,

will show that these rival plans embody abiding strategic verities conditioned by unchanging geographical facts, which will remain true in all ages. Similar plans were framed in the civil wars of 1923–30, and during every contest between the western hill provinces and the great eastern plain, the "horizontal" and "vertical" plans of the ancient Chou strategists reappear in all essentials unchanged.[7]

It was American aid to the Nationalists which alone prevented Mao from accomplishing the horizontal plan. On 30 September the U.S. 1st Marine Division landed at Tientsin; on 1 October the Marines were at Tangku; on 7 October they received, in the name of Chiang Kai-shek, the surrender of eighteen thousand Japanese troops. In a parallel move, Russian naval forces under Rear Admiral Tichanovitch landed at Port Arthur on 2 October. Chinese Red forces, armed mostly with weapons captured from the Japanese and their Chinese collaborators, were moving into Manchuria by way of Jehol; the Manchurian soviets, which had been founded in 1935 and had gone underground during the Japanese occupation, were being resurrected. On 7 October Admiral Daniel Barbey's Seventh U.S. Amphibious Force entered the harbor at Chefoo, but then withdrew in order to avoid incidents with the Reds, who controlled the city. On 9 October, two thousand American Marines arrived at Peking. The next day they occupied Tsingtao, where they established an important base. A total of 53,000 U.S. Marines took over from the Japanese in the historic key cities, to the accompaniment of mounting Com-

[7] C. P. Fitzgerald, *Son of Heaven: A Biography of Li Shih-min, Founder of the T'ang Dynasty* (Cambridge University Press, 1933), p. 51.

munist anger and incidents which flared up, almost everywhere, between their forces and the Americans.

The Americans were now too deeply involved to be completely neutral. On the contrary, General Stratemeyer, complying with Chiang Kai-shek's desire to move forces into North China as rapidly as possible, put the U.S. Tenth Air Force at his disposal. Under General Hegenberger, 235 Dakotas[8] airlifted three Chinese armies, totaling 110,000 men, from the south to the north in record time. The Ninety-fourth Army was transported from Liuchow to Shanghai, and thence to Peking, where it arrived on 26 October; the Ninety-second Army was lifted from Hankow to Peking on the 28th; lastly, the Third Army was moved from Chihkiang to Nanking. These were elite troops, equipped and trained by the Americans.

The northward movement of the Nationalists continually produced local clashes with the Communists and, as the situation became more and more confused, each side accused the other of provoking civil war. Yenan's communiqués accused the central government's troops of attacking—sometimes with Japanese assistance—and occupying Communist-liberated areas in various regions of China from Canton to the Inner Mongolian province of Suiyuan. For his part, General Fu Tso-yi, Governor of Suiyuan and commander of the 12th War Zone, on 26 October accused the Communists of attacking the government troops in his province with forces amounting to some 100,000 men. In rebuttal, a Communist communiqué claimed that the government troops had attacked Red forces as they were withdrawing from Chekiang toward the north, and that a Communist brigade had suffered severe losses in a sixteen-hour battle near Hangchow. General Ho Ying-ch'in[9] had

[8] C–47 (or DC–3) aircraft. Tr.
[9] At this time General Ho was Chief of the Supreme Staff of the Nationalist armed forces. Tr.

already stated that the Chinese Communists wanted to obstruct the movement of Nationalist troops from Chungking to Peking and Tientsin, where they were to receive the surrender of the Japanese. Battles were being waged along the Peking-Hankow railroad; localities in Hunan were under attack by the Communists, who controlled two thirds of Shantung; on 28 October new outbreaks of fighting were reported in Shansi, whose governor accused Communist forces, coming from Hopeh, Honan, and Shantung, of cutting his communications.

At the end of October the general situation was as follows: in Central China, Nationalist troops were swamping the retreating Reds, who destroyed the railroads and implanted stay-behind guerrilla cadres as they withdrew. The Nationalists occupied almost all the large cities, and were attempting to assure their control of the major lines of communication. But the big question remained that of Manchuria, for the invasion of which Chiang had concentrated in the Peking area the Third, Eighty-fourth, and Thirty-second armies. Indeed, as the Nationalist information minister once remarked to Chiang: "Without Manchuria, China is like Italy; with Manchuria, it is like India."

By virtue of its geographic position, its resources, its communications, and its ease of exploitation, Manchuria is destined to become one of the key regions of the world, like Pennsylvania, the Donets Basin, or the Ruhr. With an area of over 500,000 square miles—as large as France, Germany, and the British Isles combined—Manchuria is an immense sunken plain lying between two mountain chains: the Great and Little Khingans in the west, and the crystalline chain of the Korean and Chang Pai ranges in the east. Its exceptional importance is due, above all, to its mineral resources. It has enormous reserves of coal, estimated at ten billion tons, echeloned between Mukden, Kirin, Ningan, and the lower Sungari.

The best known of the Manchurian mines are those at Fushun, about twenty-five miles east of Mukden, which is the largest open-pit mine in the world, with reserves estimated at four billion tons; and those at Taluyentai, about twenty-eight miles south of Mukden. Before the war the annual production of coal exceeded ten million tons; under the Japanese, Manchurian coal production reached thirty million tons per year, as much as the output of all the rest of China.

Coal alone would be insufficient, but Manchuria also possesses the second element necessary to the build-up of a powerful heavy industry: iron. Although yielding only ores of low grade, the mines of Liaoning (at Anshan, Kungchuling, and Penki), and those of the Suanlung district in Chahar, have produced up to three million tons of cast-iron. Moreover, the Japanese discovered large beds of excellent ore at Tungpientao, in the valley of the Yalu in Korea, where they promptly built numerous blast furnaces and thermal electric power plants under the direction of a very powerful trust, the Manchuria Heavy Industry Company. In addition to iron and coal, Manchuria also possesses hydroelectric power (as witnessed by the dams on the Yalu and the Sungari), gold, copper, silver, lead, magnesium, and large saline deposits.

In fifty years its population had by 1945 risen from twenty to forty million inhabitants; factories of all kinds had been built; lastly, by 1939 its communications net had reached a total of over six thousand miles of railroads, eighteen thousand miles of roads, and 2,900 miles of airways.

For these reasons Chiang Kai-shek considered the conquest of Manchuria to be absolutely necessary. Despite the difficulty of achieving such a conquest, one can understand why he undertook the campaign which was to lead to his defeat.

The agreements signed on 14 August between the Chinese

Nationalists and the Russians[10] called for the evacuation of
Manchuria by Soviet troops to begin on 15 November, a pro-
vision which presupposed the arrival of Nationalist troops to
relieve the Russians. But the Communist Eighth Route Army,
by active resistance as well as destruction of railroads, effectively barred the movement of Chiang's armies into Manchuria
by land. Some other way had to be found to prevent Manchuria from falling prey to the Communists; and it was the
U.S. Navy that offered the solution to the Generalissimo's
problem. Under the command of Vice Admiral Barbey, the
transports of Admiral Kinkaid's Seventh Fleet embarked two
Chinese armies at ports in southern China and set forth for
Manchuria. The most suitable ports of debarkation were
Dairen and Port Arthur, from which the railroads would have
afforded the Nationalist divisions rapid access to the heart of
Manchuria. But the Russian authorities, taking cover in the
clause of the Sino-Soviet agreement of 14 August which
limited the use of the ports to Russian or Chinese ships, refused entry to the American transports.

There remained the small fishing ports, such as Antung,
Yingkow, and Hulutao. But here a new difficulty arose: the
Russians had evacuated these ports several days in advance of
the planned date, and had been replaced by Chinese Communist forces that were firmly determined to prevent any
Nationalist landings. Admiral Barbey, refusing to run the risk
of becoming directly involved in the struggle between the
Nationalists and the Communists, ordered his ships to withdraw. Finally, on 1 November, troops were disembarked at

[10] The Sino-Soviet Treaty was signed in Moscow by T. V. Soong. In
return for the Chinese concessions regarding Port Arthur, Dairen, and the
Manchurian railroads, the Russians agreed to evacuate Manchuria and turn
the region over to Nationalist forces. Also, Chiang Kai-shek's regime was
the only Chinese government recognized by Moscow.

Chinwangtao, which the Japanese had retaken from the Chinese Communists and turned over, in October, to the U.S. Navy. This port was located on the Tientsin-Shanhaikwan railroad, which was being guarded by American Marines as well as Nationalist troops. The Communists accused the U.S. Navy of another landing of Nationalist troops at Shanhaikwan, a port near the eastern end of the Great Wall. In this embarrassing situation, Admiral Barbey on 4 November conferred with the Nationalists and the Russian authorities regarding the possibility of his access to Yingkow, where—as at Chinwangtao—the Chinese Communists held the hinterland. On 8 November the Communist newspaper *New China Daily* declared that General Chu Teh, commander of the Communist 18th Group Army, had written to General Wedemeyer in protest against the following facts: (1) American forces had seized Communist office facilities at Tientsin, and disarmed and interrogated the office personnel; (2) American planes had strafed Communist-held Antze, in Hopeh; (3) American planes had dropped propaganda leaflets calling for Communist withdrawal from Kuan, in Hopeh.

These complaints led General Wedemeyer, on 8 November, to define the American position. He declared that for the protection of American lives he was determined to keep lines of communication open in North China with all the means at his disposal. At the same time, he specified that the American forces had no other mission than that of assisting the central government in its task of reoccupying strategic positions formerly held by the Japanese, and of disarming Japanese troops. Mr. James Byrnes[11] supported Wedemeyer by emphasizing the fact that the surrender of two million Japanese soldiers had not yet been effected. General Wedemeyer

[11] The Secretary of State at this time. *Tr.*

further specified that American forces would, in any case, stay completely out of China's civil conflict and that, beginning on 15 November, the 53,000 American Marines would evacuate North China. Despite these assurances, the Communists on 10 November appealed to President Truman and the American people to bring Wedemeyer's intervention to an end, while the *New China Daily* voiced further complaints against the alleged use of American aircraft to provide daily resupply for Nationalist troops engaged against the Communists.

As for the Russians, they carefully kept out of the conflict. On 10 November Marshal Malinovsky informed General Tu Yü-ming that the Soviet evacuation of Manchuria would be effected in three phases: (1) evacuation of areas to the south of Mukden in the period from 2 to 10 December; (2) evacuation of areas to the south of Harbin by 25 November; (3) evacuation of the remainder of Manchuria prior to 2 December. However, the Soviet command informed Chinese authorities that it would be unable to guarantee the security of Nationalist troops disembarking at Hulutao, in the Gulf of Liaotung, or near Antung, in the Gulf of Korea, due to the weakness of the small Russian detachments in these sectors. Following this phased withdrawal of Soviet troops, Chinese Nationalist forces would be free to land anywhere in Manchuria.

After all these difficulties the Nationalist forces found themselves compelled to enter Manchuria along the axis of the Tientsin-Mukden railroad which, skirting the coast beneath the steep cliffs of the Liaoning corridor, was easy to block. On 4 November some Yunnanese troops were redeployed from Indo-China and the Canton region and landed at Yingkow, which was evacuated by the Russians on the eighth; but they ran up against Communist blocking positions along the Liao River and made no progress. Along the main axis of the Nationalists' advance, fighting raged for two weeks around Shanhaikwan; on 16 November the Nationalists, who had attacked in force with tanks on the 10th, broke through the Communist defenses and resumed their slow northward advance along the railroad. Hulutao was taken on 24 November, but by now Chiang Kai-shek was beginning to realize that the occupation of Manchuria was going to be a long and arduous undertaking.

Chiang now feared that if the Russians evacuated Manchuria according to the planned schedule of withdrawal, the Chinese Communist forces that had penetrated the region by way of Chahar would have time to consolidate their hold before the arrival of his own troops—unless these were to be transported, once again, by air. Thus, he initiated negotiations with the Soviets, asking them to postpone their evacuation until the Nationalists could make good their occupation of the large cities; to permit his forces to use the airfields at Changchun, Mukden, Harbin, and Tsitsihar; and, finally, to prevent the penetration of armed Chinese Reds into the zone occupied by the Soviet Army. The Russians consented to a delay in their evacuation, a concession which permitted them to carry away with them, as prizes of war, all the heavy machinery, machine tools, railroad ties, and even office furniture —as well as 700,000 Japanese prisoners from the Kwantung Army. On the other hand, it appears that they scrupulously kept their promises, and that they refrained from any systematic aid to the lodgment of Lin Piao's Red forces in Manchuria. But the Red Chinese, proceeding as they did in the days of Japanese domination, contented themselves with infiltrating the countryside and bypassing the Russian-held population centers.

Lin Piao's forces, which had come from Yenan and the Communist base in northern Shansi, now controlled all of Chahar and rural Manchuria. As of November 1945 their strength, according to a statement by General P'eng Te-huai, was about 300,000 men, 100,000 being regulars of the Eighth Route Army or the New Fourth Army, supplemented by Manchurian volunteers and soldiers from the Tung Pei Army of Chang Hsüeh-liang, whose brother was proclaimed governor of Liaoning. These forces, gathered under the name of the "Democratic Army of the Northeast," had taken Chengteh, encircled Tatung, and occupied a large part of Jehol. Applying their methods of instituting "agrarian democracy" and popular representation, the Communists solidly established themselves in the northern and western parts of Manchuria, disarmed small groups of Japanese troops and their collaborators, and awaited only the departure of the Russians before jumping off against the cities.

Yet Chiang Kai-shek continued to rush his troops to the north: before the end of November, three Nationalist armies had been successively concentrated in the area north of Peking. On 22 November some of these forces stormed the pass at Nankow and chased the Communists out of Jehol. By the beginning of December the Nationalist advance guard was at Tahushan, about sixty miles southwest of Mukden. On 12 December the Soviets confirmed their intention to permit Nationalist entry into Manchuria by air, land, and sea; on the 13th, some air-transported Nationalist troops were landed at Mukden, which the Russians had not yet evacuated.

Two days later President Truman made an official statement on American policy in China in which he announced that, having accepted the resignation of General Hurley, he had decided to send General George Marshall, the illustrious soldier who had led the American armies to victory in World

War II, to the Far East, as an arbiter charged with the mission of making peace between the Nationalists and Communists in China.

On 23 December, the date of Marshall's arrival in China, the strategic situation was as follows: the Nationalists had regained almost complete control of the large cities to the south of the Lunghai railroad, except for a small area in Kiangsi. In North China they held Peking, Tientsin, the Mukden railroad, Taiyuan, Tatung, and the western part of the Pingsui railroad (Peking to Paotow). But they had failed to clear, in their entirety, the vital Peking-Hankow and Tientsin-Shanghai railroads, a failure which seriously handicapped the logistical support of the crack armies that the Nationalists had hurled into Manchuria. For their part, the Communists, still based primarily in the Shenkanning Border Region, remained powerful in Shansi, Hopeh, Jehol, and in Chahar, where they held Kalgan. They were strong in the western parts of Manchuria, and retained isolated but important nuclei of power in Kiangsu, Honan, and the near vicinity of Hankow.

American aid to Nationalist China continued, and the plan to equip thirty-nine divisions and eight and one-third air groups was still in effect. Without any doubt, it was the American navy and air force that enabled Chiang Kai-shek to gain the considerable Nationalist successes which marked the end of 1945. From this fact resulted the mounting exasperation of the Communists, and a clearly discernible change in the tone of their pronouncements regarding the United States. General Marshall was to find himself confronted by an insoluble problem. Rapidly realizing this, and yet faithfully striving for a solution, he was destined to end his mission in discouraged departure.

✧ PART TWO ✧

1946

THE MARSHALL MISSION, ITS
FAILURE, AND THE PERIOD OF
NATIONALIST SUCCESSES

CHAPTER V ✦

The Marshall Mission

Hurley's failure and Marshall's arrival in Chungking forced the Kuomintang—at least theoretically—into the path of reform. Chiang Kai-shek knew that he would not be able to dupe the former American Chief of Staff as he had the ex‑cowboy;[1] so he decided to play the "good democrat" in order to retain American aid and convince the new envoy of his good faith.

Thus, as early as 31 December 1945, the government announced that the Political Consultative Conference, agreed upon in principle by the Kuomintang and Yenan in October 1945, would convene on 10 January 1946. At the same time the government suggested the formation of a "Committee of Three," composed of a representative from each of the two sides with General Marshall as chairman and arbiter. Yenan accepted and designated Chou En-lai; Chungking named General Chang Chun as its representative. The committee went into action immediately, and held its first meeting on 7 January 1946. Right at the outset, General Marshall voiced his view that, given the international agreements which had been signed by the United States and the U.S.S.R., the Nationalist

[1] Before he became one of the most powerful members of the Republican party, Patrick Hurley had been a cowboy, a miner, and a lawyer.

government ought to be able to reoccupy Manchuria without any interference from the Communists. In an extraordinary development, Chou En-lai agreed. Thus, on 10 January 1946, Marshall could report to Truman that a truce had been concluded on the following bases:

All units, regular, militia, irregular and guerrilla, of the National Armies of the Republic of China and of Communist-led troops of the Republic of China are ordered to carry out the following directive:

a. All hostilities will cease immediately.

b. Except in certain specific cases, all movements of forces in China will cease. There also may be the movements necessary for demobilization, redisposition, supply, administration and local security.

c. Destruction of and interference with all lines of communications will cease, and . . . obstructions placed against or interfering with such lines of communications (will be cleared at once).

d. An Executive Headquarters will be established immediately in Peking for the purpose of carrying out the agreements for cessation of hostilities. This Headquarters will consist of three Commissioners; one representing the Chinese National Government, one representing the Chinese Communist Party, and one to represent the United States of America.[2] The necessary instructions and orders unanimously agreed upon by the three Commissioners will be issued in the name of the President of the Republic of China, through the Executive Headquarters.[3]

This declaration then went on to specify that the order did not apply to the military movements south of the Yangtze provided for in the government's plan for military reorganization, nor to movements of Nationalist forces into (or within) Manchuria for the purpose of restoring Chinese sov-

[2] Mr. Walter S. Robertson, American Chargé d'Affaires in China, became the U.S. representative. *Tr.*

[3] U.S. Department of State, *United States Relations with China, with Special Reference to the Period 1944–1949* (U.S. Government Printing Office, 1949), p. 609. *Tr.*

ereignty. This "Cessation of Hostilities Order" was made effective as of midnight, 13 January, and the Executive Head-quarters at Peking began to function as early as the 14th.

In a parallel move, the Political Consultative Conference opened its session by hearing a declaration from Chiang Kai-shek which promised the people democratic rights and freedoms and the end of the period of tutelage provided for by Sun Yat-sen. It was all there: freedom of thought, of speech, of assembly, of association; equality of rights for all; liberation of political prisoners. This magnificent program was approved by all the parties—the Communists, the Democratic League, the Young China Party—but it aroused severe criticism within the reactionary faction of the Kuomintang. Meanwhile, the Conference agreed upon numerous projects: reorganization of the government, reconstruction, revision of the draft Constitution of 1936; it set 5 May 1946 as the date for convocation of a National Constituent Assembly, to consist of 2,050 members; finally, it passed an important resolution on military problems. This resolution started off with a statement of fundamental principles: the Army belongs to the State; the soldier's duty is to protect the nation and love the people, and so on; the armed forces must be separated from the parties; they must keep out of politics; they must be under civilian control. The resolution then tackled the problem of a progressive reduction in army strength by calling for an initial cut to ninety divisions, and then reduction to a final strength of sixty divisions.

But the most difficult question was the division of troop strength between the Nationalists and the Communists. On 25 February 1946 the committee composed of Chang Chih-chung, Chou En-lai, and General Marshall[4] announced that

---

[4] This was the Military Sub-Committee, of which Marshall was the adviser, which held its first meeting on 14 February 1946. *Tr.*

agreement had been reached on this question, based upon the following points:

At the conclusion of 12 months the armies shall consist of 108 divisions of not to exceed 14,000 men each.[5] Of these, 18 shall be formed from Communist Forces.

The deployment of the armies at the end of the first 12 months shall be as follows:

NORTHEAST CHINA—5 armies, each consisting of 3 National divisions, each army with a National commander; and 1 army consisting of 3 Communist divisions with a Communist commander —total 6 armies.

NORTHWEST CHINA—5 armies each consisting of 3 National divisions each with a National commander—total 5 armies.

NORTH CHINA—3 armies each consisting of 3 National divisions, each with a National commander; and 4 army groups, each consisting of 1 National and 1 Communist army of 3 divisions. 2 army group commanders shall be National officers and 2 army group commanders shall be Communist officers—total 11 armies.

CENTRAL CHINA—9 armies, each consisting of 3 National divisions, each with a National commander; and 1 army consisting of 3 Communist divisions, with a Communist commander—total 10 armies.

SOUTH CHINA (including Formosa)—4 armies, each consisting of 3 National divisions, each with a National commander—total 4 armies.[6]

Following this initial reorganization, a second partial demobilization was to take place over a period of six months so that, within a total of eighteen months' time, the strength and deployment of the armed forces would be as follows:

NORTHEAST CHINA—1 army consisting of 2 National and 1 Communist Divisions with a National commander and 4 armies each consisting of 3 National divisions, each with a National commander—total 5 armies.

[5] The type-army was to consist of three divisions of not more than fourteen thousand men each, plus about 6,300 service troops, for a total of about 48,300 men (the rough equivalent of a U.S. corps. Tr.).

[6] U.S. Relations with China, pp. 623–624. Tr.

NORTHWEST CHINA—3 armies, each consisting of 3 National Divisions each with a National commander—total 3 armies.

NORTH CHINA—3 armies, each consisting of 1 National and 2 Communist divisions, each with a Communist commander; 1 army consisting of 2 National and 1 Communist divisions with a National commander; and 2 armies each consisting of 3 National divisions, each with a National commander—total 6 armies.

CENTRAL CHINA—1 army consisting of 1 National and 2 Communist divisions with a Communist commander and 3 armies each consisting of 3 National divisions, each with a National commander—total 4 armies.

SOUTH CHINA (including Formosa)—2 armies each consisting of 3 National divisions, each with a National commander—total 2 armies.[7]

Finally, by July 1947 the Chinese Army was to be reduced to sixty divisions, of which fifty were to be Nationalist and ten Communist. The maintenance of a "Peace Preservation Corps," in a strength not to exceed fifteen thousand men per province, was permitted, and its armament restricted to pistols, rifles, and automatic rifles. Pro-Japanese puppet troops, as well as irregulars, were to be disbanded as soon as possible.

This politico-military agreement was applauded throughout the entire country, which hoped that it would prove to be the means by which civil war could be avoided. The agreement clearly recognized the preponderant position of the Nationalists; but the Communists intended to profit from its recognition of their party by pursuing their propaganda efforts and winning the people over to their ideas. This frightened the right wing of the Kuomintang, and there were malcontents in Yenan, too; but, such as it was, the agreement was a victory for General Marshall, who sincerely believed that he had found the solution to an insoluble problem. In reality, each side remained fully determined to fight through to the complete destruction of its adversary.

[7] *Ibid.*, p. 625. Tr.

The agreement had hardly been signed when disorders broke out in Manchuria, where Nationalist troops, as agreed, were preparing to move in on the heels of a Russian withdrawal. At this time the Nationalists had only a few administrative delegates in Manchuria, charged with re-establishing the authority of the Nationalist government under the aegis of the Russian garrisons, plus some token forces in the cities. Outside the population centers, out in the countryside, the Red forces of Lin Piao were in control, and were infiltrating into all of northern and central Manchuria. Chiang Kai-shek and the Russians were playing a double game. On the one hand, Chinese public opinion clamored for the departure of the Russians, and students demonstrated in Chungking on 21 February; yet Chiang had asked the Russians to prolong their occupation until his own forces could replace them. For their part, the Soviets were quite content to prolong their sojourn in Manchuria, in such a manner as to dismantle and carry off to Siberia all the industrial machinery installed by the Japanese; yet, wishing to let the Chinese Communists take over Manchuria, they did not want to wait too long for the arrival of the Nationalists. By the end of February, Nationalist troops had occupied virtually all of the Liao Ho valley to the south of Mukden. As for the theoretically neutral Americans, they continued their aid to Chiang Kai-shek. On 10 March they transferred 271 small naval auxiliary craft to the Nationalists; they also formed at Nanking, on the same date, a "consultative commission,"[8] headed by Major General Robert B. McClure, for the purpose of reorganizing the Chinese Army along modern lines.

[8] The American designation for this body was Nanking Headquarters Command, which included the advisory groups for the three services and a Joint Advisory Staff to coordinate dealings with the Chinese government in general and the Ministry of Defense and Supreme Staff in particular. In September 1948 the designation was changed to Joint U.S. Military Advisory Group—China, or JUSMAG. See *U.S. Relations with China*, pp. 339–340. Tr.

On 23 March Chiang Kai-shek, pressed by public opinion, formally requested the Russians to evacuate Manchuria. Thanks to the American ships which had transported seven of his armies to the ports of the Gulf of Liaotung, he now felt strong enough for Manchuria. Marshal Malinovsky replied that he expected to complete his withdrawal by the end of April and, in any event, "before the Americans leave Chinese territory." The Russians did, in fact, evacuate Mukden on 12 March. Lin Piao's Communist forces immediately moved in, but were driven out on 13 March by the Nationalist Twenty-fifth Army, which was soon joined by the Fifty-second Army. Chiang Kai-shek's son, Chiang Ching-kuo, was made Governor of the Northeast Provinces. But, at the same time, the Communists were proclaiming people's governments in the provinces of Kirin and Heilungkiang.

The two sides now commenced to accuse each other of violating the truce. On 13 March, Ch'en Chi-ch'eng, the Nationalist commander in North China, claimed that the Reds had launched 220 attacks against the Nationalists, occupied 1,330 railroad stations, and invested twenty-six localities. Lu Chung-lin, the government's official representative in North China, declared that the Reds had practically isolated Peking, Tientsin, and Tsinan. For their part, the Communists charged that the Nationalists had attacked their troops in southern Manchuria and refused to send in a mixed pacification commission, or "field team,"[9] that they had encircled sixty thousand of their troops in the region of northern Hupeh and southern Honan, and, finally, that they had attempted to massacre Red forces in the Canton area. Officially,

[9] On 24 January 1946 General Marshall had proposed that a field team be sent out from Executive Headquarters in Manchuria to stop the fighting at Yingkow, and that similar action be taken in the event of further outbreaks of fighting between the Nationalists and the Communists. The Communists approved this proposal, but the National Government did not give its limited assent until 27 March 1946. See *U.S. Relations with China*, pp. 145–146. *Tr.*

Chiang Kai-shek abided by the rules of the game. On 15 March he freed General Yeh T'ing, former commander of the New Fourth Army, whom he had held prisoner since 1941; and he continued to proclaim his willingness to resolve the Manchurian problem by political means. Nevertheless, he refused to permit the entry of field teams into Manchuria, and deferred *sine die* the opening of the National Assembly. The question of Manchuria was becoming paramount, a growing seed of discord whose only fruit would be a renewed outbreak of civil war.

General Marshall, who had already begun to grasp this situation, left for Washington on 11 March to make his report to President Truman, leaving Lieutenant General Alvin C. Gillem, Jr., to represent him in the Committee of Three. Marshall had realized that American aid to the Nationalists was scarcely compatible with the position of a neutral arbiter, but he still hesitated to impose an embargo on the continuing flow of arms to Chiang Kai-shek. He also thought it necessary to withdraw American forces from China as soon as possible, and was determined to hasten their departure. But when he returned from Washington on 18 April the irreparable had occurred; open civil war had broken out on 15 April, just as the Russians were evacuating Changchun, the capital of Manchuria.

As early as the 8th, Communist forces, forewarned of the imminent departure of the Russians, moved on Changchun from the north and east. By the 9th they were in the outskirts of the capital. On 14 April at 1020 hours, the last Russian left Changchun. By the next morning the Reds had seized the airfield and infiltrated into the city, which was defended by only four thousand men of the Peace Preservation Corps, against whom the Reds had concentrated 35,000 men. After severe street fighting on the 16th and 17th, Ch'en

Chi-ch'eng's forces capitulated to the Communists on 18 April, with relieving Nationalist armies still no nearer than some 130 miles to the south of the Manchurian capital. Indeed, as late as the 15th, the New First Army had come only as far as Szepingkai, an important rail center.

Meanwhile, Nationalist forces had methodically fanned out from Mukden. The New Sixth Army and the Seventy-first and Ninety-fourth armies cleared the Mukden-Yingkow railroad by way of Liaoyang, while the Fifty-second Army advanced along the Mukden-Kirin railroad to Fushun, which it held against the attacks of five Communist divisions on 7 and 8 April. The Nationalists succeeded in running a train from Mukden to Peking on 18 April, but the line remained exposed to Red attacks in the vicinity of Shanhaikwan. While the Nationalists were trying to disengage Mukden and resume their advance upon Changchun, Lin Piao, without firing a shot, occupied all the rest of the country. Hard on the heels of the withdrawing Russians, his forces entered Kirin on 22 April, Harbin on the 25th, and Tsitsihar on the 28th. Everywhere, the representatives of Chiang Kai-shek's government were forced to flee; they sought safety with the withdrawing Russians, who later returned them, via Vladivostok and the sea, to China.

Little by little, the Nationalist armies pushed northward along the Changchun railroad. They were well equipped with heavy weapons, even with tanks, and the Communists could not stand up to them in open battle. Thus, when the New First and Fifth armies attacked on 21 April, the Communists were forced to fall back and, after a bitter, month-long resistance, to yield Szepingkai to the Nationalists on 19 May. On the 21st the government troops seized the pass at Kungchuling, about thirty-five miles south of Changchun. Finally, on 23 May, Nationalist armored units entered the Manchurian capi-

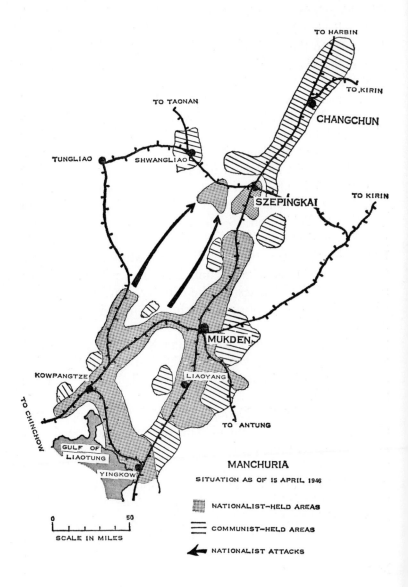

TO HARBIN

TO KIRIN

CHANGCHUN

TO TAONAN

TUNGLIAO

SHWANGLIAO

SZEPINGKAI

TO KIRIN

KOWPANGTZE

MUKDEN

LIAOYANG

TO ANTUNG

TO CHINCHOW

GULF OF
LIAOTUNG

YINGKOW

MANCHURIA

SITUATION AS OF 15 APRIL 1946

NATIONALIST-HELD AREAS

COMMUNIST-HELD AREAS

NATIONALIST ATTACKS

0   50

SCALE IN MILES

tal. Exploiting this success, they occupied Kirin on the 29th, crossed the Sungari river, and on 5 June took Schwangcheng, about thirty miles to the south of Harbin.

At this time Chiang Kai-shek was at Mukden, where he had arrived in General Marshall's personal plane for a tour of inspection. The capture of Changchun increased Chiang's confidence and his certainty of victory through force. For their part, the Communists, enraged by the fact that Chiang had flown to Manchuria in Marshall's own airplane, found it increasingly difficult to credit the impartiality of the American mediator.

While the fighting had been going on in Manchuria, two major developments had unfolded elsewhere.

In the first place, the Communists had been very active in Shantung and Kiangsu. In Shantung P'eng Te-huai's forces had come down from their mountains and, advancing along the Tientsin-Pukow railroad, had encircled Tsinan and threatened Peking. The effect of these significant successes was to force Chiang to divert forces from the Manchurian theater. In Kiangsu the Communist New Fourth Army, while retaining its hold on the coastal area between the mouth of the Yangtze and the former mouth of the Hwang Ho, took the offensive and threatened Nantung.

Secondly, the negotiations which continued throughout these operations were becoming more and more difficult for General Marshall. After proving a Communist violation of the armistice in the Red occupation of Changchun, he was obliged to recognize that the Nationalists, too, had committed numerous transgressions: encirclement, to the north of Hankow, of parts of the Communist New Fourth Army; troop movements in prohibited areas, such as Jehol; refusal of the government to report its troop movements south of the Yangtze; arrest of Communists and closing of Communist newspapers in Peking; bombing of the airfield at Yenan;[10] arrest of the Communist members of the field team at Mukden. For their part, the Communists, after their victory at Changchun, requested modification of the force ratio initially prescribed for the Northeast. General Marshall refused, pointing out that Chiang Kai-shek, in asking only for the evacuation of Changchun and not, as the initial agreements entitled him to, of all of Manchuria, was showing great good will. Moreover, fully realizing that his mediation was becoming more and more difficult, and that the field teams were never obeyed, Marshall declared his desire to withdraw from mediation.

With the Nationalist recapture of Changchun, however, Chiang became more amenable. On 24 May he proposed a truce, even though he continued his offensive against Kirin and Harbin. Returning to his restored capital at Nanking on 3 June, he approved on 5 June a cease-fire which, with Communist consent, was established for a fifteen-day period commencing 7 June 1946. Chiang declared that this truce would "give the Communist Party an opportunity to demonstrate in good faith their intention to carry out the agreements they had previously signed."[11] Invoking the Sino-Soviet treaty, he pressed his claim to Nationalist sovereignty in Manchuria. In response, Chou En-lai self-righteously recalled that the Chinese Communist Party had never ceased its efforts to bring an end to civil war.

Taking up the agreement of 25 February 1946 regarding the demobilization, reorganization, and integration of the armed forces, the two sides fruitlessly negotiated throughout the fifteen-day truce. On 22 June the truce was extended by eight days, with no results. On 30 June the Civil War, which

---

[10] The White Paper uses the term "buzzing," rather than "bombing," to describe this action of Nationalist planes over the airfield at Yenan. See *U.S. Relations with China*, p. 151. Tr.

[11] *Ibid.*, p. 641. Tr.

had never really ceased, was officially resumed—to the accompaniment of telegraphed orders from Chiang and Mao, each of whom directed his troops not to attack, but to fire only when fired upon.

Each side threw upon the other the responsibility for the failure of the negotiations. In fact, the fundamental question remained that of the areas occupied by the Red Army. The Nationalists demanded Communist evacuation of Jehol and Chahar; of the Manchurian cities of Harbin, Antung, Tunghwa, Mutankiang, and Paicheng; of the greater part of Shantung, and all of Kiangsu.[12] "This would be," declared Chou En-lai, "a return to the system of military districts, or outright annexation. It would not be a democratic measure. The demands of the government are thus unacceptable."

Regarding the reallocation of armed forces in Manchuria requested by the Communists, Chiang accepted a strength of three Red divisions in place of the one division initially prescribed, but refused the figure of five proposed by Chou En-lai. There were long discussions about the concentration zones to be left to the Communists, and about the cities the Reds were to evacuate. Chiang Kai-shek showed himself to be as intractable as his adversary. He seemed, at this time, to be absolutely sure of victory through force. As for the Communists, they were beginning to realize that, apart from his "American" divisions, Chiang's armies were really quite weak. Considering the strategic situation to be more favorable to themselves, so long as they held Shansi and Shantung, they prepared their troops, and the weapons they had taken from the Japanese in Manchuria, for the continuation of the Civil War. They, too, could see only victory as the outcome.

---

[12] The importance Chiang attached to these demands is reflected in the fact that he was to persist in his attacks until most of these objectives, announced on 17 June, were attained in November.

In July fighting resumed in earnest—despite the restraining orders which had been issued by both sides—and raged with particular severity in Shantung and Kiangsu. In Shantung the Nationalists, who had concentrated some twenty divisions in the province, succeeded in recapturing control of the Kiaochow-Tsinan railroad and regaining freedom of movement around Tsingtao and Tsinan. It proved impossible for them, however, to drive the Communists from the mountainous region of the province.

At this time (10 July) the Nationalists also launched a great offensive in Kiangsu. This operation was part of an overall, coordinated plan which aimed at the successive reduction of the Communist zones in Central China by concentration of overwhelming force upon each in turn, in such manner as to facilitate a final thrust into North China and Manchuria. This offensive, directed by General T'ang En-po, Deputy Commander in Chief of the Chinese Army, and General Li Mo-an, Commander of the First Pacification Zone, was supervised by Pai Ch'ung-hsi, the Minister of National Defense, and by General Ch'en Ch'eng, the Chief of Staff of the Chinese Army. The result of this multiplicity of chiefs was orders, counterorders, and disorder. Eight Nationalist armies (the Fifth, Seventh, Twenty-first, Twenty-fifth, Forty-ninth, Seventy-fourth, Ninety-ninth, and 100th) supported by one hundred aircraft (the Fifth Group) were launched against the 130,000 men of General Ch'en I,[13] the Red commander coordinating operations in Kiangsu and Shantung. Clearly, the

---

[13] Not to be confused with the notorious General Ch'en I who was relieved as Nationalist governor of Taiwan in 1949, and executed by the Nationalists in 1950 for his plot to kidnap Chiang Kai-shek and defect to the Communists. All subsequent references to Ch'en I in this work are to the Communist general of that name. One of the Communists' most brilliant commanders in the Civil War, this is the Ch'en I who is currently (1965) Foreign Minister of the People's Republic of China. *Tr.*

Nationalist forces possessed numerical and material superiority. But their morale was low; once again, one was to
witness inexplicable surrenders. For example, the 19th Brigade
of the 89th Infantry Division (100th Army), and part of the
Forty-ninth Army as well, laid down their arms without having
fired a shot—a capitulation which permitted the elusive Communists, who were employing guerrilla tactics *con brio*, to
conduct a successful defense along the Tientsin-Shanghai railroad between Suhsien and Nantung. The capture of Jukao
by the Nationalists failed to bring any decisive results.

Meanwhile, the Communists had vented vehement protests
against American policy in China, and Chiang's untimely
departure for Kuling[14] on 14 July led to a slowdown in negotiations. The adversaries again accused each other of violating
the truce, but now a stiffer attitude was apparent on both
sides. On the Kuomintang side the reactionary faction was
becoming, like the Communists, anti-American, and they now
viewed American mediation as positively injurious to the
Nationalist cause. At Kunming the secret police assassinated
two professors who belonged to the Democratic League, and
terrorized the liberal leaders. For their part, the Communists
provoked serious incidents with the U.S. Marines and on
29 July ambushed an American convoy at Anping, near Peking.
The convoy, consisting of members of an Executive Headquarters field team, some UNRRA supplies, and a Marine
escort detachment, lost three killed, twelve wounded, and one
jeep. The Communists alleged that the Americans had been
fighting side by side with Nationalists. The commander of the
Seventh U.S. Fleet, Admiral Charles M. Cooke, formally
denied these accusations and warned that henceforth the
Marines would fire when fired upon.

[14] Chiang's summer residence in Kiangsi, where he would take an occasional
vacation.

Meanwhile, General Patrick Hurley had yet to be replaced as American Ambassador to China. General Marshall felt a need to be backed up by a man of integrity who was an expert on China, and who would be capable of replacing him when he departed—a departure he was beginning very strongly to desire. He asked Truman to name Dr. Leighton Stuart, President of the American Yenching University at Peking, to the vacant post. Stuart arrived in Nanking on 26 July, and promptly began his efforts at mediation. Paving the new ambassador's way, Marshall warned Chiang Kai-shek against his self-delusions of rapid victory through force, pointing out to Chiang the diminution of his prestige, the deterioration of China's economic and financial situation, and the misinformation the Generalissimo was receiving from his entourage. On 1 August Dr. Stuart proposed to Chiang the creation of a Five-Man Committee, to consist of two Communists and two Nationalists, with the ambassador himself as chairman.[15]

Once again Chiang imposed preliminary conditions: withdrawal of Red forces in Kiangsu to the north of the Lunghai railroad; withdrawal from the zone of the Tsinan-Tsingtao railroad; withdrawal from all of Jehol south of Chengteh; withdrawal of all Red forces in Manchuria into the Manchurian provinces of Hsingan, Heilungkiang, and Nunkiang; finally, Communist withdrawal from all places in Shansi and Shantung occupied after 7 June. In reply, the Communists declared that they would not withdraw so long as the question of administration of their occupied territories was not resolved in a satisfactory manner. Actually, Chiang regarded the "truce" as favorable to himself, even if its terms were not respected, and he pressed on with military operations, especially in Hopeh and Jehol. The Communists having encircled Tatung at the

[15] The Nationalists were represented by two generals, Wang Ta-ch'en and Chang Li-sheng, and the Communists by Chou En-lai and Tung Pi-wu.

end of July, the government announced a Nationalist offensive against Kalgan, the only large city in the hands of the Reds. Mao Tse-tung's reply was to order, on 19 August, general mobilization in all territories under Communist control.

On 20 August the Thirteenth and Fifty-third armies advanced on Chengteh, the capital of Jehol, which they took on the 28th; the Communists, following their custom, fell back and avoided pitched battle in open country. In contrast, General Ho Lung's sixty thousand Reds tightened their grip around Tatung, despite the dispatch of a Nationalist relief column from Peking by General Fu Tso-yi. As for the stalled negotiations, nothing could break the deadlock: a message from President Truman, the explanations and supplications of Stuart and Marshall—all were to no avail. Truly, as pointed out in the American White Paper, "General Marshall was being placed in the untenable position of mediating on the one hand between the two Chinese groups while on the other the United States Government was continuing to supply arms and ammunition to one of the two groups, namely, the National Government."[16]

The American military aid program, which called for the equipping of thirty-nine Nationalist divisions and eight and one-third aviation groups, was still in effect. Thus, in order to convince the Communists of his good faith, Marshall in August imposed an embargo on American arms shipments to the Nationalists.[17] But Chiang had ample reserves of war matériel at this time, and he continued his military operations without abatement as the fruitless negotiations dragged on. On 28 August the Generalissimo proposed Red participation in a coalition government. In reply Yenan prescribed, as

[16] U.S. Relations with China, p. 181. Tr.

[17] The embargo, in the form of a ban on the issuance of export licenses for shipment of arms and ammunition, was lifted by the Secretary of State on 26 May 1947. See U.S. Relations with China, pp. 355–356. Tr.

the first condition of its acceptance, a general cease-fire; without this, the Communists feared that they would be forced by the Kuomintang, which would have a majority in the State Council,[18] to submit to conditions imposed by the Nationalists. As for Marshall, he had long since realized that there were no peaceful ways out of the Chinese impasse. He continued, however, to struggle courageously, but without hope. Session after session, the futile palaver continued, with each side always finding good reasons to reject the other's proposals.

Chou En-lai's departure from Nanking for Shanghai, on 16 September 1946, showed very clearly that the Chinese Communists regarded an agreement with the Nationalists as increasingly improbable. The Red leader released to the press a vehement protest against the aid provided the Kuomintang by the Americans, who had expended at least $600 million for the support of Nationalist China since V-J Day, and who had continued since then to supply Chiang with arms and ammunition. Nevertheless, the negotiations continued, while Nationalist attacks sought by force to obtain what the government had asked for in its June proposals. But with each defeat, the Communists only became more unyielding in negotiation. Gradually, they came to realize that they were losing far fewer men than the Nationalists, whose morale was not always proving to be of the best. And they were beginning to gather the fruits of their guerrilla campaign, which not only served to keep their regular military forces intact, but, by

[18] In January 1946 the Political Consultative Conference had passed a resolution to make an enlarged State Council, with appointed representatives of the KMT "as well as non-members of the Kuomintang," the "supreme organ of the Government" pending the convocation of the National Assembly. A major (and unfulfilled) purpose of Ambassador Stuart's August proposal for a Five-Man Committee was to reach an agreement on the organization of the State Council, which it was hoped would "give a form of genuine legislative action for control or guidance of the Government." See *U.S. Relations with China*, pp. 610, 174–175. *Tr.*

severing communications, was separating the cities from the countryside and slowly driving the government into an economic crisis.

Meanwhile, the Nationalist attack on Kalgan, the second capital of the Reds, gave Chou En-lai the opportunity to demonstrate the bad faith of Chiang Kai-shek and lodge vigorous protests with General Marshall. Marshall then asked Chiang to stop the attack and make new proposals. The Generalissimo's minimal concessions were rejected by Yenan. Clearly Chiang wanted to exploit his military superiority and resolve the issue by force. At this point Marshall threatened to withdraw from mediation and go home, thus wringing from Chiang his agreement to a truce and a halt to his advance on Kalgan. But now it was the Communists who managed to find reasons for rejecting the truce, thus leaving Marshall high and dry. In Manchuria and in all regions under Communist control, mass demonstrations against the Americans proliferated; even though the U.S. Marines had evacuated Tientsin and Chinwangtao as early as September, their continued presence at Tsingtao sufficed as fuel for these protests. On 11 October the Generalissimo, whose troops had now taken Kalgan and Chengteh, announced that the National Assembly would meet at Nanking on 12 November, whether or not the Communist Party saw fit to participate.

For the moment all was calm in Manchuria, where the Nationalists had attained almost all of their June objectives. But the Communists were preparing for open war, and they recalled the missions of negotiation they had until then maintained at Nanking, Shanghai, and Chungking, their personnel being repatriated, by courtesy of American aircraft, to Yenan. There was a last ray of hope when the "Third Party Group"[19] succeeded in persuading Chou En-lai to return to

[19] Leaders of minority parties other than the CCP. *Tr.*

Nanking and begin a last round of talks. But the Communists continued to lay down as their preliminary conditions the withdrawal of government troops to the lines of 13 January in China, and of 7 June in Manchuria. The Reds also asked for a total of fourteen seats on the State Council for the CCP and the Democratic League, thus giving them a check upon majority decisions. Chiang Kai-shek refused and presented counterproposals of his own. The situation grew worse and worse. On 24 October the Nationalists occupied the last important stations of the Kiaochow-Tsinan railroad, moved forward in southern Hopeh, and in Manchuria launched an attack on Antung. The Communists withdrew their personnel from the field teams and from the Executive Headquarters at Peking, whose activity had long been negligible at best. On 26 October Chou En-lai declared that continuation of the government attacks would mean the end of negotiations.

Announcement of the fall of Antung on 27 October filled Chiang's entourage with joy, and General Marshall felt himself bound, the very next morning, to give the Generalissimo his frank personal estimate of the general situation. In this interview with Chiang, Marshall drew his hearer's attention to the illusions nourished by his advisers. In Marshall's own view, the Nationalists had succeeded in occupying cities, but they had failed to take any weapons or prisoners from the Red forces, which remained intact. He added that even the fall of Harbin itself would solve nothing, and that the Generalissimo could not resolve the issues by force. On 8 November, Nationalist troops having occupied Tunghwa in Manchuria, Chiang declared that the time had come for a general cease-fire.

CHAPTER VI

The Military Situation at the End of October and Operations During the Last Months of 1946

A study of the zones occupied by the Communists as of the end of October 1946 shows that the situation of the Reds remained very strong in North China, owing not only to the territory they held, but to the threat they posed, from Kiangsu to Manchuria, to all the Nationalist lines of communication. They continued to implement their "horizontal plan," and to prevent the rail movement of Nationalist troops to the Northeast. Chiang Kai-shek's only important success had been the almost complete clearing of Hupeh, southern Honan, and South China; the Communists had even been compelled to evacuate their forces from Kwangtung by sea to Shantung. Those who remained, and particularly those on Hainan, had been rebaptized as "bandits" by the Nationalists, who continued to wipe out or at least neutralize the Red remnants in these areas.

The events which befell Communist forces in what had been the central zone of operations, Hupeh and Honan, can be summarized as follows: pressed by a food shortage and resupply difficulties, Li Hsien-nien, whose forces had been a source of serious trouble for the Nationalists in the Hupeh-Honan border region during the winter of 1945–1946, in April requested a truce that would permit the free passage of his troops into Kiangsu. The Nationalists refused, fearing that Li would profit from the proposed lull by moving his forces into Shantung and thence to Manchuria, where the situation was critical. Nonetheless, the Generalissimo's headquarters at Wuhan granted the hungry Reds a loan of 400 million *fapis*[1] for purposes of resupply. Early in May, General Byroade, Chou En-lai, and Hsu Yung-ch'ang arrived to investigate the situation of these troops, and signed an agreement which delimited, as a fixed zone for Li Hsien-nien's troops, an area to the east of the Pinghan[2] with Loshan as its center. But at the end of the month, Li, on the pretext that the Nationalists were attempting to encircle his forces, crossed the line of the Pinghan and marched westward, gathering up on his way other Communist elements that had survived the earlier Nationalist push and were in the process of recuperation, as well as the advance guards he had sent forward to clear the way. In one month, Li, hard-pressed as he was by the Nationalists, still managed to take a dozen towns, including Suihsien, Tsao-yang, Sinyeh, and Sichwan, and then moved northward up the valley of the Tan. In order to ease the supply problem the Reds quickly divided their forces following the fall of Suihsien, and General Wang Chen, commanding the southern column, crossed the Han and took Icheng, Nanchang, Pao-

[1] At this time the *fapi*, the Chinese nonconvertible legal-tender note, had an official exchange rate of about $2,000 Chinese to $1 U.S., and was rapidly depreciating in value. See the China Handbook Editorial Board, *China Handbook, 1950* (New York: Rockport Press, Inc., 1950), pp. 470–471, and U.S. Department of State, *United Relations with China, with Special Reference to the Period 1944–1949* (U.S. Government Printing Office, 1949), p. 221. Tr.

[2] The Peking-Hankow railroad.

kang, and Chusan. By the end of July the two Red columns had established themselves in two well-protected valleys, that of the Nan, near the Honan-Shansi-Hupeh border, and the valley of the Chu, near the Shensi-Szechwan-Hupeh border. The Communists had suffered severe losses during this march and they needed a respite in which to regroup. A new armistice of three weeks' duration, effective at midnight of 6 August and covering a zone which included Hupeh, Shensi, and Honan, gave them the needed break. Once regrouped, the Reds crossed the armistice line of the Wei River near Sian, and on 30 August entered the Shensi-Kansu-Ningsia Border Region, the official seat of Chinese communism.

Thus, at the cost of abandoning South and Central China, the Communists had succeeded in effecting a strategic concentration of their forces—a concentration which stood in marked contrast to the dispersed deployment of their adversaries.

On 15 November the National Assembly met at Nanking without the participation of the Communists or of the Democratic League, whose combined quota of seats, according to the proposals of the Political Consultative Conference, should have amounted to 610 of the total of 2,050. The Kuomintang and its affiliates should therefore have elected only 1,440 members; but the National Assembly had 1,580 of them, which gave Chou En-lai a new opportunity to protest, this time against the illegal seating of 140 representatives of the KMT.

On 19 November Chou left for Yenan. General Marshall, too, was packing his bags, for he fully realized not only that his mission had failed, but that Chiang Kai-shek, whose situation appeared to be so favorable, was actually headed for an impasse from which he had little chance of emerging. Seventy per cent of the government's budget went to the financing of the war; only twenty-five per cent of this budget was met by taxes, with another ten per cent covered by gold reserves and various fiscal devices. The missing sixty-five per cent explains an inflation that was becoming catastrophic: during 1946 prices rose by 700 per cent, while gold reserves dwindled by fifty per cent. Pleading its poverty, the government incessantly clamored for American aid, while corruption reigned unchecked at all levels of the poorly paid public service. As for the troops, they were underfed, poorly led, and without morale.

In Marshall's view the Chinese Communist Party had been sincerely desirous, in the spring of 1946, of reaching an understanding with the Nationalists; it was the Kuomintang government that had wrecked the negotiations by its incessant violations of the truce and continuation of its military action up to October, thus undermining his peace proposals even as they were being advanced. Marshall again demonstrated to Chiang that Nationalist forces were incapable, since the departure of the American Marines, of keeping open the vitally important Tientsin-Chinwangtao railroad, or of clearing the Communists from Hopeh. The Generalissimo's reply was that, in his opinion, the Chinese Communist Party had never been sincerely willing to cooperate, and that its real goal was to drive, with the help of the U.S.S.R., the Nationalists from power in China. In his view the sole solution was war, and he expected to finish off the Reds in less than a year. As for the economic situation, it did not appear so catastrophic to him, since China's compartmentalized agrarian economy made the provinces almost autarkic and only the large cities would have to be provided for.

On 4 December the Communists again demanded the dissolution of the National Assembly and withdrawal of Nationalist troops to the cease-fire line of 13 January. Stiffening more and more against the United States, they also rejected any mediation by the Americans. For the second time, Marshall, prior to his departure, personally intervened and tried to show Chiang the sensible solution. Marshall insisted upon the primordial necessity of popular support for the Kuomintang, and the consequent requirements for agrarian reform and a democratic constitution. He begged the Generalissimo to rid himself of the reactionary clique of the brothers Ch'en, and of the secret police, and to rally the liberals to his side. Quite understandably, he refused to remain in China as Chiang's adviser. With this, Chiang made what seems to have been a real effort to escape the reactionary influence of the CC clique.[3] His pro-democratic pronouncements to the National Assembly regained much of his prestige, and his efforts resulted in the adoption of a new and liberal constitution. But the Ch'en brothers continued to be active within the inner circles of the party, and maintained their hold upon the cadres of the Kuomintang.

On 6 January President Truman recalled General Marshall, who left China on the 8th. The American attempt at mediation had ended in complete failure. On the one hand, the Communists, who had long been somewhat sympathetic in their attitude toward the United States, and especially toward Marshall, had now become resolutely anti-American. On the other hand, the United States, which had proved incapable of formulating a sound China policy, now found itself more and more involved in support of the Kuomintang, when it should have been clear that its ward's chances of winning were becoming fewer and fewer. With Marshall's departure all official American organizations also left China, except for the "naval training group" at Tsingtao.

[3] The name of this clique was derived from that of the brothers Ch'en Li-fu and Ch'en Kuo-fu, Chiang Kai-shek's adopted nephews and the leaders of the KMT's extreme right.

Marshall left the Nationalists in a catastrophic position. The Communists, seeking to hasten economic collapse, were systematically destroying communications and isolating the cities from the countryside. The American dollar, worth 2,020 Chinese dollars as of 1 January 1946, had reached an exchange rate of 6,500 Chinese dollars by December of that year. Kuomintang finances were completely adrift, with no control over expenditures and each level of command indulging in embezzlement, the "squeeze," and outright theft. The enormous army—poorly employed, pent up in useless garrisons, always on the defensive—was a crushing financial burden, as was the resupply of Manchuria.

Yet, beginning as early as V-J Day, the Chinese government had received considerable foreign aid. During 1945, UNRRA had sent 300,000 tons of food, clothing, and other supplies. From 1945 to 1947, UNRRA had also contributed $685 million in financial aid, $475 million of it from the United States. Through the Export-Import Bank $82 million had been advanced to the Nationalist government, and a credit offering of $500 million had been made, for purposes of reconstruction, to Chinese companies.[4] In June 1946, Canada lent $60 million, and the United States $51,700,000, for purposes of reconstruction. Surplus military matériel of American forces in the Pacific (vehicles, spare parts, engines, electrical and medical equipment, tools, chemical products, aviation spare parts, and construction materials), worth $900 million, was turned over to the Nationalists for $175 million, payable on easy terms. Unfortunately, this enormous effort was in vain. Civil war, corruption, and incompetence prevented the Chinese government from maintaining a healthy economy and a truly strong army.

[4] The outbreak of civil war led the bank to withdraw this offer.

MILITARY OPERATIONS FROM OCTOBER
TO DECEMBER OF 1946

Military operations during the period of October-December 1946 may be described as follows: in Kiangsu, the Nationalists failed in their attempts to clean out the Communist enclave. After some success, their offensive failed when General Ho P'eng-chu, who held the eastern part of the Lunghai railroad between the Grand Canal and the sea, went over to the Communists. Although the Nationalists took Lienshui and Fowning in December, Red guerrillas reappeared behind them in the Nantung and Jukao areas. In Shantung the Communists remained invulnerable in the mountainous part of the province, while in the south they repelled a Nationalist offensive along the Taierhchwang-Yihsien front. Meanwhile, in order to separate Red forces in Shantung from those in Hopeh, the government had undertaken an enormous engineering effort. In repairing the embankments of the Yellow River which had given way, in 1938, between Kaifeng and Chengchow, they now sought to divert the river eastward into its old course. This would flood Anhwei and Kiangsu, dry the former river bed into a mud flat at best, isolate Hopeh from Shantung, and make the movement of Red troops exceedingly difficult.[5] This posed a serious threat to the Communists, for their "horizontal plan" required the maintenance of contact between the Kiangsu-Shantung region and that of Hopeh-Shansi-Shensi. In December General Liu Po-ch'eng moved to oppose the Nationalist troops of General Ku Chu-t'ung who, despite several successes which included the seizure of Taming, failed to clear the Reds from the Peking-Hankow railroad. In Hopeh the Reds continued to be extremely active, and Na-

[5] Work on this project was halted in 1947, and the river resumed its course to the Gulf of Chihli.

97

tionalist communications between Peking and Paoting, and between Paoting and Shihkiachwang as well, remained severed. By the end of December, only fifty-three of Hopeh's 133 *hsien*, or districts, were held by the Nationalists, while the Communists held forty and the other forty remained in contention. In Shansi, where the Reds were trying to lay their hands on the Luliang Shan range (the mountain chain which separates the Fen Ho from the Yellow River), the situation remained in doubt. In the Mongolian provinces, the Nationalists expanded their zone of influence to Chahar, achieving the conquest of Jehol despite the severe cold which made operations difficult and very hard on the men. In the Yenan region, General Ma Hung-ku'ei, the Nationalist governor of Ningsia, attacked the Yenchih salt-works, but was pushed all the way back to his starting point. Lastly, in Manchuria the Nationalists established lines of defense around Changchun and around their bridgehead on the Sungari, while clearing the country to the south. They were particularly successful in Liaoning, where, after encircling the Red zone around Antung, they seized practically all of the peninsula. Red guerrillas still survived in this zone, however, as well as in the Szepingkai area, where trains were continually machine-gunned by the Communists.

Toward the end of the year the Reds reorganized the five Manchurian provinces over which they held complete control: Sungkiang (with its capital at Harbin); Hokiang (Kiamusze); Heilungkiang (Lungchen); Nunkiang (Tsitsihar); and Hsingan (Hailar). This Communist zone had about twenty million inhabitants, half the total population of Manchuria, and an area of over 300,000 square miles. It was governed by a People's Council composed of twenty-seven members and directed by Lin Feng and Chang Hsüeh-szu, brother of Chang Hsüeh-liang, the young war lord who had kidnapped Chiang

Kai-shek at Sian in 1936. Theoretically, these men were not Communists, and the government was "democratic." But the presence of Lin Piao's army, 300,000 strong, gave the Reds a far from negligible instrument for the kind of pressure other Communists brought to bear in Hungary and the Balkans.

The disposition of Nationalist forces in Manchuria was now as follows: the commander in chief (General Tu Yü-ming) had established his headquarters in Changchun, and had divided his forces into two major groups. The northern group consisted of seven divisions organized in three armies. It covered the Changchun-Kirin zone, and held the Nationalist bridgehead on the Sungari. The stronger southern group, consisting of twelve divisions, was centered around Mukden and faced toward the Korean frontier; farther west, Nationalist units facing toward Jehol covered Mukden against possible attack from Inner Mongolia. Lastly, the Sixty-third Army was in process of disembarkment at Chinwangtao.

All these divisions were equipped with American weapons and vehicles; they were well supplied with ammunition; and they enjoyed considerable superiority in numbers. The Nationalist Air Force, though weak, held a self-evident mastery of the skies, since the Communists had no aircraft at all. The Nationalists could thus readily spot enemy concentrations, and rapidly airlift reinforcements or supplies to threatened points. Theoretically, then, the general situation was in their favor, so far as the pitched battles of positional warfare were concerned. But the Red armies of Lin Piao, composed of equal numbers of Manchurians and northern Chinese and supported by numerous Mongol cavalrymen, had succeeded in seizing many Japanese arms depots, particularly at Mukden, Tsitsihar, and Harbin, immediately after the Russian withdrawal. Moreover, they were in a strategically favorable position, which they improved by employing aggressive guerrilla warfare and severing the Nationalists' umbilical cord of rail communications, despite the presence of "peace preservation corps" and "pacification columns."

Finally, it must be recognized that man for man, Mao's troops were clearly superior to Chiang's. The Nationalist armies, except for those composed of the veterans of the Burma campaign, were fully representative of the classical tradition in Chinese armies: in other words, they were undisciplined, poorly trained, completely lacking in morale, and ready, from corporal on up to general, to change sides whenever circumstances beckoned. With the Communists, things were far different. Once again, the historical lesson of the wars of religion was to be repeated: the more fanatical side is always more daring, more enterprising; the majority, trusting in its superior strength, lacks nerve, and invariably garners only defeats.

Superficially, the military situation at the end of 1946 seemed very favorable to Chiang Kai-shek, and the Nationalist press services circulated a constant stream of victory bulletins. In reality, however, the Communists were as strong as ever, and the Kuomintang was digging its own grave.

CHAPTER VII ✧

The Last Attempts at
Reconciliation

THE day after General Marshall's departure from China, the State Department published a personal statement in which this great and good man analyzed, with his customary frankness and clarity, the situation in China.

In the first place, the greatest obstacle to peace has been the complete, almost overwhelming suspicion with which the Chinese Communist Party and the Kuomintang regard each other.

On the one hand, the leaders of the Government are strongly opposed to a communistic form of government. On the other, the Communists frankly state that they are Marxists and intend to work toward establishing a communistic form of government in China, though first advancing through the medium of a democratic form of government of the American or British type.

The leaders of the Government are convinced in their minds that the Communist-expressed desire to participate in a government of the type endorsed by the Political Consultative Conference last January had for its purpose only a destructive intention. The Communists felt, I believe, that the government was insincere in its apparent acceptance of the PCC resolutions for the formation of the new government and intended by coercion of military force and the action of secret police to obliterate the

Communist Party. Combined with this mutual deep distrust was the conspicuous error by both parties of ignoring the effect of the fears and suspicions of the other party in estimating the reason for proposals or opposition regarding the settlement of various matters under negotiation. They each sought only to take counsel of their own fears. They both, therefore, to that extent took a rather lopsided view of each situation and were susceptible to every evil suggestion or possibility. This complication was exaggerated to an explosive degree by the confused reports of fighting on the distant and tremendous fronts of hostile military contact. Patrol clashes were deliberately magnified into large offensive actions. The distortion of the facts was utilized by both sides to heap condemnation on the other. It was only through the reports of American officers in the field teams from Executive Headquarters that I could get even a partial idea of what was actually happening and the incidents were too numerous and the distances too great for the American personnel to cover all of the ground. . .

I think the most important factors involved in the recent breakdown of negotiations are these: On the side of the National Government, which is in effect the Kuomintang, there is a dominant group of reactionaries who have been opposed, in my opinion, to almost every effort I have made to influence the formation of a genuine coalition government. . . They were quite frank in publicly stating their belief that cooperation by the Chinese Communist Party in the government was inconceivable and that only a policy of force could definitely settle the issue. This group includes military as well as political leaders.

On the side of the Chinese Communist Party there are, I believe, liberals as well as radicals, though this view is vigorously opposed by many who believe that the Chinese Communist Party discipline is too rigidly enforced to admit of such differences of viewpoint. Nevertheless, it has appeared to me that there is a definite liberal group among the Communists, especially of young men who have turned to the Communists in disgust at the corruption evident in the local governments—men who would put the interest of the Chinese people above ruthless measures to establish a Communist ideology in the immediate future.

The dyed-in-the-wool Communists do not hesitate at the most drastic measures to gain their end as, for instance, the destruction of communications in order to wreck the economy of China and produce a situation that would facilitate the overthrow or collapse of the Government, without any regard to the immediate suffering of the people involved. They completely distrust the leaders of the Kuomintang and appear convinced that every Government proposal is designed to crush the Chinese Communist Party. I must say that the quite evidently inspired mob actions of last February and March, some within a few blocks of where I was then engaged in completing negotiations, gave the Communists good excuse for such suspicions.

However, a very harmful and immensely provocative phase of the Chinese Communist Party procedure has been in the character of its propaganda. I wish to state to the American people that in the deliberate misrepresentation and abuse of the action, policies and purposes of our Government this propaganda has been without regard for the truth, without any regard whatsoever for the facts, and has given plain evidence of a determined purpose to mislead the Chinese people and the world and to arouse a bitter hatred of Americans.

It has been difficult to remain silent in the midst of such public abuse and wholesale disregard of facts, but a denial would merely lead to the necessity of daily denials; an intolerable course of action for an American official. In the interest of fairness, I must state that the Nationalist Government publicity agency has made numerous misrepresentations, though not of the vicious nature of the Communist propaganda. Incidentally, the Communist statements regarding the Anping incident . . . were almost pure fabrication, deliberately representing a carefully arranged ambuscade of a Marine convoy with supplies for the maintenance of Executive Headquarters and some UNRRA supplies, as a defense against a Marine assault. The investigation of this incident was a tortuous procedure of delays and maneuvers to disguise the true and privately admitted facts of the case.

Sincere efforts to achieve settlement have been frustrated time and again by extremist elements of both sides. The agreements reached by the Political Consultative Conference a year ago were a liberal and forward-looking charter which then offered China a basis for peace and reconstruction. However, irreconcilable groups within the Kuomintang, interested in the preservation of their own feudal control of China, evidently had no real intention of implementing them. . .

I have never been in a position to be certain of the development of attitudes in the innermost Chinese Communist circles. Most certainly, the course which the Chinese Communist Party has pursued in recent months indicated an unwillingness to make a fair compromise. It has been impossible even to get them to sit down at a conference table with Government representatives to discuss given issues. Now the Communists have broken off negotiations by their last offer which demanded the dissolution of the National Assembly and a return to the military positions of January 13th which the Government could not be expected to accept.

Between this dominant reactionary group in the Government and the irreconcilable Communists who, I must state, did not so appear last February, lies the problem of how peace and well-being are to be brought to the long-suffering and presently inarticulate mass of the people of China. The reactionaries in the Government have evidently counted on substantial American support regardless of their actions. The Communists by their unwillingness to compromise in the national interest are evidently counting on an economic collapse to bring about the fall of the Government, accelerated by extensive guerrilla action against the long lines of rail communications—regardless of the cost in suffering to the Chinese people.

The salvation of the situation, as I see it, would be the assumption of leadership by the liberals in the Government and in the minority parties, a splendid group of men, but who as yet lack the political power to exercise a controlling influence. Successful action on their part under the leadership of Generalissimo Chiang Kai-shek would, I believe, lead to unity through good government.[1]

It is quite clear that this last sentence was no more than the expression of a pious hope, and that Marshall had fully grasped the true nature of the situation.

[1] U.S. Department of State, *United States Relations with China, with Special Reference to the Period 1944–1949* (U.S. Government Printing Office, 1949), pp. 686–688. *Tr.*

Nevertheless, the Nationalist government at the beginning of 1947 proposed an unconditional cease-fire; but the Red response was to demand, as preliminary conditions, the abolition of the constitution and the withdrawal of Nationalist forces to the line of 13 January 1946.

On 10 January, in a speech broadcast by the Yenan radio, Chou En-lai clearly indicated a reversal of Communist policy. Taking clever advantage of Marshall's criticisms of the Kuomintang, he said:

General Marshall admitted that there is a reactionary group in the Kuomintang which constitutes a dominant one in the Kuomintang government, and which includes military and political leaders. They oppose a coalition government, have no confidence in internal cooperation, but believe in the settlement of problems by armed force. They have no sincerity in carrying out the PCC resolutions. All these remarks are true. But what is to be regretted is that he did not point out that Chiang Kai-shek is the highest leader of this reactionary group. . . He continues to act against the PCC agreements in massing 280 brigades (formerly divisions), 90 percent of his total military strength, to attack the communist-held liberated areas. Up to the end of last year, his armies invaded 174,000 square kilometers and took 165 cities in the liberated areas. . . When it was advantageous for Chiang to launch an attack, he would not hesitate to attack. But when he was defeated and required time to regroup his troops, for instance (he was in such a pass last January and February), he would favor the halting of the war and conducted the so-called peace talks. . .

The Chinese Communists have unremittingly exposed and lodged protests against American aid to Chiang Kai-shek's government troops in the form of transportation, lend-lease materials, surplus property, warships and airplanes, military advisors and technical training, and the colonial policy of the American imperialists. . .[2]

At the same time, the Communist information chief, Lu Ting-i, published a memorandum entitled "Explanation of

[2] *Ibid.*, pp. 707–709. *Tr.*

Several Basic Questions Concerning the Post-War International Situation,"[3] in which the pro-Russian and anti-American attitude of the Chinese Communists was clearly spelled out. He commenced by citing Mao Tse-tung: "There is now a strong U.S.S.R. in the world, and peoples who are organized and awakened. The victory over the Fascists (Germans and Japanese) has opened the road to victory for the people's struggle in the post-war period." As a result of this post-war situation "the anti-democratic forces will be compelled to attack and the democratic forces will, inevitably, be victorious." As for the United States, "American imperialists have taken the place of German, Italian, and Japanese fascists in the world, aided by reactionaries in some countries: Churchill in England, de Gaulle in France, Chiang in China, and by Fascist remnants in others: Franco in Spain, Yoshida in Japan, Schacht and von Papen in Germany." After a violent attack against a United States which was accused of arming to the teeth, establishing its bases everywhere, and searching for ways to unleash war against the U.S.S.R., Lu asserted that "the Soviet Union is the defender of world peace" while "the real policy of the United States is to oppress the American people and the peoples of all the capitalist, colonial, and semi-colonial countries." It was the approach of an American "economic crisis" which forced the imperialists to increase the violence of their attacks, and Lu did not hesitate to declare that "the American economic crisis will come this year (1947) or the next." At this point, what were the relative strengths of the two sides in this world struggle? The people's democracies, and the Communist parties in France, in England, in the colonial and semicolonial countries, were all making progress. Strikes were spreading everywhere. "The international position of the most progressive nation in the world, the U.S.S.R.,

[3] For the full text, see *ibid.*, pp. 710–719. *Tr.*

has greatly improved." The reactionaries were still strong, but they were isolated and their strength was diminishing. "In summary, world-wide progressivism, the successes of the U.S.S.R., and the American crisis are three factors of decisive significance in the history of the future development of mankind. Let us march then," Lu concluded, "down the road to victory. The struggle will be a hard one, but we will win. We need only look at our adversaries' lack of confidence, their fear of the U.S.S.R., their abhorrence of the truth, to know that we shall prevail. It can be categorically predicted that, within three to five years at the most, the face of China and of the world will be completely changed."

Despite this public position, which should have shattered the last illusions of those who had maintained that the Chinese Communist Party was in no way an orthodox Communist party, Dr. Stuart forwarded to Yenan new truce proposals from the Nationalist government. His effort was in vain. On 1 February 1947 the Central Committee of the CCP denounced all agreements which had been signed after 10 January 1946. On 5 March the Nationalist government "invited" the last Communist representatives remaining in Nanking, Chungking, and Shanghai to leave its territory. The Communist newspaper in Chungking was shut down. Despite a last maneuver by Molotov in the Council of Foreign Ministers at Moscow on 10 March, the break was complete. Now the guns would speak: *Ultima ratio regum.*

PART THREE

1947
THE COMMUNISTS RESTORE
THE SITUATION AND
TAKE THE OFFENSIVE

CHAPTER VIII

1947: The First Six Months

Military operations in China during the first half of 1947 can be characterized as follows: strategically, the Nationalists sought to split the Communist zones in North China by gaining firm control of the main lines of communication—first of the Peking-Hankow railroad, in order to cut off Communist bases in the Shantung-Kiangsu region from the Red stronghold of Shensi-Shansi; and then of the Tsinan-Pukow and Kiaochow-Tsinan railroads, in order to slice up the Shantung zone itself. Concurrently, in Manchuria they strengthened their positions along the Sungari river and prepared an offensive against Harbin, while attempting to consolidate their rear areas in Liaoning and Jehol. Lastly, in order to obtain a spectacular success and enhance their prestige, they launched an attack against the Red capital at Yenan. This attack, mounted by the best troops the Nationalists had, was to succeed in taking the city; but it was to have no influence upon the course of operations other than to permit the Reds to perform a very pretty maneuver which put the attacking Nationalists, stranded in the wastes of Shensi, in an extremely tenuous position.

For their part the Communists, who sought to implement a strategy which would maintain at all costs the "horizontal" link between Yenan and Shantung, conducted a fiercely determined defense in North China. In Manchuria, which was to become Chiang's "strategic trap," the Reds launched diversionary offensives designed to draw and fix as many enemy divisions—which would be difficult for the Nationalists to resupply and reinforce[1]—as possible. Tactically, the Nationalists' superiority in numbers and armament[2] was to force the Reds to continue the practice of their cherished methods of guerrilla warfare: the refusal of battle in open country, the fast-moving raids on garrisons and isolated units, the rapid retreat and "disappearance" when the Nationalists concentrated in strength. For the Red leaders, the paramount point was to inflict more losses upon the enemy than they themselves suffered and, above all, to seize the maximum amount of modern arms. Remarkably well led and well trained, Communist units were to succeed brilliantly in the accomplishment of these ends. With their rapidity of movement, their discipline, their morale, their offensive spirit, the Red troops were gradually to overcome their disadvantages in matériel; by June of 1947 they would begin to abandon their guerrilla tactics, and to undertake the large-scale operations which were soon to prove decisive.

In April 1947 a French observer, commenting on Communist operations in southern Shansi, wrote:

The Communist plan clearly shows not only the sound logic of its conception, but a perfect unity of views in the Communist high command, since it calls for close coordination between the

[1] As of March 1947, 227 of Chiang Kai-shek's total of 248 regular brigades were committed either at the front or as garrisons in active theaters of operation. This left him a reserve of only twenty-one brigades.

[2] At the end of 1946 the government had 2,600,000 men under arms, against a Communist strength of 1,100,000. With regard to rifles, the Nationalists—despite the capture of large stocks of Japanese weapons by the Reds in Manchuria—still had a three- or four-to-one superiority.

theaters of operation commanded by General Ho Lung and by General Liu Po-ch'eng. This is in marked contrast to the Nationalists, who have always found it extremely difficult to get their generals to work together, and even more so to get them to do it on their own initiative.

As regards tactical operations, this observer gave the following examples:

The capture of Houma cost the Reds two hundred killed and wounded, but brought them eighteen hundred prisoners, including a brigadier general. The capture of the town of Sinkiang cost them four wounded, and they took six hundred prisoners from the seven hundred militia who tried to defend the place. The capture of Kuwo, defended by two Nationalist regiments and attacked by three Red regiments, yielded the Communists two thousand prisoners—the entire garrison. Taking into account the fact that the Nationalists do not bother to destroy their weapons before they surrender, these operations were the kind of "paying propositions" General Chu Teh likes to talk about. The lack of fighting spirit shown by the common soldier demonstrates the degree to which the Nationalist army has disintegrated. The easy successes of the Communists can be explained only by their superior morale. After Communist indoctrination and political instruction, the ex-Nationalist soldier, typically passive and disheartened until then, becomes an enthusiastic and aggressive fighting man.

And this perspicacious observer concluded:

When they are not positively hostile, the people show no sympathy at all for the Nationalists. Nationalist generals pay no attention to one another. Their troops do not want to fight. They have no effective weapon against a resolute and elusive enemy. The American aid they get ends up in the hands of the Communists, often right after the first fight. If military factors alone were involved, there would be no doubt at all about the outcome of this war.

OPERATIONS IN MANCHURIA

After the operations of late 1946, the front in northern Manchuria stabilized along the arc of the Sungari River. But within the triangle Taolaichao-Changchun-Kirin, during the first half of 1947, the Reds were to launch, one after the other, five offensives. Originally diversionary in nature, these offensives were at first designed to diminish Nationalist pressure in Shantung; but they were to end in a major Communist victory. General Lin Piao, who had only about 300,000 men for this vast Manchurian front—a relatively small force, despite the almost total support of the population—launched his first attack, with sixty thousand men, on 6 January 1947. Three groups crossed the frozen Sungari and headed for Changchun and Kirin. Advancing southward down the Harbin-Changchun railroad from Wukoshu, the northern group isolated Nationalist garrisons, cut communications, and by 13 January reached Chengtzekai, about fifty miles north of Changchun. The second group, which moved out to the west from Paikitun, located on the Sungari to the south of the Willow Wall, seized the power station at Kiutai on the 15th, thus depriving the Manchurian capital of light and water. Finally, the third group, which departed from Wulakai, advanced southward to the immediate vicinity of Kirin.

The success of the Reds was short-lived. As early as 15 January the Nationalists, having concentrated their forces at Kirin, unleashed a counteroffensive which, moving northward along both banks of the Sungari, threatened to trap the advancing Red forces. Retiring in haste but leaving few prisoners to the Nationalists, the Communists were forced to recross the Sungari, pursued by forces from Changchun. On the twenty-fifth Wukoshu was retaken by the Nationalists. Lin

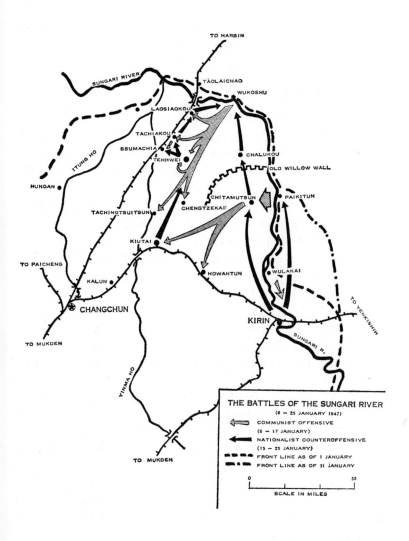

TO HARBIN

SUNGARI RIVER

TÀOLAICHAO

WUKOSHU

LAOSIAOKOU

TACHIAKOU

SSUMACHIA

TEHHWEI

CHALUKOU

OLD WILLOW WALL

ITUNG HO

NUNGAN

CHITAMUTSUN

CHENGTZEKAI

PAIKITUN

TACHINGTSUITSUN

KIUTAI

TO PAICHENG

KALUN

HOWANTUN

WULAKAI

CHANGCHUN

KIRIN

TO MUKDEN

SUNGARI R.

TO YENKISHIN

YINMA HO

THE BATTLES OF THE SUNGARI RIVER
(6 – 25 JANUARY 1947)

COMMUNIST OFFENSIVE
(6 – 17 JANUARY)

NATIONALIST COUNTEROFFENSIVE
(15 – 25 JANUARY)

FRONT LINE AS OF 1 JANUARY

FRONT LINE AS OF 31 JANUARY

TO MUKDEN

0   30

SCALE IN MILES

Piao had been completely defeated. The Nationalists, noisily optimistic, announced a forthcoming attack on Harbin.

Nevertheless, on 16 February the Reds launched a new attack to the northwest of Changchun, and then crossed the Sungari on the 23rd at the same places as in January. Moving as rapidly as they had in their first offensive, the Reds by the 24th again threatened to deprive Changchun of light and water. Severe fighting took place around Kirin and along the Kirin-Changchun railroad. But once again Red strength proved to be insufficient and, after a lull in the fighting, the government's New First Army counterattacked along the three railroads running from Changchun to Taoan, Harbin, and Kirin. The Reds were thrown back to their positions behind the Sungari, and the Nationalists again cried victory.

But Lin Piao left them little respite. Renewing his attack on 10 March, a three-day advance again found him a few miles from Changchun; but once again, as in some figure of a well-rehearsed ballet, Lin was forced to fall back to his starting point. This third failure was balanced, however, by Communist successes in the area to the east of Kirin and Mukden near the Korean border, where the Reds invested Tunghwa, and in the Tungliao valley, about seventy-five miles west of Changchun.

The Manchurian front remained quiet in April, and the Nationalists were able to effect a change of command in which General Sun Li-jen,[3] the defender of Changchun and commander of the New First Army, was replaced by General P'an Yü-kun. The Red offensives during the first three months of the year had worn out the Nationalist troops. Dissension among their commanders, poor leadership, the insecurity which prevailed outside the cities, had sapped their morale.

---

[3] A V.M.I. graduate and veteran of the Burma campaign, Sun was regarded by Stilwell as the ablest of the Nationalist field commanders. *Tr.*

Thus the Red offensive in May, perfectly prepared and executed, was to be an overwhelming success.

For this offensive, Lin Piao divided his forces into four groups. The first, in the north, commanded by Lu Cheng-ts'ao, was composed of two columns which were concentrated to the west of the Sungari between Talai and Fuyu, along the Changchun-Taoan railroad. The second group was north of the Sungari in the Yushu area. The third group was concentrated in the Hweinan area to the east of the Mukden-Kirin railroad, about fifty miles to the east of Szepingkai. Finally, a fourth and weaker group, consisting of Mongolian cavalry, was concentrated to the west of Mukden. To these regular forces were added the Red guerrillas, who were already in action along the railroads. On the Nationalist side, part of the forces were concentrated as garrisons for Changchun, Kirin, and Mukden, but a large number were scattered along the railroads to defend the stations and bridges.

The Red offensive, their fifth, was launched on 10 May 1947. The northern column marched south, isolated Nungan, and threatened Changchun by seizing, as early as the 18th, the city's airfield. Continuing its advance, it took Kungchuling on the evening of the 19th, but the Seventy-first Army retook the city on the 23rd. Szepingkai was encircled by the Reds on the 25th. Simultaneously, the southwest group, in a move designed to prevent the Mukden garrison (New Sixth Army) from coming to the aid of Changchun, attacked and took Faku and Kangping on the 24th. A state of siege was proclaimed at Mukden. The eastern group reduced the Nationalist bridgehead on the Sungari, to the east of Kirin, crossed the river, and on 17 May encircled Kirin, whose garrison shut themselves up in the city and proclaimed martial law. Lastly, the Communist group in the southeast cut the Mukden-Kirin railroad at Tsingyuan on 15 May and took Tunghwa on the

25th. Confronted by this catastrophic situation, the Nationalists made a grave decision: they abandoned the Liaotung Peninsula and concentrated their forces around Mukden. Thanks to a massive effort by their attack aircraft and their unhindered use of air transport, the Nationalists succeeded in the resupply and reinforcement of their encircled garrisons, and finally managed to re-establish a precarious link between Mukden, Changchun, and Kirin.

The Communists used the early days of June to exploit their successes. By 10 June, only Szepingkai still held out in the area between Mukden and Changchun. In the southeastern sector the Fourteenth and Fifty-second armies, which had held Liaotung for the Nationalists, succeeded in making their way north and concentrating anew at Mukden; but this success, requiring as it did the abandonment of Antung, led to the fall of that city, and of considerable matériel, to the Reds on 10 June. On the 20th Liaoyang, in its turn, succumbed to the Reds. By 16 June the Communist tide was at its height. Kirin and Changchun had been isolated. The Reds had entered Szepingkai. Mukden was now threatened from the north, the east, and the south. Finally, all of Liaotung was now in Communist hands.

Nevertheless, the arrival of the Fifty-second and Fourteenth armies at Mukden now permitted the Nationalist high command to retake the offensive. These two armies attacked along the railroads leading out of Mukden, while the New First Army and the Eighth Army (formerly a puppet army of the Japanese) launched similar attacks from Changchun and Kirin. Jumping off simultaneously from Mukden and Changchun, the attacking Nationalist forces succeeded in linking up on 2 July, after retaking Szepingkai. On 9 July the Nationalists announced the "liberation" of the Mukden-Changchun railroad. Contact between Changchun and Kirin had been restored on 29 June; but the greater part of the Kirin-Mukden railroad remained in the hands of the Reds, who also retained their hold on the line from Yingkow to Tashihkiao.

As of 10 July, when torrential rains brought operations to a halt, the balance sheet of battle reveals the disaster that had befallen Chiang Kai-shek: loss of half the Nationalist-occupied territory in Manchuria; abandonment of two thirds of the railroads; enormous losses of matériel, weapons, and supplies of all sorts. The low morale of the government's troops had caused a great number of desertions which, when added to combat losses, had reduced the strength of all Nationalist units by an average of over fifty per cent. Some units had been particularly hard hit: after the battles at Hwaite and Kung-chuling, the 88th Infantry Division of the Seventy-first Army, for example, had been reduced to the strength of a battalion. All the fleeing garrisons had abandoned considerable amounts of matériel, leaving entire depots and supply trains to the Reds, and many organic vehicles and weapons as well. Along the railroads, bridges had been destroyed, the ties torn up and burnt, the rails thrown into the fires and twisted into uselessness.

Although the Reds were not yet capable of standing up against continuous and massive attacks employing modern matériel and air power, they showed a degree of mobility and flexibility which enabled them to evade most of the blows leveled against them. Their discipline and morale were incomparably better than the Nationalists'. This is proved by the ratio between the weapons lost by the Communists and the number of Red prisoners and dead: one rifle, five prisoners, fifty dead.[4] If after two months of uninterrupted operations they stood in need of a certain amount of regrouping and re-

---

[4] It is interesting to note that figures from Nationalist sources, though undoubtedly exaggerated in absolute terms, reflect the same ratio.

equipping, they had lost little of their combat effectiveness. This fact is even more remarkable when it is realized that in Manchuria the great majority of Communist troops, cadre as well as fillers, were local recruits whose training, in theory at any rate, could not be compared with that of Chiang's "Burma veterans" or the Japanese-trained puppet troops of what had formerly been Manchukuo.

The American Consul General at Mukden reported the real situation at the end of May 1947:

In past two months [the] morale [of] Nationalist forces has deteriorated at rapidly accelerating pace. Present serious state of their demoralization has been confirmed to us by many sources . . . and has become matter of wide public knowledge and talk. It is reflected in jumpy nerves of military garrison, efforts to evade conscription, and reliable information from all sectors of Nationalist territory (including points distant from current fighting) indicating that Nationalists in a panicky state are feverishly building trench systems everywhere with only "Maginot" defense strategy in mind. There is good evidence that apathy, resentment, and defeatism are spreading fast in Nationalist ranks causing surrenders and desertions. Main factors contributing to this are Communists' ever-mounting numerical superiority (resulting from greater use [of] native recruits, aid from underground and Korean units), National soldiers' discouragement over prospects [of] getting reinforcements, better solidarity and fighting spirit of Communists, losses and exhaustion of Nationalists, their growing indignation over disparity between officers' enrichment and soldiers' low pay, life, and their lack of interest in fighting far from home among "alien" unfriendly populace (whereas Communists being largely natives are in position of fighting for native soil).[5]

Confronted by such a situation, it would appear that Chiang Kai-shek should have written off Manchuria com-

<hr>

[5] U.S. Department of State, *United States Relations with China, with Special Reference to the Period 1944–1949* (U.S. Government Printing Office, 1949), pp. 315–316. *Tr.*

pletely, in order to concentrate all his forces in North China while he still had a certain superiority in numbers and armament. But the Generalissimo did not want to "lose face." He satisfied himself with firing a scapegoat, General Tu Yü-ming. Persisting in his attempt to hold on in Manchuria, an increasingly difficult operation, he was to bury his best troops in this "far-off land." As the American White Paper so rightly concludes, the Communist victories must be attributed primarily to the "military ineptness of the Government,"[6] reflected by this overextension in Manchuria; and it was in Manchuria that the Kuomintang cause was lost.

THE BATTLE OF SHANTUNG

While these disasters were befalling the Nationalists in Manchuria, a bitter struggle was raging in Shantung, a major Communist stronghold which the Nationalists wanted to seize before moving on into Hopeh, Shansi, and the Red "Border Region" of Shenkanning. Once again the struggle centered around the control of the railroads. Shantung is crossed from north to south by the Tsinpu railroad (Tsinan-Pukow), and from east to west by the Kiaotsi (Kiaochow-Tsinan) and the eastern part of the Lunghai (Sian-Kaifeng-Suchow-Tunghai). The Nationalists had controlled almost all of the last two lines since late 1946; they now sought to open a way to the north, so as to link the Tsinan-Tsingtao corridor to the rest of the territories under their control.

But Chiang, always seeking particularly prestigious successes, decided to commence his campaign with the capture of Lini, an important commercial center, the capital of the Communist zone in Shantung, and the headquarters of General Ch'en I. The battle, which pitted eight Nationalist divisions

[6] *Ibid.*, p. 314. *Tr.*

—half of them mechanized and American-equipped—with air support, against no more than six Red divisions, opened in December with a Nationalist advance which carried as far as Tsangshan. But on 1 January the Reds counterattacked with their customary dash, hitting the Nationalist flanks with night and dawn attacks boldly executed after rapid marches and carefully coordinated with guerrilla harassment of the Nationalist rear. By 23 January the Reds were threatening Taierhchwang and the Grand Canal; they had also made prisoners of several Nationalist generals, cut the Lunghai railroad, and seized the mining center of Tsangshan. The situation of the Nationalists had clearly become critical when a new defection of General Ho P'eng-chu, who suddenly changed sides and went back to Chiang Kai-shek on 23 January, forced the Communists to break off their attack toward Suchow. During the war against the Japanese, Ho P'eng-chu had commanded the Nanking puppet government's forces in the Shantung region; he had rallied to Chiang in 1945 and then, on 9 January 1946, had gone over to the Reds with his four divisions, totaling forty thousand men, who held the coast of Shantung between Liangcheng and the mouth of the Shu. Although Ch'en I had never really trusted Ho's "New United Army of Central China" and was quickly able to react to its loss, the new threat to his capital from the east forced him to abandon his offensive.

The defection of Ho P'eng-chu brought with it an inordinate increase in the confidence of the Nationalists, who now wanted to do three things all at once: capture Lini; clear the Tsinpu railroad to the north; and trap Ch'en I's troops between the Kiaotsi rail line and the Nationalist troops advancing from the east and south. Despite a vigorous Communist counterattack in the first days of February, Ch'en I was forced to evacuate his headquarters, and the victorious Nationalists entered Lini on 15 February. As usual, they found their prize to be completely devoid of Red troops, all of whom had vanished. Once again the Nationalists were faced with the same dilemma: they had either to mass their forces, in order to push the Reds back and seize the cities—a ponderous solution incapable of bringing the elusive enemy to decisive battle; or they could scatter out to clear the countryside—a hazardous solution which ran the risk of exposing thinly deployed forces to defeat in detail. In view of General Ch'en I's exceptional talents, this last possibility became a strong probability.

In 1947 Ch'en I was forty-eight years old, a short, stubby man, quick-moving and quick-talking. He always wore a beret, pulled down almost to his ears; beneath a scraggly moustache a cigarette perpetually protruded from his mouth, one side of which continually drooped in a sardonic sort of half-smile. At first sight he gave, with his rough manner, an impression of coarseness; but this impression would soon yield to an awareness of the lively intelligence reflected in his eyes. And this man, a master of disconcerting irony, was also a poet and an ardent lover of art and the theater. He had studied in France, where he won his degree in electrical engineering. His inquiring mind had led him to take a job as a common workman in the Michelin plant at Clermont-Ferrand, where he worked for some time, and in the Creusot works as well: it also led him into a new belief in Communist doctrine. Upon his return to China he immediately joined the Red troops in the Kiangsi-Fukien region,[7] where he commanded a band of guerrillas. When the Chinese Red Army started off on its "Long March," Ch'en was left behind with General Yeh T'ing, and took command of one of the divisions in Yeh's newly organ-

---

[7] According to several other authorities, Ch'en returned to China in 1921, and did not join the Red Army until 1927, at the time of the Nanchang Uprising. Tr.

ized Fourth Army. He also became Yeh's second-in-command, and took over the New Fourth Army as its acting commander when Yeh was arrested by the Nationalists in 1941. Upon Yeh's death in a plane crash in 1946, after his release from Nationalist captivity, Ch'en was officially confirmed as commander of the Communist New Fourth Army. He also confirmed his reputation as a master in the art of prompt retreats and unexpected reappearances, becoming so famous for this in Shantung that the peasants would say, of each Red victory: "Ch'en I is back at the front."

Meanwhile, following their capture of Lini, the Nationalists undertook to move back up the Tsinpu railroad, and entered Yihsien on 17 February, Tenghsien on the twenty-fourth, and Tsowhsien on the 25th. They found nothing before them but a void, the Reds having suddenly withdrawn to the east. On the 28th, Kufow, the home of Confucius, fell into their hands. To the Nationalists, everything now seemed to be going their way. In a move designed to trap Ch'en I's elusive forces, the government's Twelfth and Seventy-third armies, under General Wang Yao-wu, now pushed southward from Poshan, near the Kiaotsi rail line, toward a link-up at Lini with the Nationalist forces in the south.

The Red reaction was truly remarkable. While Ch'en I's troops hit hard at the flanks of the Nationalist armies moving southward and also harassed the Kiaotsi railroad in their rear, the Red forces of General Liu Po-ch'eng, coming all the way from Hopeh, crossed the Lunghai railroad and threatened Suchow from the southwest in a move calculated to compel the Nationalists to withdraw from northern Shantung.

In the face of the concurrent Communist threats to Tsinan and Suchow, the Nationalists were forced to abandon their southward march on Lini and pull back for the defense of the Kiaotsi railroad. They tried in vain to trap the forces of Liu Po-ch'eng, which had ventured far from their base in Hopeh;

but Liu, after having saved Ch'en I from a serious threat of encirclement, at the end of February withdrew to the north of the Lunghai rail line. Better yet for the Reds, they had succeeded in cutting the Kiaotsi railroad between Weihsien and Yehsien, thus restoring a direct link between their zones in Hopeh and northern Shantung.

In March, however, a mighty effort by the Nationalists brought their southern forces, which took Tawenkow on 27 March and arrived at Taian on 1 April, to a successful linkup with the forces of General Wang Yao-wu, who pushed southward from Tsinan to meet them at Taian on 2 April. A precarious connection was thus established between Tsinan and Suchow, but the rail line continued to be subjected to the unceasing attacks of Communist guerrillas. In April the Nationalists attempted a link-up at Mengyin, moving Ou Ch'en's forces eastward from the Tsinpu railroad and T'ang En-po's troops northward from Lini; the attempt failed under the counterattacks of ten Communist columns, numbering about ten thousand men each. Ch'en I's skillful maneuvering had denied the Nationalists any decisive results.

Resuming their efforts on 1 May, Ou Ch'en and T'ang En-po finally succeeded, at the price of considerable losses, in effecting their junction in the Mengyin area. In the erroneous belief that they had destroyed the enemy, they made the dangerous mistake of dividing their forces and venturing forth in divergent directions. Ou Ch'en moved northward toward Poshan, while T'ang En-po charged off to the east against Ishui, which he attacked in conjunction with other Nationalist forces moving northward from Lini. On 16 May, the left flank of the forces which were moving on Ishui from Mengyin was hit by a Communist counterattack that threw the troops of T'ang En-po into a complete rout. The Nationalists were forced, at least temporarily, to give up their attempts to cut off the Shantung peninsula from the rest of China. Moreover, the following months saw them become bogged down in a series of difficult mountain operations which cost them enormous losses in men and matériel and brought them nothing in the way of really positive results. As of 1 July the Communists still retained their hold upon the peninsular portion of Shantung, more than half of the central plain, and the Weihsien-Yehsien isthmus.

But also by 1 July the Nationalists, for their part, had succeeded in completely clearing the Tsinpu railroad between Tsinan and Suchow and carving out a large corner of southern Shantung. This dearly bought success led Mao and Chu Teh to decide upon a major redisposition of Red forces. In Shantung, Red guerrillas, militiamen, and newly formed regular columns were left with the task of spreading confusion throughout the enemy's rear areas and harassing the Kiaotsi and Tsinpu railroads. From Hopeh, Liu Po-ch'eng attacked southward along a broad front. Since this attack denuded southern Hopeh of Red troops, Ch'en I's regulars were moved out of Shantung to replace Liu Po-ch'eng's forces in southern Hopeh. The Nationalists were unable to prevent this major shift of Communist forces. Although Ch'en I's departure permitted them to reach the Gulf of Laichow and thus, in theory, to accomplish their mission, they never really conquered peninsular Shantung. This hard campaign, which cost the Nationalists considerable losses, did little to diminish the Communists' powers of resistance.

OPERATIONS IN HOPEH AND SHANSI, AND THE ATTACK ON YENAN

During the first half of 1947 the struggle in Hopeh and Shansi was characterized by the inability of the Nationalists to exert effective control in the territories which, theoretically, were under their authority, and by the ease with which Communist guerrillas severed communications and gradually became a threat even to the large cities. In Hopeh, a key position which permitted the Reds to implement their "horizontal plan" and maintain contact between the Shenkanning Border Region and Shantung, General Liu Po-ch'eng had no difficulty in repelling the attacks of Hu Tsung-nan, whose twelve divisions were little more than equal in strength to Liu's. As for General Fu Tso-yi, who held Peking for the Nationalists, he kept open the Peking-Paoting-Chengting portion of the Pinghan railroad; but he never succeeded in clearing even a short stretch of the Tsinpu line.

In Shansi, General Hu's government troops received no support at all from the forces of Yen Hsi-shan, who was satisfied merely to protect the Chengtai railroad (Chengting-Taiyuan). This inaction delivered almost all of the province into the hands of the Reds, who also seized the arsenal at Chaoyi on 21 January 1947. When they perceived that the Nationalists, inspired only by the desire to obtain a prestigious success, had made the strategic error of committing considerable force to the sterile conquest of Yenan, the Reds gradually built Shansi into their principal base of maneuver. Repeated Red attacks hemmed Nationalist forces in Shansi into a few cities, whose garrisons were resupplied only by air. The Communists also harassed Yen Hsi-shan's troops along the Chengtai railroad and launched violent attacks against Shihkiachwang, near Chengting.

The Nationalist attack on Yenan was long in the making. For several months there was indecisive fighting around the fringes of the Shenkanning Border Region, particularly in the southern salient of the area. On 20 January the Nationalists seized the town of Malanchen, in the center of the salient, declaring that this operation was purely defensive in nature. In reality, major troop concentrations were effected there by the Nationalists, who then launched simultaneous attacks from four directions. In the north, the 22nd Infantry Division, operating under the orders of General Fu Tso-yi, pushed southward from Yulin. In the west, General Ma Hung-ku'ei's troops advanced eastward from Ningsia. From the southwest two cavalry divisions, based at Kingchwan, pushed to the north along the valley of the Tung. And from the south, General Hu Tsung-nan, with five well-trained and Russian-equipped divisions, on 15 March attacked in force northward between the Lo Ho and the Yellow River.

Facing these forces the Communists had barely half-a-dozen poorly equipped brigades, two of which were training units; they also had some militiamen, armed only with pikes, or rifles of venerable vintage. The Communists had long since anticipated the attack and were well prepared to evacuate the miserable "Border Region" and set themselves up in Shansi, where they now decided to establish the new seat of their government. Ho Lung's defending Red troops were therefore quite content to fight only delaying actions.

The Nationalists' main effort attacked in two columns, the right wing moving up the Yellow River and the left advancing directly upon Yenan from Lochwan. The left wing took Fuhsien on 15 March and Kanchuan on the 16th, and on the 18th was stopped at the Tahsiaolao pass by the last fortified position in front of Yenan. The right wing took Linchenchen on 15 March, veered to the left to seize Chengchiakou on the 17th, infiltrated the Yen Shui hills on the 18th, and arrived, during the night of 18–19 March, on the heights which dominate Yenan from the southeast. At 0800 hours on 19 March the 1st Division (of the left wing) led the Nationalist entry into Yenan, which was found to be completely empty. By this time the party's Central Committee was at Wayaopu, about

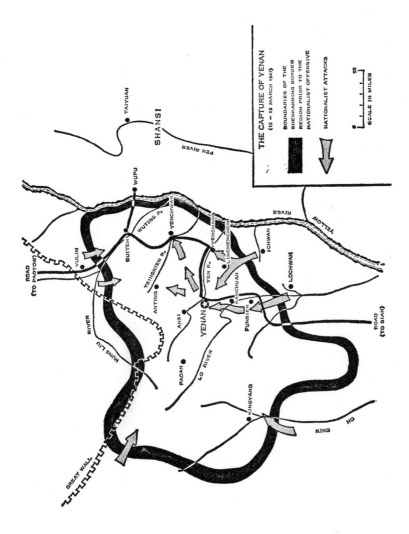

THE CAPTURE OF YENAN
(15 – 19 MARCH 1947)

BOUNDARIES OF THE
SHENKANNING BORDER
REGION PRIOR TO THE
NATIONALIST OFFENSIVE

NATIONALIST ATTACKS

SCALE IN MILES

fifteen miles north of their "capital," heading for a leisurely withdrawal down the Suiteh-Wupu road toward Shansi; the families were already at Suiteh, the radio transmitter at Wayaopu, and the administrative services at Anting.

The capture of Yenan, the capital of Chinese communism, was proclaimed to the world as a great triumph for Chiang Kai-shek. In reality it was only another false victory. The Nationalist armies had cast and drawn their net around a void. Henceforth, as they ventured forth into northern Shansi, they were to find themselves in a strategic situation which would lead only to their defeat.

CHAPTER IX

1947: The Last Six Months

Two Communist campaigns constituted the major developments of the last half of 1947. On the one hand, there were Lin Piao's sixth and seventh offensives in Manchuria which, without being decisive, achieved appreciable results and drained the Nationalists of their last reserves; on the other, southward envelopments by the armies of Ch'en Keng, Liu Po-ch'eng, and Ch'en I succeeded, to everyone's amazement, in establishing new Communist bases in Central China, near the north bank of the Yangtze itself. By the end of 1947 the Communists were to have almost made up their previous inferiority in numbers and armament, and were ready to undertake massive offensive operations.

THE NORTHEASTERN THEATER OF OPERATIONS

Following their defeat in the summer of 1947, the Nationalists had reorganized their high command in the Northeast, and the dualism that had existed between the Peace Preservation command (General Tu Yü-ming) and the Generalissimo's headquarters in this region (General Hsiung Shih-hui) had been suppressed through dissolution of the former. Both generals had been relieved of their commands and replaced by Chiang's Chief of the Supreme Staff, General Ch'en Ch'eng. The new commander had twenty-five divisions, divided into four groups; some of these troops were cooped up in the cities—Changchun, Kirin, Szepingkai, Mukden, and Fushun—which were the Nationalists' centers of resistance, and the rest were scattered among the isolated strong points along the railroads. No reserves were available, but Chiang had promised to send ten to twenty divisions as reinforcements.

On the Communist side, Lin Piao had somewhere between 250,000 and 300,000 men, twenty-five divisions, twenty of which were concentrated to the east of the Mukden-Changchun line around Meihokow, plus five "independent divisions." Supplementing these purely Chinese forces were some Koreans (who arrived, in fully trained and organized units, direct from North Korea), some Mongols, and some Japanese. The Communists were armed with Japanese matériel, taken from the Kwantung Army with Russian permission, and with weapons captured from the Nationalists. The Reds were well trained, fairly well supplied in ammunition by their arsenals, and well led. Their artillery consisted of horse-drawn 75 mm., 105 mm., and 155 mm. pieces, which they employed, following Russian practice, in massive concentrations. Gradually, they increased recruitment and training of Manchurian peasants to the point where they were to have no difficulty in replacing their losses.

During the breathing spell that remained to them, the Nationalists made feverish efforts to re-establish rail communications between Peking and Mukden, which were absolutely necessary to them if they were to receive reinforcements and resupply. Unfortunately, it is much easier to sabotage a railroad than it is to repair it or, what is even more difficult, to protect it. Despite the construction of thousands of pill boxes, and the parceling-out of tens of thousands of troops to man them, the Communists practically always succeeded in their sabotage, either by raids against small stations and bridges, or by mine-laying, rail removal, and razing of telephone poles. According to a Nationalist officer, there were, in September 1947, no more than one hundred Communists engaged in sabotage against the Peking-Paoting, Peking-Tientsin-Shanhaikwan, and Peking-Kupehkow railroads. Yet, during this single month, sixty-two successful sabotage operations, which destroyed 201 rails and 876 ties, were carried out by the Reds against these three lines.[1] Despite these difficulties, Nationalist railroadmen, with astonishing patience and great ingenuity, persisted in repair work which permitted the passage of several trains. But the necessary materials became increasingly scarce, and eventually the Nationalists were to find it impossible to assure the proper functioning of their transport services.

The sixth Communist offensive in Manchuria began on 15 September 1947. Carried out by troops of the Hopeh-Jehol-Liaoning military zone, it was directed at the Peking-Mukden railroad, between Chinchow and Shanhaikwan, with the isolation of Manchuria from North China as its strategic objective. Despite the reinforcement of the defending Nationalists the offensive was a complete success for the Communists, who cut the railroad about ninety-five miles south of Mukden and seized the molybdenum mines at Chinsi as well.

The second phase of the offensive opened on 1 October. Its objectives were to isolate the cities of Changchun, Kirin, and Szepingkai from Mukden, and to cut Mukden itself off from the ports at Hulutao and Yingkow. At the same time, the Communists organized foraging sweeps to seize the harvest in the areas controlled by their adversaries. In accordance

[1] Earlier, in July, comparable figures were: twenty-nine sabotage operations, fifty-five rails, and 534 ties.

133

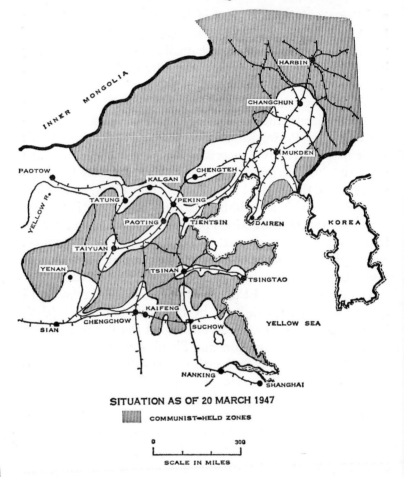

SITUATION AS OF 20 MARCH 1947

▥ COMMUNIST-HELD ZONES

0   300

SCALE IN MILES

with their plans for a hedgehog defense, the Nationalists, as
expected by the Reds, withdrew into the cities, which were
rapidly surrounded by the Reds. Kungchuling, a town halfway
between Szepingkai and Changchun, fell to the Communists
on 4 October. South of Szepingkai, the Reds took Changtu
and Kaiyuan on the 5th, but were stopped at Tiehling by

fierce resistance from the forces of General Liao Yao-hsiang.[2] Between Mukden and the sea the Nationalists lost Tashihkiao and Haicheng, but continued to resist at Yingkow. In the face of arriving Nationalist reinforcements (one division came from Jehol and two divisions from North China were disembarked at Hulutao) the Communists—who had not yet committed the bulk of their forces, which remained to the east of the Mukden-Changchun line—broke off their attacks and momentarily withdrew. But the Reds maintained their grip upon the large cities they had previously surrounded; and it was only by the most painful effort that the Nationalists, during the two-month lull (15 October–15 December) that followed the sixth Red offensive, succeeded in establishing a precarious link between Szepingkai and Mukden by retaking Kungchuling on 1 November. The same kind of effort was required for the relief of Kirin, which was accomplished on 13 November.

The Reds launched their seventh offensive on 15 December. It soon became evident that, once again, Lin Piao's goal was the isolation of Mukden from the rest of Manchuria. In order to strengthen the defense of the city, General Ch'en Ch'eng was forced to shift there from Changchun two good divisions of the New First Army (the 30th and the 38th), which were replaced by two divisions airlifted from Fukien. This shift prevented the Communists from taking Mukden, but it permitted them to concentrate the bulk of their forces—eight columns of regulars, reinforced by independent units—well to the south of Changchun, in an area northwest of Mukden and between the main north-south railroad and the border of Jehol.

[2] General Liao Yao-hsiang, born in 1906, was a product of French training, including the Military Academy at St. Cyr (1931–1933), the Cavalry School at Saumur, and service with a French cavalry regiment at Strasbourg. During World War II, he commanded the New Sixth Army in Burma. He took command of the 4th Group Army at Mukden shortly before the Communists launched their sixth offensive in Manchuria.

Adhering to the strategic precepts of their great leader, Mao Tse-tung, the Communists did not yet attempt to reduce the large cities, such as Changchun and Mukden; but one could sense that an all-out Communist offensive would not be long in coming.

On 1 January 1948 Chiang Kai-shek reassuringly declared that "the threat of Mukden's encirclement" had "disappeared." On the same day, General Chang Chun[3] proclaimed that the critical period in the Northeast had passed and that "Nationalist troops were ready to launch their winter offensive." He added that the Reds had made a great mistake in overextending their lines of communication, and in ignoring the rigors of winter; as for the Nationalists, concentrated at several well-defended points, they could "contemplate the future with serenity." Nothing could have been further from the truth. The Communists, who lived off the land and obtained their arms and ammunition from the enemy, did not even have, properly speaking, lines of communication, which were so important to the Nationalists. And far from being spent, the Communist columns ceaselessly grew in strength. Very soon, on 5 January 1948, the Nationalists—who had hoped for a respite of two months—were to undergo an eighth Communist offensive in Manchuria.

OPERATIONS IN NORTH CHINA

Manchuria, where the Nationalists continued to pour in their best troops and use up what remained of their transport aircraft in extremely costly operations, was not the only scene of Nationalist reverses during the last half of 1947. The period also witnessed the Communists' consolidation of their great

[3] At this time Chang Chun was President of the Executive Yüan, or premier, of the National Government. *Tr.*

base in Shansi; the Nationalists' loss of Hopeh, and their failure to clear Shantung; the breakout of Communist forces to the south of the Lunghai railroad; and, finally, the establishment of a Red base in Honan, high in the Tapieh mountains to the northeast of Hankow.

Operations in Shansi and Shensi

Following their loss of Yenan to the forces of General Hu Tsung-nan, the Communists maneuvered very skillfully in Shansi. While Ho Lung's forces in the northeast of the province conducted delaying actions in their slow withdrawal to the north, General Ch'en Keng, in the south, launched an attack westward toward the Yellow River which threatened to take Hu Tsung-nan's forces in the rear. The Nationalist commander in Shansi was still, as always, the old war lord Yen Hsi-shan, whose sole thought was to hold on to Taiyuan, his capital, with his own private army; he cooperated little, if at all, with Hu Tsung-nan, or with Fu Tso-yi, who commanded in Chahar as well as in Suiyuan and Hopeh. Having isolated Taiyuan, Ch'en Keng's Red forces took Yicheng on 5 April and crossed the Fen river, after defeating the Nationalist reinforcements sent out from Shensi by Hu Tsung-nan.

The Red forces in northern Shansi, aided by forces from Inner Mongolia and Suiyuan, pushed northward and threatened Tatung with encirclement. In the eastern part of Shansi, the Reds further protected their grip on the province by mounting a bold attack against the Chengtai railroad, an attack coordinated with a threat to Shihkiachwang by their forces in Hopeh. By May, practically all of Shansi was in Communist hands, except for a strip along the Peking-Suiyuan railroad in the north, a few Nationalist strong points undergoing gradual reduction, and the beleaguered capital at Taiyuan.

In the neighboring province of Shensi the Nationalists, after their capture of Yenan, had been stopped by the threat of a westward movement against their rear by Ch'en Keng's forces in southern Shansi. A link-up between the forces of Fu Tso-yi and those of Hu Tsung-nan, along the line Yulin-Yenan, was now the goal of the Nationalists. This goal seemed to be in sight in July, after the capture of Suiteh and Micheh, but the Nationalists' successes had overextended their highly vulnerable lines of communication, and they failed to reach it. Moreover, Red forces moved up the Yenan-Yulin road from Yuhopao in March 1947 and attacked Yulin, reaching its outskirts on the 27th. This town, which Fu Tso-yi's forces seemed incapable of defending, was saved by a relief column of thirty thousand men dispatched by the governor of Ningsia (General Ma Hung-ku'ei), who until then had refused to commit his troops outside his own province. The Red forces pulled back to the western border region of Shensi, south of the Great Wall.

Operations in Hopeh

In Hopeh the Nationalists were exposed to unceasing guerrilla warfare within the triangle Peking-Tientsin-Paoting and, as early as 9 April 1947, to the attacks of Liu Po-ch'eng's regulars in the Shihkiachwang area. As of September the Nationalists still had a firm grip on the Peking-Suiyuan railroad, the Peking-Tientsin-Mukden line, and the Pinghan (Peking-Hankow railroad) as far as Paoting. But Paoting itself was almost completely encircled by the Reds, who also took Chengting, in the vicinity of Shihkiachwang.

In the last months of the year the situation took a sudden turn for the worse, changing the forced optimism of Nationalist officers into the darkest pessimism. The principal causes of this abrupt change were the fall of Shihkiachwang and

Yuanshih to the Communists, and the reinforcement of General Nieh Jung-chen's forces by two Communist columns which had hitherto been part of Li Yung-chang's command in eastern Hopeh and southeastern Jehol. The fall of Shihkiachwang, taken by the Communists after the crushing defeat of General Lu Li-fung's forces in a pitched battle fought in open country, was a heavy loss for the Nationalists. It not only freed large numbers of Red regulars for further operations; the loss of this important town also meant the loss of much railroad matériel to the Communists. And Mao Tse-tung, moving in behind his conquering troops, soon established his new capital at Shihkiachwang.

Thus, as of 1 January 1948, except for the Tientsin-Peking-Kalgan-Tatung corridor, still firmly held by Fu Tso-yi, and the encircled cities of Taiyuan, Paoting, and Anyang, the Reds were in possession of all of Shansi and Hopeh. For the Nationalists this was a major defeat.

Liu Po-ch'eng's Offensive in Central China

During the night of 11–12 August 1947 the Red columns of General Liu Po-ch'eng, about fifty thousand strong, crossed the Lunghai railroad to the east of Kaifeng and, meeting with no resistance, flooded southward toward Honan. Advancing at the rate of thirty miles per day, they reached the mountainous Tapieh Shan region where, in conformity with classic Communist doctrine, they established a new base. Swerving then to the east, their advance guards reached the heights overlooking the Anking-Hofei highway on 11 September. While passing through Liuan,[4] Liu's columns cleaned out the Nationalist arsenal there, carrying off some 150,000 rifles. Almost simultaneously, on 22 August, the twenty thousand troops of General Ch'en Keng, one of Liu Po-ch'eng's prin-

[4] A town in Anhwei, about 130 miles west of Nanking.

cipal subordinates, crossed the Yellow River in the vicinity of Yuanku, cut the Lunghai railroad between Loyang and Shanhsien, and marched east to join up with Liu. To counter this perilous threat, the Nationalists reinforced the Hankow region with units from Chungking and Canton. But the ceaseless growth of Communist strength, fed by numerous volunteers, soon made it apparent to the Nationalists that a major operation would be required if they were to succeed in wiping out the new Communist base. Thus, the center of gravity of the fighting had suddenly moved south, almost to the Yangtze. For Chiang Kai-shek, who managed to keep up a show of optimism, this was a very severe blow.

Meanwhile, Liu Po-ch'eng's movement to the Tapieh mountains had left a gap in southern Hopeh. The forces of General Ch'en I, based in Shantung and threatened by a Nationalist offensive against Chefoo, received Chu Teh's order to fill this gap. Crossing the Lunghai rail line on 27 September with five columns, Ch'en I bypassed Suchow and on 8 October cut the Tsinpu railroad on either side of Suhsien, as well as the Pinghan line in the vicinity of Hsuchang.

During December the struggle raged in the region between the Yellow River and the Yangtze, where three Communist armies were now in action. Ch'en I's force of seven columns was operating on both sides of the Lunghai line, to the east and south of Kaifeng. Liu Po-ch'eng's six columns were in the Tapieh mountains and adjacent areas to the south and west. Ch'en Keng, with two columns and the Thirty-eighth Army, was fighting in the area west of the Pinghan line up to the Honan-Shansi border.

The activity of these three groups was both intense and important. They severed Nationalist lines of communication, interdicted river traffic on the Yangtze, and destroyed protective outposts along the Lunghai and Pinghan rail lines, all in order to isolate the cities and aggravate the supply problems of the Nationalists. In December Liu Po-ch'eng further widened the action by thrusting two columns, against stiff Nationalist opposition, to the west of the Pinghan railroad near Liulin. And everywhere the presence of these Red forces gave rise to numerous guerrilla bands which threatened the large population centers and spread anarchy and desolation throughout the region.

The End of the Shantung Campaign

Having failed in their attempt to conquer Shantung by land, the Nationalists organized an amphibious operation. On 27 August a landing took place at Shihkiuso, about sixty miles southwest of Tsingtao, followed by another at Chefoo. A third landing, at Weihaiwei on 30 September, was repulsed by the Reds.[5] The capture of Chefoo was hailed as a great victory by the Nationalist press; but it brought no decisive results and, in spite of Ch'en I's departure for the Kaifeng area, the remaining Red columns in Shantung escaped the Nationalist pincers. Moreover, the forces of General Su Yü, who had replaced Ch'en I as Red commander in Shantung, succeeded in maintaining control of the peninsula, Weihaiwei included, and of their important bases in the Chucheng area. In November the Reds retook Laiyang, Chiaohsien, and Kaomi and then, pushing southward, reoccupied all the ground they had lost as far as the borders of Anhwei and Kiangsu. The Shantung campaign, into which the Nationalists had poured up to half-a-million men, ended in bitter defeat. And they were never to regain the initiative.

---

[5] The Nationalists took only Linkung, the island off the port of Weihaiwei.

CHAPTER X

Political Developments in 1947

On 2 March 1947 T. V. Soong resigned his post as premier,[1] very probably because he felt that China's financial situation was incapable of sustaining Chiang Kai-shek's program for all-out war, which in Chiang's view would be "all over in three months."[2] Increasingly influenced by the reactionaries of the CC clique, Chiang refused to give credence to the demoralization of his troops; in his view, the reason for their defeats was always treason. His response, in the face of student demonstrations against the Civil War, was to intensify the repressive action of the secret police.

To Chiang the capture of Yenan came as a ray of hope; but for the liberals in the Kuomintang, Nationalist defeats in Manchuria soon led to a realization that the situation was continuing to worsen. The government's only real solution was to take the road of radical reform. The Americans did all they could to bring this about. But such reforms as the reorganization of the Council of State, the naming of Dr. Sun Fo as Vice President and of General Chang Chun as premier,

[1] Soong's official title was President of the Executive Yüan. *Tr.*

[2] It should also be noted that the Constitution of 1947, under which the President of the Executive Yüan is appointed by the President of the Republic with the consent of the Legislative Yüan, was promulgated before Soong's resignation, on 1 January 1947. *Tr.*

effected in April 1947, were to mean little in actual practice. The CC clique continued to dominate the party, and the corruption and inefficiency of the Nationalist officials, who were miserably paid, led to a total lack of popular confidence in the party and in the Generalissimo himself. In an attempt to galvanize the troops the Standing Committee of the party's Central Executive Committee on 30 June decided to integrate the *San Min Chu I* Youth Corps into the Kuomintang, and to intensify punitive action against the Communists. At the same time an anti-Kuomintang plot was uncovered at Peking, and numerous arrests were made; the Democratic League, the left wing of which was indeed communistic, was compromised by the plot and subsequently outlawed. On 4 July the Communists were proclaimed to be "in open rebellion," and a general mobilization of all Nationalist resources was ordered.

Yet, while the Americans could see no other solution than far-reaching internal reforms, the Nationalists saw American aid as their sole source of salvation. This is why General Wedemeyer's arrival in China was greeted with satisfaction by the Nationalists. Charged by President Truman with a fact-finding mission covering the entire situation—political, economic, psychological, and military—Wedemeyer arrived at Nanking on 16 July and remained in China until 24 August. Upon his departure he summed up his findings in a public statement that came as a severe blow to Chiang Kai-shek. In it Wedemeyer criticized "the abject defeatism of many Chinese, who are normally competent and patriotic, and who instead should be full of hope and determination."[3] He declared that "the existing Central government can win and retain the undivided, enthusiastic support of the bulk of the

[3] U.S. Department of State, *United States Relations with China, with Special Reference to the Period 1944–1949* (U.S. Government Printing Office, 1949), p. 763. *Tr.*

Chinese people by removing incompetent and/or corrupt people who now occupy many positions of responsibility in the government, not only national but more so in provincial and municipal structures."[4] He insisted upon the urgent necessity of radical reforms in the army (equalization of the burden of conscription, increase in pay), and in the administration as well (pay increases for officials, lowering of taxes, and so on).

In the lengthy report presented to President Truman by Wedemeyer on 19 September, the general examined the problem in all its aspects. From a purely military point of view, he found the situation to be extremely serious:

> Total Nationalist forces of about a million and a half combat troops plus another million service troops are opposing less than a million Communist combat troops and militia supported by an unknown number of service troops . . .
>
> The underlying military reason for Communist success is that they retain the initiative, striking at places of their own selection with local superiority of forces and with a mission of *destruction* [author's italics]. Nationalist forces, on the other hand, with a mission of *protection* [author's italics], are forced to what amounts to a perimeter defense of scattered areas and of long connecting lines of communication. Such widespread defense offers little chance of lateral coordination and mutual support, thus immobilizing forces that would otherwise be available for offensive action. Communist drives appear to meet with little substantial resistance, while Nationalist withdrawals are generally premature and the words "strategic retreat" have lost all significance . . .
>
> All in all, the military situation in China appears to be governed predominantly by Communists enjoying substantial military successes in Manchuria, in Shantung and in Hopeh. These successes can be attributed mainly to the lightness and efficacy of their hit-and-run guerrilla type forces, to their mission of destruction as opposed to the Nationalist mission of protection, to the ineptitude and incompetence of Nationalist high command, to the shrinkage of Nationalist communications, to the general depreciation and

[4] *Ibid.*, p. 764. Tr.

depletion of Nationalist equipment and supplies, both ground and air, to increased friction between military forces from the south and civil administration in the areas under attack, and to the stigma attached to troops which so often live off the local civil population.[5]

After describing the situation, Wedemeyer came to the important matter of recommendations. He recommended:

That the United States provide as early as practicable moral, advisory and material support to China in order to prevent Manchuria from becoming a Soviet satellite, to bolster opposition to Communist expansion and to contribute to the gradual development of stability in China.

That China be advised to request the United Nations to take immediate steps to bring about a cessation of hostilities in Manchuria and request that Manchuria be placed under a Five-Power Guardianship (the U.S.S.R., the U.S.A., Great Britain, China and France) . . .

That China be advised to take steps to reduce its military expenditures in the national budget and at the same time increase the effectiveness and efficiency of the military establishment.

That China give continuing evidence that urgently required military reforms are being implemented.

That China, with the advice and support of the United States, develop and implement a sound program of equipment and improved logistical support.

That arrangements be made whereby China can purchase military equipment and supplies (particularly motor maintenance parts), from the United States.

That China be assisted in her efforts to obtain ammunition immediately.[6]

That the 8⅓ Air Group Program be completed promptly and that consideration be given to expansion of its air transport (two groups of C–47 aircraft).

[5] *Ibid.*, pp. 808–809. *Tr.*
[6] The embargo on arms shipments imposed by Marshall in August 1946 had been lifted in May 1947.

That the China Mapping Program be extended in scope where practicable.

That the program for transfer of ships to China be completed as rapidly as China is able to utilize them effectively ...

[That] military advice and supervision be extended in scope to include field forces, training centers and particularly logistical agencies[7] ...

Thus Wedemeyer, recognizing that the National Government was "incapable of supporting an army of the size it now has in the field,"[8] was led to propose to Truman intensification of American aid to Chiang Kai-shek. In view of the Generalissimo's increasingly slim chances of victory, this proposed action risked troublesome consequences for the future course of Sino-American relations. As Brigadier Field, the British military attaché at Nanking, remarked at this time: "I would be most embarrassed if my government, finding itself in the situation of the United States, were to ask me to propose a solution to the problem."

American hopes for a sound and reasonable response from Chiang Kai-shek were soon dashed. The fourth session of the KMT's Central Executive Committee, which opened at Nanking on 9 September 1947, was to see the triumph of the reactionary clique and the consolidation of its hold upon the Youth Corps. The appointment of T. V. Soong as governor of Kwangtung was without doubt the result of a deal with the brothers Ch'en, who wanted to get Chiang Kai-shek's brother-in-law out of the way. It is true that Chiang tried to combat corruption, to put real power into the hands of the Control Yüan, and to re-establish, by augmenting the authority of the local police at the expense of the secret police, a certain degree of individual freedom. These fragmentary measures proved to

[7] *U.S. Relations with China*, p. 814. *Tr.*
[8] *Ibid. Tr.*

be insufficient. In October 1947 the military situation became increasingly bad; turning in anguish to the United States, Chiang met a deaf ear from the Americans, who held fixedly to their own plan. On 28 October, the Democratic League was outlawed. Carson Chang's Democratic Socialist Party rapidly crumbled. The political situation degenerated into anarchy. Eroded by factional intrigue, the political power of Chiang Kai-shek was steadily diminishing.

In contrast, Mao Tse-tung's power over the Communist movement became ever greater. In November 1947 he had established his capital at Shihkiachwang, reorganized his services, and placed political commissars at the side of the generals who were in command of armies. In the Central Committee, where he continued to lean upon the faithful shoulders of Liu Shao-ch'i, Jen Pi-shih, Lu Ting-i, and K'ang Sheng, his authority was never questioned; events had always borne him out, and his methods were showing themselves to be victorious. Following the successes of the last half of 1947, Mao on 25 December gave a speech to the Central Committee of the CCP that was a veritable victory chant. He proclaimed his conviction that the Communists now possessed all that was needed for the final victory he foresaw in 1949. Magisterially, he prescribed the strategy and tactics of the Red Army, and the necessity of agrarian reform. Finally, he violently attacked the United States, declaring that "reactionary American imperialism was the great enemy of humanity and the agent responsible for the continuation of the Chinese civil war." From a military viewpoint the principal passages of Mao's speech are well worth quoting at length.[9]

[9] The quoted passages are from the English translation of Mao's speech of 25 December 1947, "The Present Situation and Our Tasks," in *Mao Tse-tung: Selected Works*, vol. V: *1945–1949* (New York: International Publishers, 1956), pp. 157–163. Quoted by permission of International Publishers. *Tr.*

I. A *Turning Point in History*

The Chinese people's revolutionary war has now reached a turning point. That is, the Chinese People's Liberation Army has beaten back the offensive of several million reactionary troops of Chiang Kai-shek, the running dog of the United States of America, and gone over to the offensive. Already in the first year of the present war, from July 1946 to June 1947, the People's Liberation Army beat back Chiang Kai-shek's offensive on several fronts and forced him onto the defensive. And beginning with the first quarter of the second year of the war, July-September 1947, the People's Liberation Army went over to the offensive on a national scale and wrecked Chiang Kai-shek's counter-revolutionary plan of continuing to carry the war into the Liberated Areas in order to destroy them completely.

Now the war is no longer being fought chiefly in the Liberated Areas but in the Kuomintang areas; the main forces of the People's Liberation Army have carried the fight into the Kuomintang areas. In this land of China, the People's Liberation Army has turned back the wheel of counter-revolution—of U.S. imperialism and its lackey, the Chiang Kai-shek bandit gang—and sent it down the road to destruction and has pushed the wheel of revolution forward along the road to victory.

This is a turning point in history. It is the turning point from growth to extinction for Chiang Kai-shek's twenty-year counter-revolutionary rule. It is the turning point from growth to extinction for imperialist rule in China, now over a hundred years old.

This is a momentous event. It is momentous because it is occurring in a country with a population of 475 million and, having occurred, it will certainly culminate in victory throughout the country. Furthermore, it is momentous because it is occurring in the East, where over 1,000 million people—half of mankind—suffer under imperialist oppression. The turn of the Chinese People's War of Liberation from the defensive to the offensive cannot but gladden and inspire these oppressed nations. It is also of assistance to the oppressed people now struggling in many countries in Europe and the Americas.

II. *Chiang Kai-shek's Counter-Revolutionary War and Its Direction by American Imperialism*

From the day Chiang Kai-shek started his counter-revolutionary war we said that we not only must defeat him but can defeat him. We must defeat him because the war he started is a counter-revolutionary war directed by U.S. imperialism against the independence of the Chinese nation and the liberation of the Chinese people. After the conclusion of World War II and the overthrow of Japanese imperialism, the task of the Chinese people was to complete the new-democratic transformation politically, economically and culturally, to achieve national unification and independence and to change China from an agricultural into an industrial country. But at that time, after the victorious conclusion of the anti-fascist Second World War, U.S. imperialism and its lackeys in various countries stepped into the shoes of German and Japanese imperialism and their lackeys and formed a reactionary camp against the Soviet Union, against the People's Democracies in Europe, against the workers' movements in the capitalist countries, against the national movements in the colonies and semi-colonies and against the liberation of the Chinese people. At such a time the Chinese reactionaries headed by Chiang Kai-shek acted as the running dog for U.S. imperialism, just as Wang Ching-wei had done for Japanese imperialism, sold out China to the United States and unleashed a war against the Chinese people to check the advance of their liberation. At such a time, if we had shown weakness or given ground and had not dared to rise resolutely to oppose counter-revolutionary war with revolutionary war, China would have become a world of darkness and the future of our nation would have been forfeited. The Communist Party of China has led the Chinese People's Liberation Army in firmly waging a patriotic, just and revolutionary war against Chiang Kai-shek's offensive.

The Communist Party of China, having made a clear-headed appraisal of the international and domestic situation on the basis of the science of Marxism-Leninism, recognized that all attacks by the reactionaries at home and abroad not only had to be defeated but could be defeated. When dark clouds appeared in the sky, we pointed out that this was only temporary, that the darkness would soon pass and the sun break through. When the Chiang Kai-shek bandit gang launched the country-wide counter-revolutionary war in July 1946, they thought it would take them only three to six months to defeat the People's Liberation Army. They reckoned that they had a regular army of two million, more than a million irregulars and another million or more men in the military establishments and armed units in the rear, making a total military strength of more than four million; that they had taken time to complete their preparation for the offensive; that they had regained control of the big cities; that they had a population of more than 300 million; that they had taken over all the equipment of a million Japanese invading troops; and that they had received huge military and financial aid from the U.S. government. They also reckoned that the People's Liberation Army was tired after fighting for eight years in the War of Resistance Against Japan and was far inferior to the Kuomintang army in numbers and equipment; that the population of the Liberated Areas was only a little more than 100 million; and that in most of these areas the reactionary feudal forces had not yet been cleaned up and the land reform had not yet been universally and thoroughly carried out, namely, that the rear area of the People's Liberation Army had not yet been consolidated.

Proceeding from this appraisal, the Chiang Kai-shek bandit gang ignored the Chinese people's desire for peace, finally tore up the truce agreement signed by the Kuomintang and the Communist Party in January 1946, as well as the resolutions adopted by the Political Consultative Conference of all parties and launched an adventurist war. We said then that Chiang Kai-shek's superiority in military forces was only transient, a factor which could play only a temporary role, that U.S. imperialist aid was likewise a factor which could play only a temporary role, while the anti-popular character of Chiang Kai-shek's war and the feelings of the people were factors that would play a constant role, and that in this respect the People's Liberation Army was in a superior position. Patriotic, just and revolutionary in character, the war waged by the People's Liberation Army was bound to win the support of the people of the whole country. That was the political foundation for victory over Chiang Kai-shek. The experience of eighteen months of war has fully confirmed our judgment.

III. *The Military Principles of the People's Liberation Army*

In seventeen months of fighting (from July 1946 to November 1947; December figures are not yet available), we killed, wounded and captured 1,690,000 of Chiang Kai-shek's regular and irregular troops—640,000 killed and wounded and 1,050,000 captured. Thus we were able to beat back Chiang Kai-shek's offensive, preserve the main territories of the Liberated Areas and go over to the offensive. Speaking from the military aspect, we were able to do this because we employed the correct strategy.

Our principles of operation are:

1. Attack dispersed, isolated enemy forces first; attack concentrated, strong enemy forces later.

2. Take small and medium cities and extensive rural areas first; take big cities later.

3. Make wiping out the enemy's effective strength our main objective; do not make holding or seizing a city or place our main objective. Holding or seizing a city or place is the outcome of wiping out the enemy's effective strength, and often a city or place can be held or seized for good only after it has changed hands a number of times.

4. In every battle, concentrate an absolutely superior force (two, three, four and sometimes even five or six times the enemy's strength), encircle the enemy forces completely, strive to wipe them out thoroughly and do not let any escape from the net. In special circumstances, use the method of dealing crushing blows to the enemy, that is, concentrate all our strength to make a frontal attack and also to attack one or both of his flanks, with the aim of wiping out one part and routing another so that our army can swiftly move its troops to smash other enemy forces. Strive to avoid battles of attrition in which we lose more than we gain or only break even. In this way, although we are inferior as a whole (in terms of numbers), we are absolutely superior in every part and every specific campaign, and this ensures victory in the campaign. As time goes on, we shall become superior as a whole and eventually wipe out all the enemy.

5. Fight no battle unprepared, fight no battle you are not sure of winning; make every effort to be well prepared for each battle, make every effort to ensure victory in the given set of conditions as between the enemy and ourselves.

6. Give full play to our style of fighting—courage in battle, no fear of sacrifice, no fear of fatigue, and continuous fighting (that is, fighting successive battles in a short time without rest).

7. Strive to wipe out the enemy through mobile warfare. At the same time, pay attention to the tactics of positional attack and capture enemy fortified points and cities.

8. With regard to attacking cities, resolutely seize all enemy fortified points and cities which are weakly defended. Seize at opportune moments all enemy fortified points and cities defended with moderate strength, provided circumstances permit. As for strongly defended enemy fortified points and cities, wait till conditions are ripe and then take them.

9. Replenish our strength with all the arms and most of the personnel captured from the enemy. Our army's main sources of manpower and matériel are at the front.

10. Make good use of the intervals between campaigns to rest, train and consolidate our troops. Periods of rest, training and consolidation should in general not be very long, and the enemy should so far as possible be permitted no breathing space.

These are the main methods the People's Liberation Army has employed in defeating Chiang Kai-shek. They are the result of the tempering of the People's Liberation Army in long years of fighting against domestic and foreign enemies and are completely suited to our present situation.

The Chiang Kai-shek bandit gang and the U.S. imperialist military personnel in China are very well acquainted with these military methods of ours. Seeking ways to counter them, Chiang Kai-shek has often assembled his generals and field officers for training and distributed for their study our military literature and the documents captured in our war. The U.S. military personnel have recommended to Chiang Kai-shek one kind of strategy and tactics after another for destroying the People's Liberation Army; they have trained Chiang Kai-shek's troops and supplied them with military equipment. But none of these efforts can save the Chiang Kai-shek bandit gang from defeat. The reason is that our strategy and tactics are based on a people's war; no army opposed to the people can use our strategy and tactics.

On the basis of a people's war and of the principles of unity between army and people, of unity between commanders and fighters and of disintegrating the enemy troops, the People's Liberation Army has developed its vigorous revolutionary political work, which is an important factor in winning victory over the enemy. When we abandoned many cities on our own initiative in order to evade fatal blows from superior enemy forces and shift our forces to destroy the enemy in mobile warfare, our enemies were jubilant. They took this to be their victory and our defeat. They became dizzy with this momentary "victory." On the afternoon of the day he seized Changchiakou (Kalgan), Chiang Kai-shek ordered the convening of his reactionary National Assembly, as though his reactionary regime had from that moment become as stable as Mount Taishan.[10] The U.S. imperialists, too, danced with joy, as though their wild scheme for converting China into a U.S. colony could now be realized without obstruction.

But with the lapse of time, Chiang Kai-shek and his U.S. masters began to change their tune. Now all our enemies, domestic and foreign, are gripped by pessimism. They heave great sighs, wail about a crisis and no longer show any sign of joy. In the past eighteen months, most of Chiang Kai-shek's high-ranking field commanders have been replaced for losing battles . . . Ch'en Ch'eng, too, was relieved of his post as Chiang Kai-shek's chief of staff in over-all command of operations and demoted to command a single front in the Northeast. However, it was in the very period when Chiang Kai-shek himself assumed over-all command in Ch'en Ch'eng's place that the situation changed and that his armies shifted from the offensive to the defensive, while the People's Liberation Army went over from the defensive to the offensive. By now the reactionary Chiang Kai-shek clique and its U.S. masters should have realized their mistake. They had regarded as signs of cowardice and weakness all the efforts for peace and against civil war which the Communist Party of China, representing the wishes of the Chinese people, had made over a long period after the surrender of Japan. They had overestimated their own

[10] One of the five legendary mountains of ancient China.

strength, underestimated the strength of the revolution and rashly unleashed the war and so were caught in their own trap. Our enemy's strategic calculations failed completely.

These remarkably sound principles were very skillfully applied by Red armies that were manifestly well trained, well led, and possessed of an iron-like morale. And their victories were made all the easier by the fact that they were opposed by Kuomintang armies whose disintegration was becoming increasingly widespread.

✧ PART FOUR ✧

1948

THE DECISIVE YEAR

CHAPTER XI

The Situation at the Beginning of 1948

THE decisive year of the Civil War was 1948. On the one hand, Chiang Kai-shek's last attempts to renovate the economy failed, and President Truman refused to renew an American effort foredoomed to failure by the deepening disintegration of the Nationalist regime and its increasing unpopularity. On the other hand, the wear and tear on Nationalist forces was such that the Communists, having attained numerical parity, were now able to launch truly coordinated offensives, to attack large cities, and to fight and win pitched battles in open country; lastly, by securing all of Manchuria, the Reds were able to redeploy the additional forces that were to assure their final victory. There being no need for the Communists to guard conquered areas with regular troops, they could free such troops for further operations elsewhere; but Nationalist-conquered areas, because of guerrilla activity and the hostility of the populace, required enormous garrisons.

It is difficult to study simultaneously operations that were as entangled and confusing as those of the year 1947, which saw the Reds reach the Yangtze, continued fighting in Manchuria, Communist guerrilla activity in Kwangtung, and the

GENERAL DISPOSITION AND STRENGTH OF NATIONALIST AND COMMUNIST FORCES AS OF 1 JANUARY 1948[a]

Theater of operations	Nationalists	Communists	Nationalist margin of superiority
Manchuria	TOTAL: 400,000 men Nine armies under General Ch'eng	TOTAL: 320,000 men General Lin Piao	80,000 men (25%)

Yellow River Valley	TOTAL: 280,000 men (28 divisions)
	
	1. *Forces of Ku Chu-t'ung:*
	  a) 75,000 men (8 infantry divisions), in the Suchow area.
	  b) 75,000 men (8 infantry divisions), in the Kaifeng area.
	  c) 70,000 men (7 infantry divisions), in Shantung.
	
	2. *Forces of Hu Tsung-nan:*
	  60,000 men (5 infantry divisions).
	
	Note: all of these were reorganized divisions
		TOTAL: 180,000 men
		
		1. 60,000 men under Ch'en I in Shantung, western Honan, northern Anhwei.
		2. 40,000 men under Ch'en Keng in western Honan.
		3. 40,000 men under Ho Lung in southern Shansi.
		4. 40,000 men under Su Yü in Shantung.
			100,000 men (55.6%)

North China	TOTAL: 430,000 men	TOTAL: 120,000 men
	1. 230,000 men under Fu Tso-yi (20 to 25 divisions, not reorganized) in Hopeh, Chahar, Jehol, Suiyuan, northern Shansi. 2. Fu Tso-yi's "personal" troops amounted to 100,000 men. 3. 200,000 men under Yen Hsi-shan in central Shansi (inactive troops).	1. 60,000 to 80,000 men under Nieh Jung-chen in Hopeh and Chahar. 2. 40,000 men under P'eng Te-huai in northwestern Shansi.
		310,000 men (258%) Exclusive of Yen Hsi-shan's troops, the difference is 110,000 men (92%)
Yangtze Valley	TOTAL: 140,000 men	TOTAL: 80,000 men
	Twelve divisions under Pai Ch'ung-hsi, whose command extended to the valley of the Hwai.	1. 40,000 men under Liu Po-ch'eng in the Tapieh Shan. 2. 20,000 men under Li Hsien-nien in the valley of the Han. 3. 20,000 men under Wang Hung-kun in the area northwest of Hankow.
		60,000 men (75%)

RECAPITULATION: Communists: 700,000 men   Nationalists: 1,250,000 men

[a] Nationalist strength figures are exclusive of troops located to the south of the Yangtze and in Szechwan. The Communist strength figures are for regulars only, and do not include guerrillas or militia.

faithful adherence of the northwestern provinces (Ningsia and Kansu) to the Nationalist cause. It is clear, however, that numerical parity between the two armies had not yet been arrived at as of 1 January 1948. The table on pages 158–159 gives the strength and general disposition of the opposing forces at this time. It shows that the Nationalists still had a two-to-one superiority. Nevertheless, they had suffered enormous losses. Even though Mao Tse-tung's claims of 640,000 killed or wounded and 1,050,000 prisoners for the period July 1946–November 1947 were doubtlessly exaggerated, the government itself admitted Nationalist losses of 400,000 killed, wounded, and missing during 1947. As for the Nationalist claims of 638,000 Communist dead and 127,000 prisoners, it is certain that they were far more exaggerated than those of the Communists. In any event, the really important factors were the cohesion of Communist troops, their discipline, and their tremendous moral superiority over their adversaries.

. Mr. M. Keon,[1] a reliable non-Communist newspaperman from Australia who spent several months of 1947 with the Reds in Shantung, has provided extremely interesting information on this subject. As soon after each engagement as the situation permitted, a small unit would assemble to listen to its leader's explanation of the operational results obtained, his criticisms, and his answers to the questions all were free to ask. Mr. Keon once witnessed the return of a small detachment from the front with half its strength wounded; one of the casualties had lost an arm and was still in tourniquet, and another had a bad stomach wound; the customary critique

---

[1] Michael Keon, in 1947 a correspondent for the Melbourne newspaper *The Age*, later served as Press Attaché of the Australian Embassy in China. He also covered the guerrilla war in Malaya. He is the author of two novels dealing with Communist guerrilla warfare, *The Tiger in Summer* (1953), and *The Durian Tree* (1960), and is currently news editor of the *Rome Daily American*. Tr.

took place anyway, and the wounded asked questions like everyone else. In another case, a telephone line was being strung over a fast-flowing river by a fifteen-man detail; when three of the men fell and drowned, they were rapidly replaced, without the others ever faltering in their task. Numerous other incidents testifying to the energy and courage of Communist troops appear to have deeply impressed Mr. Keon, especially after what he had seen on the Nationalist side.

The behavior of the Red Army toward the population was always scrupulously correct, and its soldiers everywhere received a joyful welcome. Red troops were forbidden to interfere in village politics, and they actively aided the peasants whenever help was needed. Products of the same political education, soldier and peasant thought alike, and the Red Army was truly one with the *lao pai hsing.*[2]

Although there was conscription, the great majority of Communist soldiers were volunteers. Of peasant origin, the volunteer valiantly defended the lands newly acquired by his own kind, and fought with an enthusiasm heightened by awareness of the honor now accorded the role of soldier. He could also derive some degree of material or educational advantage from service with the Red Army. He was generally well armed with either Japanese or captured American weapons, and large stocks of Japanese small-arms and artillery ammunition came from Manchuria, by junk, for distribution to all units. Locally manufactured hand grenades were favorite weapons, but there was also great stress on bayonet training. Radio and telephone communications, benefiting from Japanese and American equipment, were excellent, with some telephone lines extending over hundreds of miles. Motor vehicles were quite plentiful, and fuel was supplied as needed by whole convoys of wheelbarrows (Mr. Keon saw convoys

2 The "hundred thousand," or common people.

of up to three thousand wheelbarrows, each with a two-man team). The Communists continued to free their prisoners en masse, even the officers, usually after a period of political indoctrination; by this means, they riddled the Nationalist zone with spies and agitators.

There is no doubt that the Nationalist Air Force hampered the movement of Communist troops, which almost always took place under the cover of darkness. Bombing of villages by B-25's was seldom effective, especially since the bombings always occurred at regular, set times; strafing attacks, usually by P-51's, were feared far more by the Communists. The Reds had no active antiaircraft defenses, but an excellent warning system existed in all the villages.

At this time (late 1947), Mr. Keon estimated that at least sixty per cent of the peasants were pro-Communist, most of the others being neutral and a few discreetly hostile. Essentially, the Communists' success with the peasantry was due to their program of land redistribution and to the relief they promptly provided whenever scarcity threatened; it was also the result of a state of mind which Communist propagandists so well knew how to create. For the first time in Chinese history, the peasantry had become the object of attention and intensive education. Mr. Keon has described a typical village of the time: schoolchildren, like ambulant apostles, would teach the elders, read the wall newspapers to them, help with the household chores and sometimes in the fields, and set up mutual aid and cooperative organizations. The Communists found their most ardent adherents among young children and adolescents, upon whom they bent their greatest efforts. The younger generation was especially useful in keeping tabs on public opinion, and frequently practiced a familial sort of espionage. There was also a great change among women, most of whom came to be strong supporters of the Communist Party.

Although there was an active political life in the villages, complete with elections, town meetings, and leaders who very often were non-Communists, the all-powerful political commissar was always there to rectify errors and maintain adherence to the party line. This kind of politico-administrative organization of the village tended to supplant the traditional family organization; thus the village, where every measure was discussed and decided upon in common, was replacing the family as the basic unit of Chinese society. At higher levels of government, such as the provincial, there was a large proportion of non-Communist administrators; former officials of the Kuomintang's central or provincial regimes, they were kept on by the Communists because of their technical skills. They were what the Russians call "specialists." Staying on because of sentimental regional attachments, job interest, or a taste for responsibility, most of them were remarkable individuals who indirectly did much to help a movement whose own administrative personnel were still lacking in experience.

Both in theory and in apparent practice there was a complete separation between administration and politics. There were, however, numerous propagandists, ninety per cent of whom were students, both male and female. These young people, nourished on Marxist literature and fluent in classical Communist phraseology, were the "pure ones," the "believers," always ready to sacrifice themselves, as well as others, to the continued functioning of a machine they themselves had helped to set in motion. Their energy and devotion to the people were limitless. Together with the army's political commissars, they constituted the vital force of the Chinese Communist Party. But, deeply influenced as they were by the Soviet Union, they were already *more Marxist than Chinese.* Hatred of Americans and admiration for the U.S.S.R. constituted the core of their opinions on foreign affairs. Apart from anti-American slogans and the arguments employed by party leaders, the attacks by Nationalist aircraft—the American origins of which were known to all—resulted in resentments which considerably facilitated the agitators' task. The name of General Marshall was rendered particularly infamous: he was denounced as a double-crosser who had deliberately disguised the machinations of the American "imperialists." It is likely, however, that the real target of this agitation against Marshall was the head of the State Department, responsible as he was for American foreign policy.

In brief, according to Mr. Keon, communism had brought to China a mystique, a faith, which had enraptured Chinese youth and infused them with an extraordinary dynamism classically based upon two slogans: for internal use, "Land Reform"; for external use, "Liberation of the Fatherland from the Imperialists." The success of this propaganda was astounding. And to oppose it there was no real counter-mystique; there was only a decadent and fossilized political party.

By the end of 1947 the Kuomintang was finished, and far beyond redemption by any amount of aid from abroad.

CHAPTER XII

1948: The First Six Months

OPERATIONS IN MANCHURIA

On 5 January 1948 General Lin Piao launched his eighth offensive, with seven columns, to isolate Mukden from China Proper and the rest of Manchuria as well.

In order to isolate Mukden from China, Lin had to do three things: maintain, and if possible enlarge, the incision his forces had made in the Peking-Mukden railroad; cut the Mukden-Dairen railroad; and close off the port of Yingkow. At the first news of Lin's entirely unexpected attack, Chiang Kai-shek hastened to Mukden on 10 January. Here he replaced General Ch'en Ch'eng by General Wei Li-huang, and decided to reinforce the new commander with two divisions transported by sea from Shantung to Hulutao and Chinwangtao; the "Liaoning corridor" had to be held at all costs. Despite these enemy reinforcements, Lin Piao succeeded in taking Kowpangtze on the Peking-Mukden line, and cutting, with the fall of Liaoyang on 4 February, the Mukden-Dairen railroad. The port of Yingkow, which came under heavy attack at the end of January, fell to the Reds on 27 February. Mukden, however, was staunchly defended by its Nationalist garrison, which received strong reinforcement by air.[1] Early in March, Lin Piao shifted the bulk of his attacking forces to the north and displaced his headquarters from Liaochung, about thirty-five miles southwest of Mukden, to Faku, some fifty miles to the north of the city. Although the Red offensive against Mukden had not been decisive, it had forced General Wei to weaken his garrisons at Kirin, Szepingkai, and Changchun in order to strengthen Mukden; and the Nationalists had failed in their attempts to maintain a link between Mukden and North China.

Breaking out anew in the north, the Communist offensive took Kirin—abandoned by the Sixty-ninth Army for Changchun[2]—on 9 March, and Szepingkai on the 13th. Changchun, some 120 miles to the north of Mukden, was now completely isolated; and Mukden itself was now the center of a circular Nationalist-held area no more than sixty miles in diameter.

The situation in Manchuria was desperate. Unwilling, at any price, to lose face, the Generalissimo had refused to evacuate his troops while there was still time, as he had been advised to do by General Barr, the director of JUSMAG.[3] The garrisons of Mukden and Changchun were now being re-supplied only by air (seven to ten aircraft per day), and it was clear that such airheads could not be held indefinitely. Consequently, a Nationalist offensive to reopen the Liaoning corridor, at all costs, was clearly necessary. But to the Nationalists, frozen as they were in a defensive mentality, no attack was conceivable without a numerical superiority of at least three to one. None of General Barr's suggestions was accepted.

---

[1] Following the fall of Liaoyang, General Wei had assigned forty C–47 "Dakotas" to the transport of troops from northern Manchuria to Mukden.

[2] This shift came about at the insistence of Chiang's American advisers, who felt that all of Manchuria should have been evacuated at this time. Chiang, however, consented only to the evacuation of Kirin.

[3] The Joint U.S. Military Advisory Group to China.

To his increasingly strong and even angry representations, the sole response was new requests for more weapons and matériel. Yet the Mukden garrison, consisting of the Fifty-second Army, the Thirteenth Army, and the New Sixth Army— 200,000 men, well trained, well armed, supported by ample artillery and even tanks—could easily have broken out to link up with relieving forces from Chinchow. But General Wei Li-huang could think only of static defense.

Thus, for two months all was quiet on the Manchurian front. Only the Nationalist Air Force was active, bombing— to no great effect—Tsitsihar, Meihowkow, Hailung, Tunghwa, and Yingkow, and attacking trains on the Harbin-Kirin, Kirin-Tunghwa, and Tashihkiao-Yingkow lines, which had been restored to operation by the Reds. Profiting from the inaction of his adversaries, Lin Piao sent part of his forces to the aid of his comrade Li Yung-chang in Jehol, and devoted his time to training his troops and organizing new columns. As the summer went by there were only small skirmishes, with the Nationalists attempting a sortie to the south in May and the Reds continuing their close investment of Changchun, where famine gradually set in. Yet one could sense that the last round in Manchuria was drawing near.

OPERATIONS IN NORTH CHINA

In North China, at the beginning of 1948, General Fu Tso-yi, with his headquarters at Peking, kept a firm hold upon the Tientsin-Peking-Kalgan-Tatung-Paotow line with 230,000 troops of his own private army. His forces thus were able to maintain contact with the troops of Ma Hung-ku'ei, the governor of Ningsia, who had won the battle of Yulin. In contrast, the situation in Shansi was much less favorable to the Nationalists: Marshal Yen Hsi-shan, with 200,000 men, was practically encircled at Taiyuan, and Nationalist forces in the south of the province now held no more than the town of Linfen and a small bridgehead across the Yellow River. In Shensi, General Hu Tsung-nan[4] still held Yenan, but was experiencing difficulties accentuated by Communist guerrilla attacks which gradually wore down his forces. Finally, three fourths of Jehol and Chahar was in the hands of the Communists. Here the Reds had reinforced Nieh Jung-chen, who had eighty thousand regulars, while in Shansi and northern Shensi, Ho Lung and P'eng Te-huai together had only fifty thousand men.

THE BATTLE OF ICHWAN AND THE RED DEFEAT AT PAOKI

The first important operation was the battle of Ichwan, in Shensi, which ended in the recapture of Yenan by the Reds. The offensive was launched on 29 February 1948 by General P'eng Te-huai, who had spent most of January and February in reorganizing his twelve columns along the regulation lines prescribed for Communist columns. Debouching from the Anyi area and attacking toward the northwest, P'eng's forces encircled and annihilated four brigades of the Twenty-ninth Army; the army commander, General Liu Kan, who had taken Yenan the year before, was killed on the battlefield, and numerous other generals were killed or captured. Ichwan fell on 3 March, its capture by the Communists accompanied by their destruction of a new brigade of the 76th Infantry Division. Kanchuan fell to them on the 5th and Fuhsien the next day. By 10 March the Reds had arrived in front of Loch-

---

[4] It is interesting to note that this Nationalist commander's troops were equipped with *Russian* matériel, given to Chiang Kai-shek by the U.S.S.R. at the beginning of the war against Japan.

wan where the Nationalists, pulling themselves together, managed to put up a staunch resistance. In the belief that he had sufficiently weakened the enemy, P'eng Te-huai left the siege of Lochwan to part of his forces and, concentrating four of his columns and two cavalry divisions about sixty miles north of Sian, on 17 April launched an audacious raid toward Szechwan, with only his 3rd Column as rear guard.

The Nationalists then decided to evacuate Yenan and abandon the city to the Reds. At the price of this hard blow to their prestige, they were to gain a real success. After leaving Yenan and relieving and gathering up the defenders of Lochwan, the 27th and 17th infantry divisions set off in pursuit of P'eng Te-huai. It was high time: the Communists had by now crossed the King river at Pinhsien and cut the Lanchow-Sian road between Changwu and Kienhsien; by 27 April, they had taken Paoki, on the Wei river at the western extremity of the Lunghai railroad, a town in which the Reds found much valuable booty. P'eng now posed a direct threat from the north to the province of Szechwan, the Nationalists' holy of holies, and they bore in on him from all sides. A division coming from the east retook Paoki on 28 April. A Moslem cavalry division from General Ma Pu-fang's command rushed down the Lanchow-Sian road from Tsinghai. Finally, the divisions moving down from Yenan cut off P'eng Te-huai's retreat. A decisive battle then ensued within the triangle Linyu-Fengsiang-Kienyang; the Reds lost half their strength, and were forced to pull back into northern Shensi. Despite this defeat, the Communists managed to keep their hold on almost all of Shensi, and their base in Shansi remained sheltered from Nationalist attacks. And even P'eng's defeat itself had served to demonstrate that, henceforth, Szechwan was vulnerable to Communist attack.

THE BATTLE OF LOYANG

The second major operation was the battle of Loyang, a strategically important city on the Lunghai railroad taken by Ch'en Keng's army in a northward attack from Honan. Loyang fell to the Reds on 12 March, only to be retaken by the Nationalists on 18 March; it changed hands for the last time when the Reds, in their turn, retook the city on 7 April 1948. Thus, the Communist base in Shansi was now and henceforth linked to Liu Po-ch'eng's newly organized Red base in Central China. The Reds rounded out their victory at Loyang by taking Linfen, the last island of government resistance in southern Shansi; the city and its 25,000-man garrison fell to the Communists on 17 May. The Red troops freed by its fall immediately moved north to join in the siege of Taiyuan.

OPERATIONS IN SHANTUNG AND KIANGSU

Despite the departure of Ch'en I's forces from Shantung, the Communists, during the first half of 1948, continued to gnaw away at Nationalist strength in the province. This strength was further reduced by the need for Nationalist reinforcements in Manchuria, and for the formation of a reserve against the threat of Liu Po-ch'eng's columns along the Yangtze. Slowly, the Red guerrillas regained the upper hand. They reduced, one by one, the Nationalist strong points along the Kiaotsi railroad. On 27 April they seized Weihsien and entered Weihaiwei, which had been "voluntarily" abandoned by the Nationalists; they now could block off Tsinan, defended by 100,000 men, and Tsingtao, still occupied by American forces (a naval task force, three thousand Marines, and fifty combat aircraft).

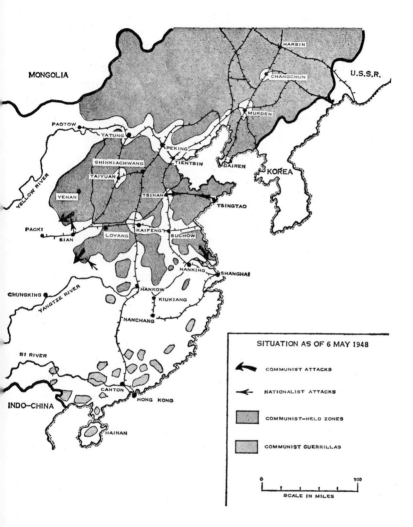

SITUATION AS OF 6 MAY 1948

COMMUNIST ATTACKS

NATIONALIST ATTACKS

COMMUNIST-HELD ZONES

COMMUNIST GUERRILLAS

SCALE IN MILES

While their leaders argued among themselves, the Nationalist soldiers gradually fell prey to Communist propaganda. By the end of April the Shantung peninsula, except for Chefoo, had been completely mopped up by the Communists. The last of Ch'en I's columns were now free to move westward and isolate Suchow, as Su Yü's forces made their appearance in southern Kiangsu with the capture of Honancheng, about sixty miles to the east of Nanking.

THE BATTLE OF KAIFENG

Following the fall of Loyang the Communist objectives in Central China became Chengchow and, above all, the city of Kaifeng. The battle of Kaifeng is of capital importance in the history of the Civil War. For the first time, the Reds, abandoning guerrilla tactics for positional warfare, were to join battle with the Nationalists in open country and maneuver large masses of infantry, artillery, and even some tanks.

Preceding this major milestone, some interesting politico-military developments took place within the Nationalist camp during May 1948. After the re-election of Chiang Kai-shek as President by the National Assembly at Nanking in April, the Vice Presidency became the object of a bitter struggle. The election of General Li Tsung-jen, who was not the Generalissimo's candidate for this post, appeared to be a sure index of Chiang's waning influence. The political crisis which followed this election was ended, on 24 May, only by the naming of Dr. Wong Wen-hao as premier,[5] with General Ho Ying-ch'in as Minister of National Defense and Dr. Wang Shih-chieh as Minister of Foreign Affairs. Simultaneously, General Ku Chu-t'ung became Chief of the Supreme Staff, and was replaced as Commander in Chief of the Army by General

[5] Or President of the Executive Yüan. Tr.

Yü Han-mou. These two generals were known for two principal characteristics: their professional mediocrity, and their fierce loyalty to Chiang Kai-sek. Their incompetence was promptly proved by the battle of Kaifeng.

Kaifeng, the capital of Honan province, is a city of about 300,000 inhabitants, surrounded by ramparts and served by two airfields. Its military significance lies in its covering location to the east of Chengchow, the strategically important junction of the Lunghai and Pinghan railroads. In May 1948 the Nationalists had twenty-five brigades in the Chengchow-Kaifeng area, about 250,000 men; added to these regular troops were about fifty thousand men of the Peace Preservation Corps, railroad guards, and various auxiliary units. These forces were divided into three group armies, commanded by generals Chiu Ching-chuan, Huang Po-tao, and Ou Shou-nien. Against these considerable numbers the Reds threw eighteen columns, about 200,000 regulars, supported by guerrillas, and organized into five groups assigned to the armies of Ch'en I, Ch'en Keng, and Liu Po-ch'eng. General Ch'en I had over-all command of the entire operation.

The Red attack started at the end of May. One group moved down from Shantung, took Taian on 30 May, and advanced southward along the Tsinpu railroad, while another group, coming from Shansi, crossed the Yellow River at Puhsien and advanced as far as the area around Kinsiang and Chengwu. The latter group was then blocked by the Nationalist Fifth Army, which sought to prevent the junction of the two Communist groups. The Fifth Army being thus engaged, Ch'en I moved from the center of Honan toward Chengwu with a third Red group, his initial idea being to hit the Fifth Army from the rear. In pursuit of this plan he crossed the Lunghai railroad, reaching the Lanfeng-Kaocheng area on 15 June. Then, receiving intelligence on the weakness of the

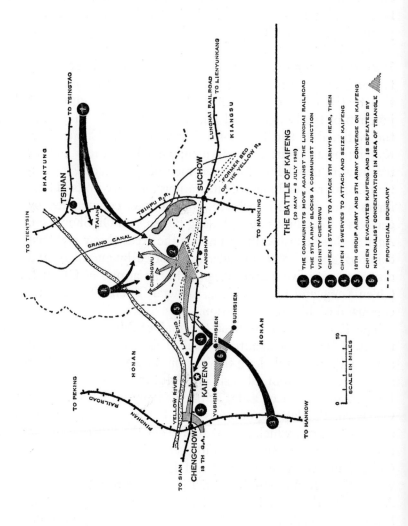

THE BATTLE OF KAIFENG
(30 MAY – 8 JULY 1948)

1 THE COMMUNISTS MOVE AGAINST THE LUNGHAI RAILROAD
2 THE 5TH ARMY BLOCKS A COMMUNIST JUNCTION
   VICINITY CHENGWU
3 CHEN I STARTS TO ATTACK 5TH ARMY'S REAR, THEN
4 CHEN I SWERVES TO ATTACK AND SEIZE KAIFENG
5 18TH GROUP ARMY AND 5TH ARMY CONVERGE ON KAIFENG
6 CHEN I EVACUATES KAIFENG AND IS DEFEATED BY
   NATIONALIST CONCENTRATION IN AREA OF TRIANGLE

▨ NATIONALIST CONCENTRATION
‒ ‒ ‒ PROVINCIAL BOUNDARY

SCALE IN MILES
0   50

garrison at Kaifeng, Ch'en abandoned his initial scheme of maneuver and improvised a swift descent upon the capital of Honan, with the aim of looting its large depots and gaining a success of enormous psychological value. He thus launched his three columns against Kaifeng and, after a brief struggle against weak resistance, took the airfields on 17 June and the city itself on the 19th.

The capture of Kaifeng did indeed produce a considerable effect: since the fall of Kalgan, it was the first provincial capital to be taken by the Reds. The Generalissimo himself hastened by air to Chengchow, where he took over personal direction of operations. At his orders Kaifeng was bombed by the Nationalist Air Force which, flying much too high, obtained no militarily significant results and contented itself with killing civilians. Meanwhile, the Nationalists hurried their troops to the scene of Ch'en's audacious victory. The Fifth Army and part of the 16th Group Army closed in on Kaifeng from the east and west. In the face of this threat, Ch'en I slipped smoothly out of the city on 25 June and, well covered by the columns of Ch'en Keng and Liu Po-ch'eng, withdrew his forces eastward to the south of the Lunghai railroad. Within a triangular area bounded by Suihsien-Kihsien-Yushih there now took place a great battle. It lasted until 8 July and ended in a partial defeat for the Communists who, seeing clearly that they could not win, rapidly dispersed to the north, south, and southeast, leaving a void before the victors. But the Reds had inflicted ninety thousand casualties upon their foes; and the Nationalists, despite their final success, had shown in this battle a marked tactical inferiority to an adversary who had continually kept the initiative and dominated the situation.

Moreover, the behavior of Communist troops at Kaifeng had greatly impressed the populace: perfect discipline, no pillage, no arbitrary arrests, the helpfulness constantly shown by the Red soldiers to the sorely tried inhabitants of the city —all this added to the prestige of the Communists. And the Reds now had well-organized fifth columns in all the cities. As soon as they arrived in Kaifeng, for example, they readily found the local personnel needed for the establishment of a provisional administration; the Nationalists discovered, to their angry consternation, that even the head of the Kuomintang's propaganda office in Kaifeng was a Communist agent!

With respect to the Nationalist high command, the record of an interview with one of the Nationalist field army commanders[6] after the Kaifeng offensive is of interest:

In March 1948, Ch'en I moved north of the Yellow River to regroup. Three months later we were warned that he was preparing an offensive. At this time we were south of the Yellow River, facing the 1st, 4th, 6th, and 11th columns, plus the Two Kwangs Column and the Rapid Column. Then two of Ch'en I's columns south of the Lunghai railroad, the 3rd and the 8th, started moving west toward Shangkiu. Those *fumbling bunglers* in the National Defense Ministry ordered me to displace to the south to intercept these two columns. I wired back that if I were to do so, the Communists would move the main body of their forces south of the Yellow River. They replied that if the Reds were to do this, I would still be able to get back in time to stop them. So I obeyed the order and moved south. We marched over thirty miles a day, getting only two hours' sleep out of the twenty-four, but before we could catch up with the 3rd and 8th columns, Ch'en I slipped across the Yellow River with his main body. The Defense Ministry then ordered me back to my former positions. My soldiers were furious, but we turned around and went back. . .

On 26 June, I was all set to move into Kaifeng. The Generalissimo wired me from Sian: "Enter Kaifeng." But the Ministry of Defense panicked: before I ever got the Generalissimo's message about Kaifeng, the Ministry ordered me to move south imme-

[6] The energetic General Chiu Ching-chuan (who was later killed in the fighting around Suchow in January 1949. Tr.)

diately to Kihsien, and ordered Ou Shou-nien to displace from Shangshui to Suihsien. . .

On 30 June the Ministry ordered me to go to the rescue of General Shen.[7] I started moving out toward the east on 1 July, with my 83rd Infantry Division taking heavy losses. On 2 July a plane dropped a message to me from the Ministry: five new Communist columns, under Liu Po-ch'eng, were about to hit me from the rear. I turned around, but there was nothing there. This false report must have been put out by the Communists . . . and the Ministry, as usual, fell for it.

THE RELATIVE SITUATION OF EACH SIDE AS OF 1 JULY 1948

In a secret session of the Legislative Yüan on 24 June 1948, generals Ho Ying-ch'in and Hsiao Yi-shu, the Minister and Deputy Minister of Defense respectively, revealed some very interesting information regarding long-term changes in the strength of the two sides. At the time of Japan's surrender, the government had had 3,700,000 men, of whom 1,620,000 were armed, and six thousand artillery pieces.[8] Against these, the Communists had had 320,000 regulars, of whom 166,000 were armed, and six hundred artillery pieces. By late June 1948 the situation had changed drastically. While the strength of regular troops in the Nationalist Army had been reduced by about one third, the number of Red regulars had quintupled, and the Communists had attained parity with their adversary in combat matériel. The Nationalists now had no more than 2,180,000 men, 980,000 of them armed, and 21,000 artillery pieces. Opposing them now were 1,560,000 Red regulars and 700,000 guerrillas, with a total of 970,000 rifles and 22,800 artillery pieces. And it is easy to guess where the

[7] Commander of the Nationalist 75th Infantry Division, then engaged at Suihsien.
[8] Including 37mm. guns and mortars.

greater part of all this Red matériel came from: it had been captured from the Nationalists.

For their part, the legislators sharply criticized the poor organization of the high command, the unfair rewards and punishments, the favoritism and empire-building of influential generals. They broke out in particularly harsh denunciation of the officers who set themselves up in business with military funds, and used army trucks for the transport of their "merchandise."

In reply, General Ho Ying-ch'in declared that he was sending inspectors to all troop units in an effort to restore proper discipline; he had prohibited the trafficking denounced by the legislators; he was struggling against the practice of officers to pad payrolls and pocket the pay of nonexistent enlisted men; he was seeking to raise the pay of officers and men alike, which by now had dwindled to one fourth and one fifth, respectively, of prewar levels.

This memorable session clearly revealed the deep malaise and discouragement which prevailed among the Nationalists, at a time when their adversaries were gaining one success after another—as shown by the appearance of Communist guerrillas in every province of Nationalist China, and especially in Kwangsi, in Kwangtung, and even in Szechwan.

It was in North China that the situation of the Nationalists, thanks to the quality of Fu Tso-yi's troops and his good administration, remained the most stable. But the government's need to withdraw troops from Chahar and Jehol, in order to reinforce Manchuria, had permitted the Reds to intensify increasingly numerous attacks against the Tatung-Kalgan-Peking-Tientsin railroad and the Tientsin-Shanhaikwan and Peking-Kupehkow lines, which were repeatedly cut, and to keep the entire region south of Peking in a permanent state of confusion. At the end of the first half of 1948 the government still held its essential bastions in North China (the quadrilateral Peking-Tientsin-Mukden-Chengteh) and in Central China (Suchow, Chengchow, Sian), in this manner covering the valley of the Yangtze. Nonetheless, the situation south of the Great Wall was back where it had been in January of 1946. Indeed, the Communists had made appreciable gains since that time:

(a) Occupation of all of Shantung except Tsinan, the Lini salient near the Kiangsu border, and the two hemmed-in ports at Chefoo and Tsingtao; the Nationalists, moreover, had suffered enormous losses in the battles of Weihsien (45th Infantry Division) and Kiaohsien (32nd Infantry Division);

(b) Occupation of all of Shansi, except for the besieged capital at Taiyuan; the capture of Linfen, where the Nationalists' 30th Infantry Division was completely destroyed; the capture in June 1948 of all the towns in the central plain, and the destruction of two thirds of Yen Hsi-shan's forces;

(c) Reoccupation of Yenan and occupation of western Honan, including Loyang.

To offset these Red victories the Nationalists could claim only meager successes: incomplete reduction of Liu Po-ch'eng's bastion in the Tapieh Shan; P'eng Te-huai's check at Paoki; and the reoccupation of Kaifeng.

In the first half of 1948 the directives of Mao Tse-tung and Chu Teh brought about a complete change in the nature of Communist operations. During the first year of war (generally speaking, the period from July 1946 to July 1947), the course of operations had followed an almost immutable pattern. The Nationalists would concentrate their forces in a zone of particular interest, and launch a powerful and sometimes rapid push along the axis of a major road or railroad. Normally, they would reach their objective against little or no resistance. Communist units would then stage only brief and limited attacks against such vulnerable targets as isolated strong points, displacing units, or lines of communication. In nature if not in degree, their actions differed very little from those of guerrillas who attempt to make an occupied region untenable for the enemy. Except for the first battle of Szepingkai, this early period saw the careful avoidance by the Communists of any prolonged, positional battle, and very few sieges on their part. Only in regions of reputedly impregnable terrain did the Reds ever seek to make a serious stand.

September and October of 1947 marked the beginning of a profound change in this pattern, not only in Manchuria but in China Proper as well. Without renouncing its traditional hit-and-run tactics, the Red Army now showed that it no longer feared to undertake sieges: Weihsien, Linfen, Tzeyang, and Loyang were taken; Tatung, Changchun, Chengteh, and Tsinan were attacked; Kaifeng, though subsequently retaken by the Nationalists, had fallen to the Reds. But of far greater significance was the increasing frequency of Communist operations in open country, at first in Manchuria and then in China Proper. And these movements were being made in ever greater strength: P'eng Te-huai attacked between Lanchow and Sian with six columns, and no fewer than sixteen Red columns had been concentrated in the course of the battles at Kaifeng and Kihsien. Communist operations now appeared to be better coordinated, more precise in their goals, more extensive in the choice of their objectives. Although they could not yet be compared to the operations which have unfolded upon the battlefronts of Europe, they at least showed an evolution in Communist strategy and tactics which more and more approached the scale and level sustained by their adversaries in the early months of the war.

A second important development was the southward shift in the war's center of gravity. The main theater of operations in 1946 had been in Manchuria; in 1947, Manchuria and, above all, Shantung, were the great cockpits of conflict. In October 1947 the strength of Red regulars to the south of the Lunghai railroad had totaled no more than eighty thousand men (forty thousand under Ch'en I, twenty thousand under Liu Po-ch'eng, and twenty thousand under Ch'en Keng). Now, in July 1948, official Nationalist estimates put the strength of regular Red troops in Central China at 450,000 or 500,000 men—a five-fold increase in less than one year. Where, in the previous year, Communist units had been chased from both sides of the Lunghai and Pinghan railroads, it was now they who were doing most of the chasing, and who penned the Nationalists into the few population centers which remained to them. Three or four times in the past the Nationalists had pushed the Communists back into western Honan, and restored the Chengchow-Hankow section of the Pinghan rail line. Now they seemed too tired to do so, or incapable of doing so—even during the Kaifeng crisis, when they were stopped in their northward advance from the Sinyang area. As of 1 July 1948, *fully half the strength of both the Communists and the Nationalists was now in Central China.* This region had become the main theater of operations, without any lessening of previous activity along the northern fronts. And the regular forces of the Reds, as always under the supreme command of Chu Teh,[9] had now been organized into six field armies: the People's Liberation Army of Northwest China, commanded by P'eng Te-huai, with Wang Wei-chou and Chao Shou-shan as his deputies; the People's Liberation Army of North China, com-

[9] Mao Tse-tung remained Chairman of the Revolutionary Military Council. Yeh Chien-ying was Chief of Staff of the Red Army (by late 1947 known by its present name of "People's Liberation Army." Tr.)

manded by Nieh Jung-chen (deputy commander, Hsü Hsiang-ch'ien); the United Democratic Army of the Northeast, commanded by Lin Piao (with Lü Cheng-ts'ao and Hsiao Ching-kuang as deputies); the Shansi-Suiyuan-Shenkanning Field Army, commanded by Ho Lung (with Chang Tsung-hsun as deputy); the Liberation Army of the Central Plains, under Liu Po-ch'eng; and the People's Liberation Army of East China, commanded by Ch'en I, with Su Yü as deputy commander and Chen Shih-chu as Chief of Staff.

CHAPTER XIII

1948: The Last Six Months

THE second half of 1948 was to see the collapse of the Nationalists in Manchuria, the loss of their last stronghold in Shantung, and the fall of Kaifeng, Chengchow, Paoting, and Taiyuan to the Communists. The loss of these cities was in turn to bring about the total isolation of Fu Tso-yi's forces in the Peking-Tientsin-Kalgan area. And this area, in turn, was thenceforth cut off from Central China and the two provinces of the West, Ningsia and Tsinghai, which still remained faithful to the Nationalists.

THE BATTLE OF TSINAN

Tsinan, the capital of Shantung, is a city of about 700,000 inhabitants. The old walled city is adjoined, to the west, by a modern industrial section with many textile factories. On the north, the city is bordered by the lower course of the Yangtze. It is on the Tsinpu and Kiaotsi railroads, and until April 1948 the trains were still running between Tsinan and Suchow. There were two airfields, one to the northwest of the city and the other to the south, which were dominated by hills the Nationalists had taken care to enclose within the defensive perimeter they had set up around the city. Held by the Nationalists since the surrender of the Japanese, Tsinan had played an important role in their operations in Shantung. At first it had been a base of departure for Nationalist offensives; but it gradually became a refuge for the badly mauled units from the central part of the province. Since the Communist offensive of April-May 1948 the city had been completely isolated, except by air. Its garrison, about sixty thousand strong, was commanded by General Wang Yao-wu, who was also the governor of Shantung.

At the beginning of September all of Ch'en I's columns that had taken part in the operations in Honan rejoined his forces in Shantung. These were formed into three groups: one group, composed of four columns, acted as a blocking and screening force to the east and south of Tsinan; the second group echeloned its three columns along the Tsinpu railroad between Taian and Tzeyang; the third group, with seven columns, concentrated in the Kinsiang-Chengwu area. Farther south, the Reds posted two columns around the Nationalist stronghold at Lini. And to the west of the Pinghan railroad, midway between Chengcow and Sinyang, the Communists concentrated eight columns, in groups commanded by Liu Po-ch'eng, Ch'en Keng, and Li Hsien-nien.

The Nationalist reaction to this threat has been described by General Barr:

Decision was made by the Generalissimo to defend isolated Tsinan to the last. (Such decisions have been costly to the Nationalists in troops and supplies.) I pointed out again to the Generalissimo and to the Supreme Staff the futility of attempting to hold cities from within restricted perimeters by purely defensive measures against overpowering enemy forces. Tsinan at this time was isolated from Suchow by Communist forces at Yenchow and Taian. Although in considerable strength in this area the main Communist force was still on the Honan plains, southeast of Kaifeng. An opportunity existed to do one of two things. By offensive action north from Suchow and south from Tsinan, the Nationalist forces were capable of destroying the Communists and reopening the corridor between Suchow and Tsinan. The Nationalists were also capable at this time of evacuating Tsinan and withdrawing into Suchow. Having no confidence in the will to fight of the Tsinan garrison after their ineffective attempt to recapture Weihsien, and having heard reports of the questionable loyalty of some of the senior commanders, I recommended that the city be evacuated, and the troops be withdrawn to Suchow. Again, as in the case of Changchun, I was told that because of political reasons, Tsinan, the capital of Shantung Province, must be defended. . .

At a meeting in the Ministry of National Defense War Room on 14 September 1948, the following observations were made by the Chinese:

The G3[1] stated that although completely surrounded and isolated, food was still coming to Tsinan from the countryside. He believed that an additional division could be air-lifted into Tsinan to assist in the defense. I recommended strongly against this, believing that the city was lost and that it only meant the loss to the Nationalists of an additional division. One had already been air-lifted in from Tsingtao. I recommended that rather than fly in additional troops, the present Tsinan garrison be air-lifted to Suchow.[2]

Unfortunately, this wise counsel was not followed. In the face of the Nationalists' inertia, Ch'en I—who had nothing to fear from the north, was well covered to the south, and protected, by the latent threat of Liu Po-ch'eng's forces, against any Nationalist counterattack from Kaifeng—launched his eight columns against Tsinan at midnight, 14–15 September. The attacking Reds rapidly seized the airfield to the northwest of the city, interdicted the southern airfield with their

[1] On the Nationalists' Supreme Staff, the G3 was the general staff officer for war plans.
[2] U.S. Department of State, *United States Relations with China, with Special Reference to the Period 1944–1949* (U.S. Government Printing Office, 1949), pp. 330–331. *Tr.*

fire, and hustled the defenders back from the perimeter into the city itself. General Wu Hua-wen, commander of the Nationalist 84th Division and—either through conviction or corruption—a hitherto secret Communist, tried to bring his entire division into the enemy camp. Although his plan was partially foiled by the fidelity of the 155th Brigade's commander, the Communists promptly profited from the confusion produced among the defenders by Wu's treason, and penetrated into the new part of the city. Successively the Two Kwangs Column, the Rapid Column, the 7th Column, launched their assaults; on 24 September, they stormed the north gate of the old city, and Tsinan was engulfed by Red troops who rapidly mopped up the last resistance. On 25 September the Nationalist high command admitted, in veiled terms, the loss of the city, estimating that it had cost the Communists fifty thousand casualties against a Nationalist loss of twenty thousand. But the fact was that the Reds took fifty thousand rifles at Tsinan, and large stocks of ammunition.

In a message to his superiors, the American Consul General at Tsingtao described the causes of the Nationalists' defeat:

Prime cause for swift loss of city is *psychological* [author's italics] rather than material or military. Nationalist garrison had been isolated for two months with no possibility ground support. Previous Nationalist defeats in which Nationalist troops *failed to fight* [author's italics] known to Tsinan garrison and people. Communist victory at Tsinan felt inevitable in view record of failure of Nationalists and consistent victories of Communists who at Tsinan used many of best troops. Nationalist soldiers and population Shantung in general no longer consider Nationalist Government merits continued support in civil war, loss of lives and economic chaos. These factors expressed themselves in outright defection to Communists, immediate surrenders, and failure to stand and fight. Those soldiers willing to fight were unable to trust other units to support them. No mutuality of feelings between regular forces and local Peace Preservation Corps troops. Nationalist regulars were largely from Central and South China and had little interest in defending strange city and people. Communists undoubtedly had organized support within city. No real attempt made to defend perimeter at distance outside of city wall. Antiquated custom of falling back to city walls was speedily observed by Nationalist defenders. Other military causes were poor intelligence, failure to take initiative against Communists when concentrating for campaign and thus keeping them off balance. Belated inadequate improper air support.

In summary, majority troops at Tsinan did not want to fight while those that did fight found their position made impossible by the disaffected. Defection of Wu Hua-wen was merely the manifestation of a general phenomenon. His treason was not of itself the cause of defeat.

Nationalists at Tsinan had ample ammunition and food and assurance of further supplies in event protracted siege.[3]

Disastrous as it was, the fall of Tsinan was only the harbinger of the catastrophe to come in Manchuria.

THE MANCHURIAN CATASTROPHE

The final Communist offensive in the Northeast was launched on 12 September 1948. For this climactic effort Lin Piao had assembled a total of 600,000 men:[4] 65,000 around

---

[3] U.S. Relations with China, pp. 319–320. Tr.

[4] This figure reflects the fact that the strength of Lin's forces had doubled within one year. This increase, moreover, had been achieved through the formation of new units whose personnel came from Manchuria itself. As for his concept of operations, Lin's major goal was to unhinge the remaining Nationalist communications in southern Manchuria. So long as they held their bridgehead at Chinchow, to the north of the Great Wall, and maintained their garrisons between Chinchow and Mukden, it would always be possible for the Nationalists to restore contact between North China and South Manchuria. But the capture of Chinchow by the Communists would result in the confinement of Nationalist forces to the narrow corridor between the mountains and the sea, and the complete encirclement of Mukden: it would then be all over for the Nationalists in Manchuria.

Changchun, 183,000 around Mukden, 179,000 between Mukden and Chinchow, and 180,000 in reserve. To these 600,000 Reds the Nationalists could now oppose only 300,000 men: 60,000 at Changchun, 200,000 at Mukden, and only 40,000 between Chinchow and Chinsi.

Lin Piao threw thirteen columns of Red regulars into his victorious battle of Chinchow. Covering himself against a possible sortie from Mukden, he first snapped up, in succession, the last Nationalist garrisons between Mukden and Chinchow. He then turned the full weight of his attacking forces upon Chinchow. The attempts of the Nationalist high command to relieve the beleaguered city were all in vain. Leaving too late from Hulutao, elements of the Thirty-first Army, which had come all the way from Formosa, were stopped before they could reach Chinchow. The same thing happened to a relief column sent out from Mukden[5] which, instead of heading straight for Chinchow, divided its forces in divergent attempts to re-establish contact with Changchun, on the one hand, and to retake Yingkow on the other. In the meantime Chinchow, together with General Fan Han-chieh and a garrison of 100,000 men, yielded to the Communists on 17 October 1948. With its fall came the destruction of the entire system of Nationalist communications, and the loss of immense supply stocks to the Reds. On 20 October a last attempt to retake Chinchow was shattered by Lin Piao's powerful forces. And the same day saw the fall of Changchun, the capital of Manchuria: part of its garrison, the Sixtieth Army, refusing to attempt a break-out toward Mukden, had turned upon and disarmed, with Communist cooperation, the New Seventh Army. General Cheng Tung-kuo, the garrison

---

[5] General Wei Li-huang, commanding at Mukden, received Chiang Kai-shek's order to go to the relief of Chinchow on 25 September. Wei did not move out until 7 October.

commander, was a prisoner; five divisions, with all their equipment, had fallen into the hands of the Reds.

After so disastrous a defeat the Nationalists now had no other alternative than to evacuate from Mukden, if possible, the bulk of their remaining forces. Earlier, on 11 October, the Mukden garrison had succeeded in retaking Yingkow and reopening the Mukden-Anshan-Yingkow rail line. But instead of capitalizing on this by using the last way open to them to evacuate their main body from Mukden, and fastening a firm grip around the port of Yingkow, the Nationalists persisted in their attempts to retake Chinchow. While most of the Mukden garrison moved out down the Mukden-Chinchow rail line toward the rail center at Kowpangtze, the eleven Nationalist divisions at Hulutao, by attempting to move on Chinchow from the south, sought to link up with the forces coming from Mukden and assure their evacuation by way of Hulutao.

On 27 October the bulk of the Mukden garrison, which had been formed into a group army commanded by General Liao Yao-hsiang and made up of the New First, Third, and New Sixth armies, plus the Seventy-first Army and elements of the Forty-ninth Army, reached Tahushan, about halfway to Chinchow. Mukden itself was now held by nothing more than the Fifty-third Army and two brigades of the 207th Youth Infantry Division. The Fifty-second Army was strung out along the Mukden-Yingkow rail line. This inviting strategic situation was immediately exploited by Lin Piao, who now maneuvered in a manner worthy of Napoleon's first Italian campaign, or of the Germans at Tannenberg. Leaving only two columns (the 9th and 11th) to watch the Nationalist forces moving northward from Hulutao, the Red commander slipped his main body of eleven columns, some 200,000 men, to the southeast of Liao's advancing group army, and hit it

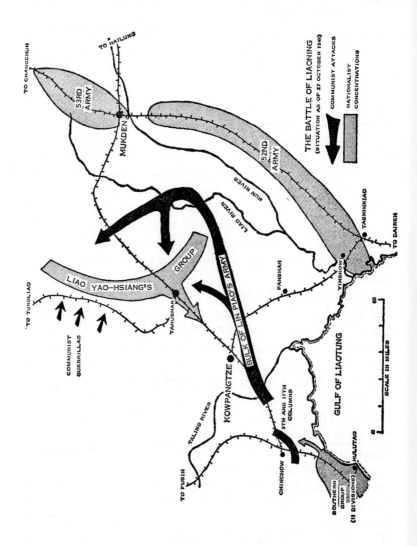

THE BATTLE OF LIAONING
(SITUATION AS OF 27 OCTOBER 1948)

COMMUNIST ATTACKS

NATIONALIST CONCENTRATIONS

TO CHANGCHUN

TO HAILUNG

53RD ARMY

MUKDEN

52ND ARMY

HUN RIVER

LIAO RIVER

TASHIHKIAO

TO DAIREN

YAO—HSIANG'S GROUP

LIAO

TAHUSHAN

PANSHAN

YINGKOW

TO TUNGLIAO

COMMUNIST GUERRILLAS

BULK OF LIN PIAO'S ARMY

KOWPANGTZE

GULF OF LIAOTUNG

SCALE IN MILES

TALING RIVER

9TH AND 11TH COLUMNS

TO FUSIN

CHINCHOW

SOUTHERN GROUP (11 DIVISIONS)

HULUTAO

190

from the flank and rear. As the Nationalist troops in Mukden looked on, the Red columns in seventy-two hours of furious fighting dispersed, destroyed, or captured Liao's entire group army. General Liao, killed in the early hours of the battle, was spared the end of the debacle, which came on 30 October. For the Fifty-third Army, shut up in Mukden, there was now nothing to do but surrender—a fall facilitated by the defection of General Chou Fu-cheng, the garrison commander, to the Reds. As for the Fifty-second Army, it was only the twenty thousand men in the port of Yingkow who were able to escape, by sea, the Red avalanche which flowed over Yingkow itself on 5 November.

This series of disasters had far-reaching effects. The battle in western Liaoning had cost the Nationalists eleven infantry divisions, one Youth Brigade, and three regiments, either captured or destroyed; three generals had been made prisoner, and General Liao Yao-hsiang had been killed. At Mukden, the equivalent of seven divisions had been taken by the Reds. At Chinchow, the Nationalists had lost eight infantry divisions, or 122,000 men—some 88,000 of them, including thirty-six generals and 197 field-grade officers, taken as prisoners. Added to these losses were the division and a half lost at Yingkow and the five divisions lost at Changchun, plus an immense amount of matériel. In total, the loss of Manchuria cost the Nationalists seven armies[6]—some twenty-nine infantry divisions, three Youth Brigades equaling three infantry divisions in strength, two cavalry brigades, four regiments, and numerous nondivisional units—a total of at least 400,000 men. Lost with them were all their weapons, of which about one third were of American make; to these losses were added the

[6] These were the following: New First Army, New Third Army, New Sixth Army, Sixth Army, Forty-ninth Army, Fifty-third Army, and Seventy-first Army.

enormous stocks of military supplies, the entire arsenals—including the one at Mukden, the best-equipped of all—which also became the booty of the Reds. And now the Communists, henceforth relieved of any concern regarding their rear, were free to move Lin Piao's forces to the south of the Great Wall; after losing their last reserves, the Nationalists, driven from Manchuria by Lin Piao's well-trained and combat-tested columns, were again to be confronted by this formidable force of 400,000 crack Red regulars.

Chiang Kai-shek did not, of course, give up. Hastily withdrawing from Hulutao the eleven divisions[7] whose culpable passivity had partially provoked the disaster in Manchuria, he reassigned some of them (General Li Wen's corps) to Fu Tso-yi's command; the remainder, some eighty thousand men of the Fifth, Ninth, and Fifty-fourth armies, went to the Central China command. "The loss of Manchuria," declared Chiang, "is discouraging; but it relieves the government of a formidable burden, so far as military defenses are concerned, and allows it to concentrate its war effort to the south of the Great Wall."

But Lin Piao's forces were already pouring into Hopeh, where they regrouped to form front against the Peking-Tientsin line. Chiang's fate was sealed.

THE BATTLE OF SUCHOW

After the fall of Tsinan, the only important bastions remaining to keep the Red armies from the Yangtze and Nanking were Suchow, the Nationalists' main base in Central China, and Pengpu, a city in Anhwei situated on the Tsinpu

---

[7] These forces did not include the divisions of the Ninety-third Army, which had been annihilated, or of the Sixtieth Army from Yunnan, which had gone over to the Reds.

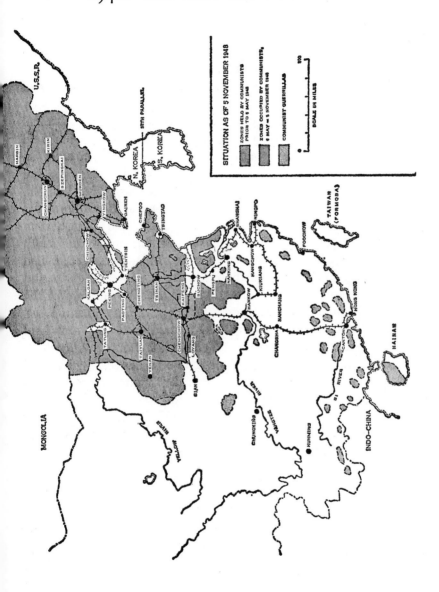

railroad and the river Hwai, at the southern edge of the central plain. Deciding upon a decisive battle and the annihilation of the Nationalist forces in Central China, General Chu Teh concentrated almost 600,000 men—all the columns of Ch'en I, Liu Po-ch'eng, and Ch'en Keng—in the vicinity of Suchow.

To face these Red forces the Generalissimo gave General Pai Ch'ung-hsi[8] fifty-five divisions, organized into ten field armies and four group armies, totaling some 600,000 men. To the west of Suchow was General Chiu Ching-chuan's 2nd Group Army. The 13th Group Army, under General Li Mi, held the city itself. General Huang Po-tao's 7th Group Army was concentrated to the east of Suchow, and General Sun Yuan-ling's 16th Group Army was strung out to the south along the Pengpu-Suchow railroad. All of these forces had ample artillery, both medium and light, as well as tanks and the support of an air force that had absolute mastery of the air. In order to reconstitute a reserve, the Generalissimo had evacuated his troops from Chefoo and Lini, and now held nothing in Shantung except Tsingtao. Possessing as he did a fairly strong and completely unopposed air force, which at will could bomb and strafe the villages and Communist troop concentrations so easily discernible on the open plain, the general situation seemed favorable to Chiang Kai-shek.

But poor morale, inept command, and a fixedly defensive frame of mind were to bring the Nationalists to another terrible disaster. Right at the beginning they adopted a dubious, "mushroom"-type disposition, with part of their forces deployed along the Lunghai railroad, and the rest, like a dangling stem,

---

[8] According to F. F. Liu, Pai Ch'ung-hsi, "the best of the Nationalist strategists," was not offered this command by Chiang until the "eleventh hour," when he turned it down. It went instead to General Liu Chih, "a man of no particular ability," who had General Tu Yü-ming, "fresh from defeats in Manchuria," as his deputy. See F. F. Liu, A *Military History of Modern China* (Princeton University Press, 1956), p. 261. *Tr.*

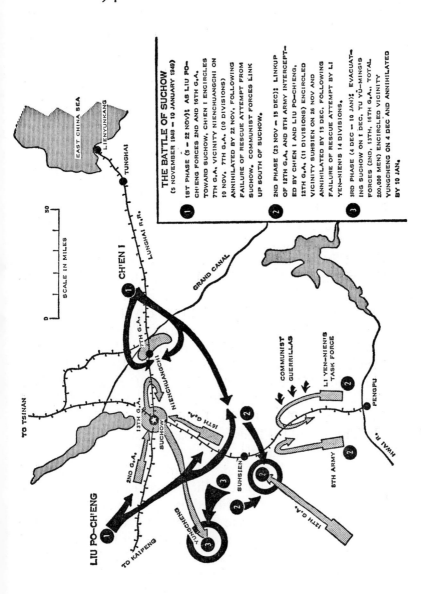

THE BATTLE OF SUCHOW
(5 NOVEMBER 1948 — 10 JANUARY 1949)

1ST PHASE (5 — 22 NOV): AS LIU PO—CHIENG FORCES 2ND AND 16TH G.A. TOWARD SUCHOW, CHIEN I ENCIRCLES 7TH G.A. VICINITY NIENCHUANGCHI ON 10 NOV. 7TH G.A. (10 DIVISIONS) ANNIHILATED BY 22 NOV, FOLLOWING FAILURE OF RESCUE ATTEMPT FROM SUCHOW. COMMUNIST FORCES LINK UP SOUTH OF SUCHOW.

2ND PHASE (23 NOV — 15 DEC): LINKUP OF 12TH G.A. AND 8TH ARMY INTERCEPT—ED BY CHIEN I AND LIU PO—CHIENG. 12TH G.A. (11 DIVISIONS) ENCIRCLED VICINITY SUHSIEN ON 26 NOV AND ANNIHILATED BY 15 DEC, FOLLOWING FAILURE OF RESCUE ATTEMPT BY LI YEN—NIEN'S 14 DIVISIONS.

3RD PHASE (4 DEC — 10 JAN): EVACUAT—ING SUCHOW ON 1 DEC, TU YÜ—MING'S FORCES (2ND, 13TH, 16TH G.A., TOTAL 200,000 MEN) ENCIRCLED VICINITY YUNGCHENG ON 4 DEC AND ANNIHILATED BY 10 JAN.

deployed along the Pengpu-Suchow rail line to the south. Frozen in their defensive fixation, they awaited the Communist attacks. The first of these came from the east on 8 November. Defending the eastern approaches to Suchow were the ten divisions of Huang Po-tao's group army, in position along the Grand Canal and the Lunghai railroad. The position was a strong one; but the sudden defection to the Reds of two Kuomintang generals, together with 23,000 men of the army in the northwestern sector, forced Huang to abandon it and attempt a withdrawal to Suchow. Unfortunately, the way was barred by Red columns, as well as by the 23,000 turncoats. Attacking with the 13th, 4th, 2nd, 8th, 9th, and 6th columns, Ch'en I encircled Huang's 7th Group Army at Nienchuangchi, to the west of the Grand Canal and about thirty miles east of Suchow. At the same time, the 2nd Group Army, which defended the western approaches to Suchow, and the 16th Group Army, defending the southern approaches, were forced back into the city itself, where panic rapidly spread. Six regiments went over to the Reds, who momentarily threatened the airfield on the southern outskirts of the city. Fortunately for the Nationalists, the energetic General Chiu Ching-chuan restored the situation, while the massive intervention of the Nationalist Air Force, which flew from four hundred to five hundred sorties per day from Nanking, forced the Reds to fall back and momentarily loosen their grip around Suchow.

Meanwhile, Chiang Kai-shek ordered the 16th and 2nd group armies to send part of their forces eastward to the rescue of Huang Po-tao's encircled group army at Nienchuangchi. Fifteen divisions were assembled for this task, but the movement was so slowly executed that, after having advanced only eight miles in ten days and losing half their tanks, these forces were stopped about twelve miles west of Nienchuangchi. Here they met no more than three thousand survivors of a new Nationalist disaster: Huang's entire 7th Group Army, ninety thousand strong, had been torn to bits; the Reds had captured one thousand artillery pieces; Communist tanks had swept into Nienchuangchi; all the Nationalist generals were prisoners.[9]

On 22 November Ch'en I's victorious forces pressed rapidly southward from Nienchuangchi. Chiang had meanwhile ordered Liu Ju-ming's Eighth Army and Huang Wei's 12th Group Army, located to the south of Suchow, to go to the aid of that city, where there were still twenty-five divisions under Tu Yü-ming.[10] But here again Nationalist execution was pitifully poor. The two forces failed to effect their planned junction at Suhsien, and were soon trapped between Ch'en I's columns, coming from the north, and the forces of Liu Po-ch'-eng, which cut them off from the south. On 26 November it became the turn of General Huang Wei's 12th Group Army, with 125,000 men and many mechanized troops, to be encircled by the Reds at Shwangchiaochi, about fifteen miles southwest of Suhsien.

The Nationalists now made the decision to abandon Suchow and march southward, in order to prevent the annihilation of the 12th Group Army and join up with Liu Ju-ming, who was hastily retiring toward Pengpu. The three group armies at Suchow, with General Tu Yü-ming in over-all command, abandoned the city on 1 December; the Reds entered Suchow the next day. Once again the Nationalists, poorly led and with low morale, let themselves be outmaneuvered by the Reds, who pushed them gradually westward and ended by encircling them in the vicinity of Yungcheng.

As of 6 December the situation was as follows: Tu Yü-ming's twenty-five infantry divisions, some 200,000 men, with

[9] Except for Huang Po-tao himself, who had been killed in action. *Tr.*
[10] The Generalissimo had put Tu Yü-ming in command of all troops who had taken refuge in Suchow, and of the city's garrison as well.

all their artillery and tanks, were encircled to the west of Su-chow; Huang Wei (whose 110th Division had deserted to the Reds on 30 November) now had eleven infantry divisions, totaling 110,000 men, which were surrounded to the southwest of Suhsien; nine infantry divisions were still at large, and holding the Hwai river along the line Fenyang-Pengpu-Hwai-yuan. The difficulties of the encircled group armies rapidly worsened: the men were eating potatoes stolen from the fields of the peasants, and fought like dogs over the meager rations parachuted to them each day. The morale of the troops sank ever lower and, one after the other, whole divisions went over to the enemy.

Meanwhile Chiang Kai-shek had brought up some troops from the Yangtze region, and had ordered Li Yen-nien's Sixth Army, based at Pengpu, to go to the aid of Huang Wei's encircled forces with fourteen divisions.[11] In fifteen days Li advanced only seventeen miles against the furious resistance of Red guerrillas and village militiamen, who savagely contested every foot of his advance; without reaching Suhsien, Li's forces turned around and retraced their steps. The Reds then launched their final assault against Huang Wei's encircled group army. The attack was preceded by an intensive artillery preparation from howitzers, mortars, and mountain guns, which threw the defenses into complete disorder; when the Red assault detachments attacked, the shaken and demoralized defenders immediately surrendered. By 15 December the 12th Group Army had ceased to exist and Huang Wei was a prisoner of the Reds.

The fate of Tu Yü-ming was even more disastrous. His three group armies[12] encircled by the Reds to the northwest

[11] This task force included Liu Ju-ming's Eighth Army, as well as Li's Sixth Army. *Tr.*
[12] The 2nd, 13th, and 16th.

of Yungcheng, he had already lost more than half his forces on 17 December. As demoralization visibly spread, the commanders fell to wrangling among themselves. Earlier, on 6 December, Tu Yü-ming had ordered Sun Yuan-liang, whose forces had already covered the retreat from Suchow, to attempt a sortie; Sun's resentful troops had obeyed only with reluctance, and ended by surrendering to the Reds. Soon all was chaos. Prompted by continual Communist propaganda, desertions multiplied among the now starving defenders. Finally, on 6 January, the Red armies, after twenty days of rest and reorganization, launched their final assault. The encircled Nationalist forces were torn to pieces. In attempting to escape this final debacle, Tu Yü-ming disguised himself as a common soldier and posed as a "prisoner" of his own bodyguards, whom he had disguised as Red soldiers; the subterfuge failed, and he became the real prisoner of real Reds.

By 10 January 1949 the battle of Suchow,[13] which had lasted sixty-five days, was over. The Reds had taken 327,000 prisoners, and Nationalist losses had totaled 600,000 men. The entire region between the Hwai and the Yangtze had been "liberated" by the Reds, and their passage of the historic river barrier was now possible. The Kuomintang had lost its last chance.

THE POLITICAL AND ECONOMIC SITUATION

On 19 August 1948 the Nationalist government, in a desperate effort to check the ruinous inflation, the rise in prices, hoarding, corruption, and famine, decreed a number of stringent measures which, had they been strictly applied and received with confidence by the people, could have succeeded. The first measure taken was to replace the *fapi*, the Nationalist

---

[13] The Reds call this battle, which in the future will be considered one of the decisive battles of history, the Hwai-Hai Campaign.

monetary unit which had sunk to a value of zero, with a new currency backed by gold: the gold *yüan*, which was to represent 0.222 grams of gold, with a conversion rate of four *yüan* to one American dollar. The old currency was to be replaced at an exchange rate of one gold *yüan* for three million *fapis*. This monetary reform was accompanied by other strict measures, such as the freezing of wages, prices, and foreign exchange rates. Severe penalties were prescribed against black marketeers, and General Chiang Ching-kuo, the Generalissimo's son and a forceful personality, was charged with applying the reforms first in Shanghai and then in Nanking and the neighboring provinces.

Despite vigorous action by Chiang Ching-kuo, who conducted a "tiger hunt" against the big black marketeers and speculators of Shanghai, and also succeeded in gaining the support of the workers, the reforms rapidly failed. One reason for this failure was that the younger Chiang was ordered by his father to be "less severe" toward certain tigers, such as David Kung, the president of the Yangtze Development Corporation; but the major reason was that the government, having achieved no increase in revenue or decrease in expenditure, was obliged to print bills which rapidly reduced the value of the gold *yüan*. Prices skyrocketed. On 31 October the ceilings on wages and prices were removed. Resigning in disgust, Chiang Ching-kuo apologized to his fellow citizens in an open letter, characteristically Chinese, to the people of Shanghai:

After the past seventy days of my work, I feel that I have failed to accomplish the duties which I should have accomplished. Not only did I not consummate my plan and mission, but in certain respects I have rather deepened the sufferings of the people which they experienced in the course of the execution of my task ... Today, aside from petitioning the government for punishment so as to clarify my responsibility, I wish to take this opportunity of offering my deepest apology to the citizens of Shanghai. But in so doing . . . I sincerely wish the citizens of Shanghai to use their own strength to prevent unscrupulous merchants, bureaucrats, politicians and racketeers from controlling Shanghai.[14]

China now found itself back in the vicious circle of rising prices and wages. In the provinces everything was disintegrating. Banditry broke out everywhere, and fifty-five million refugees rendered the food problem insoluble. It was only unconditional and permanent aid from the United States which could prevent an immediate collapse. But General Marshall, now the American Secretary of State, in October 1948 redefined American policy toward China: there was to be no more mediation, no more direct intervention in Chiang's favor, but strict application of the China Aid Act of 1948.[15]

Marshall declared:

To achieve the objective of reducing the Chinese Communists to a completely negligible factor in China in the immediate future, it would be necessary for the United States virtually to take over the Chinese Government and administer its economic, military and governmental affairs. . . It would be impossible to estimate the final cost of a course of action of this magnitude. It certainly would be a continuing operation for a long time to come. It would involve the United States Government in a continuing commitment from which it would practically be impossible to withdraw, and it would very probably involve grave consequences to this nation by making of China an arena of international conflict.[16]

This was indeed a grave decision. At the United Nations, Dr. T. F. Tsiang, China's representative on the Security Council, pronounced these prophetic words: "The fate of the entire

[14] *U.S. Relations with China*, p. 880. Tr.
[15] Of the $125 million voted by Congress for special grants to China, the Nationalists used $37,800,000 to buy munitions which were delivered to them in December 1948.
[16] *U.S. Relations with China*, p. 281. Tr.

Far East is linked to that of China, because the Chinese Communists will help the Communists in Indo-China, in Malaya, in Burma, in India, in all the Far East. Against this tide, you have built in the West a solid dike, in the form of material aid, from Scandinavia to the Persian Gulf. But now this tide will overflow in another direction."[17] But was it possible to do anything useful, considering the actual state of things? General Marshall had no illusions: "The present regime has lost the confidence of the people, reflected in the refusal of soldiers to fight and the refusal of the people to co-operate in economic reforms."[18]

Chiang Kai-shek continued to ignore the advice of General Barr, refusing even to hear it. He wished to direct everything himself, and he was surrounded, as always, by old comrades who were as incompetent as they were corrupt. In the face of a degenerate Kuomintang, the Communists boldly and successfully proceeded to organize the zones under their control. On 1 September 1948 they announced the formation of a People's Government for North China, to include the provinces of Hopeh, Chahar, Shensi, Shansi, and Shantung.[19] Their policy continued to be flexible and adaptable enough to avoid frightening the people, and their establishment of an agrarian democracy which eschewed collectivization and confiscated only the property of landlords, gave satisfaction to the majority. Cer-

[17] For a summary of Tsiang's speech, see *Plenary Meetings of the General Assembly: Official Records of the Fourth Session of the General Assembly, 20 September–10 December 1949* (Lake Success, N.Y.: United Nations, 1949), pp. 15–16. Tr.

[18] *U.S. Relations with China*, p. 282. Tr.

[19] Nine of the twenty-seven members of the government council were Communists. The Chairman of the North China People's Government was Tung Pi-wu, one of the founders of the CCP, a graduate of the Lenin Academy, and a Communist representative at Chungking from 1937 to 1945. The Vice Chairman was General Nieh Jung-chen. The non-Communist members were from the Democratic League, the National Salvation Association, and the Non-Party Democrats.

tain now of victory, Mao Tse-tung toughened even more against the Kuomintang, and published a list of "war criminals" which included all the KMT party chieftains. As his columns prepared for the liquidation of the forces of Fu Tso-yi, Mao's last serious adversary in North China, he tranquilly awaited the peace proposals of his enemies.

In a last effort, Chiang Kai-shek sent his wife to the United States to seek an increase of American aid. Arriving in Washington on 1 December 1948, Mme. Chiang did not get to see Marshall, who was ill, until the 3rd, and was not received by President Truman until the 10th. The visit soon showed itself to be fruitless. Indeed, Mr. Hoffman,[20] who had come to Shanghai on 11 December, went back to Washington on 20 December, and the next day the United States government announced the suspension of its reconstruction aid program for China.

[20] Paul G. Hoffman, head of the Economic Cooperation Administration. *Tr.*

✧ PART FIVE ✧

1949
THE END OF THE CONQUEST

CHAPTER XIV

The Surrender of Fu Tso-yi
and
Chiang Kai-shek's Departure

As the last act opened, it was clear that the Nationalists had no real basis for further hope. On 1 February 1949 the American Department of the Army reported:

The Nationalists entered 1948 with an estimated strength of 2,723,000 troops. Recruitment and replacement of combat losses kept this figure constant through mid-September. By 1 February 1949, however, heavy losses had reduced Nationalist strength to 1,500,000, of which approximately 500,000 are service troops. This represents a reduction of 45 percent of the Nationalist Government's total troop strength, in a 4½-month period.

Communist strength, estimated at 1,150,000 a year ago, has mounted to 1,622,000, virtually all combat effectives. This increase of approximately 40 percent represents the creation of new units, particularly in Manchuria and East Central China. Whereas the Nationalists began 1948 with almost a three-to-one numerical superiority, the Communist forces now outnumber the total Nationalist strength and have achieved better than a one-and-a-half-to-one superiority in combat effectives.[1]

---

[1] U.S. Department of State, *United States Relations with China, with Special Reference to the Period 1944–1949* (U.S. Government Printing Office, 1949), p. 322. *Tr.*

The American military attaché at Nanking estimated that, from September 1948 to February 1949, the Reds had captured 400,000 rifles, some 140,000 of which were of American origin; and they had integrated 600,000 ex-Nationalist troops into their own forces, using 400,000 of them as service troops.[2] Moreover, twenty arsenals, including fifteen of major importance, had fallen into Mao's hands.

At about the same time the Communists published their own claims of losses inflicted upon the Nationalists since the beginning of the war. For the period 1 July 1946 to 31 January 1949 these were:

a) *Personnel:* 4,959,000 killed, wounded, or taken prisoner, with the proportion of prisoners seventy-five per cent. Of this total, 2,641,000 casualties had been inflicted upon the Nationalists during the period July 1946 through July 1948, and 2,318,000 in the seven months preceding January 1949. The Nationalists had lost 869 generals; 697 of them had been taken prisoner, sixty-seven killed, and 105 had gone over to the Communists.

b) *Units:* According to the Communists, they had destroyed during this period 380 entire divisions, 615 regiments, and 760 battalions; and the Nationalists had lost the headquarters of two theaters of operations, fifteen group armies, and eighty-six field armies.

c) *Matériel:* The Communists claimed to have captured 1,709,000 rifles, carbines, and pistols; 193,000 automatic weapons; 37,000 mortars and artillery pieces; 250 million rounds of small-arms ammunition; 2,580,000 shells; and 1,900,000 hand grenades. They had taken 513 tanks, and destroyed 140 more. Other booty included 289 armored vehicles; twelve thousand motor vehicles; 857 locomotives; and eighty-six aircraft, more than fifteen of whose pilots had deserted, with their planes, to

[2] *Ibid.,* p. 323. *Tr.*

the Communists. The capture of this matériel by the Communists—especially the American matériel—for the first time gave Red armies an ample margin of material superiority over the Nationalists, who now retained only naval and air superiority.

THE SURRENDER OF FU TSO-YI

Throughout the fighting in Manchuria and Central China, General Fu Tso-yi, at the head of the Nationalists' best troops, had held firm control of a zone centered around the Tientsin-Suiyuan railroad. This zone included the cities of Peking and Kalgan, through which Fu was able to maintain contact with his province of Suiyuan and with General Ma Hung-k'uei. In the north he held Chengteh, the capital of Jehol, which covered the pass at Kupehkow; to the south, he held Paoting and the port of Tangku. General Fu Tso-yi, whose merit was but little appreciated by Chiang Kai-shek, had long been known as one of the few Kuomintang generals who had the support of the population. Applying Communist methods, he had set his troops to work with the peasants in the fields, and to the repair of the railroads. An excellent strategist, he had succeeded in maintaining effective control over his zone of responsibility, repelling the Red columns of Nieh Jung-chen and Lin Piao.

When Lin Piao attacked in Manchuria, Fu had been compelled to dispatch large forces to Chinchow. The Communists profited from this development by attacking in Jehol, Chahar, and Hopeh. Paoting succumbed to the Reds on 23 October. Immediately after the fall of Yingkow to the Communists on 5 November, Lin Piao and Nieh Jung-chen launched simultaneous attacks against Fu. On 9 November Nieh took Chengteh, the capital of Jehol. On the 18th Lin Piao, in his turn, seized Shanhaikwan; on 2 December, he took Kupehkow, on the Peking-Chengteh railroad. Lin then attacked the defense lines established by the Nationalists to the north of Peking, along the Sino-Manchurian border. Breaking through Fu Tso-yi's front, Lin's forces on 7 December seized Miyun and Hwaiju, about forty miles north of Peking.

Little by little, the front drew ever closer to Tientsin, Peking, and Kalgan; yet Fu Tso-yi, despite his considerable superiority in numbers, fought nothing more than delaying actions. The plain fact was that the Nationalist general had been in secret contact with the Communists since the beginning of December, and was now in the process of negotiating his surrender to the Reds. Following the fall of the coal-mining center at Tangshan on the 13th and of Tungchow on 15 December, Fu permitted Peking to be "encircled" by eight Communist columns and four independent infantry divisions, even though the city was garrisoned by twenty-five Nationalist infantry divisions, of which five belonged to Fu's own personal army.

As for the Communists, their problem was to choose between a conciliatory attitude toward Fu Tso-yi, or the refusal of any concessions. Mao well understood that a bloodless capture of Peking, the ancient capital, plus control of the Tientsin-Suiyuan railroad, were well worth compromise. The necessary assurances were accordingly transmitted to Fu Tso-yi, who continued to withdraw before the outnumbered Red forces. He abandoned Tangku on 19 December, and on the 26th withdrew from Kalgan the garrison of seven infantry divisions supposedly "blockaded" there by Nieh's six columns. Fu, a former governor of Suiyuan, pulled these troops back toward Tsining and Paotow. The westward withdrawal of the Kalgan garrison clearly indicated Fu Tso-yi's intentions: early in January the Nationalist leader officially opened negotiations with Lin Piao, using Chang Tung-sun, a professor at Yenching University and former Secretary-General of the defunct Democratic League, as his intermediary.

Vice President Li Tsung-jen paralleled this move by sending to Peking a former mayor of that city, Ho Ssu-yuan; but anything this envoy might have done was forestalled by his assassination, on 16 January, at the hands of the Ch'en brothers' secret police. Chiang Kai-shek and the Sun Fo cabinet then called a meeting, at Nanking, of the regime's leading generals: Pai Ch'ung-hsi, war lord of Kwangsi and Nationalist commander in Central China; Lu Han, the governor of Yunnan; Yen Hsi-shan, from the beleaguered city of Taiyuan; Hu Tsung-nan, from Sian; Ma Hung-k'uei, from Ningsia; and Chu Shao-liang, from Szechwan. Fu Tso-yi, of course, prudently refrained from attending. During this meeting Chiang decided to entrust each governor with responsibility for the defense of his own province, relying upon the formation of local militia units and appeals to the patriotism of the inhabitants. For all practical purposes this meant the end of coordinated resistance against the Communists.

Nevertheless, Chiang clearly indicated at this meeting his intention to defend the Nanking-Shanghai area to the very end. Throughout Nationalist China this decision was received with dismay by a public opinion which longed only for peaceful compromise. Thus it was that the news of Fu Tso-yi's capitulation at Peking brought forth no great popular indignation. After letting Tientsin go to the Communists on 15 January, Fu had signed a "compromise" with Lin Piao on the 23rd, following a token siege of Peking in which the Communists had done nothing more than sprinkle the city with about 150 seventy-five millimeter shells—most of which failed to explode.

The compromise of 23 January, very moderate in its terms, was to become the "model" for other Nationalist governors. Its thirteen conditions were the following:

1. Hostilities would cease immediately.
2. The two sides would appoint delegates to a joint commission in charge of military and political affairs during the "period of transition."
3. Nationalist troops within Peking would move to the outskirts of the city. Although permitted to retain their original unit designations and insignia, they would be reorganized one month later.
4. For the maintenance of peace and order, some of the Nationalist troops would remain within the city to assist the police and troops already provided for the protection of shops and stores.
5. All government offices, public enterprises, banks, stores, cultural institutions, and schools would retain their current status pending further instructions from the joint commission.
6. The provincial government of Hopeh would retain, at all echelons, its current status, pending further instructions from the joint commission. The personal safety of its officials would be guaranteed.
7. The currency in use, the gold *yüan*, would continue in circulation.
8. All military construction in progress would be suspended.
9. The consular personnel and property of foreign powers in Peking would be protected.
10. Postal and telegraph services would continue without interruption.
11. All newspapers would continue publication, but would be required to renew registration and submit, at a later date, to censorship.
12. Cultural relics, shrines, and historical monuments would be safeguarded, and freedom of worship guaranteed.
13. The normal existence of the population would remain undisturbed.

Promptly, as early as 23 January, a Communist regiment entered Peking and established itself within the city.

The Peking compromise having been arrived at with the assent of Li Tsung-jen and over the opposition of Chiang Kai-shek, the latter now realized that the game was lost; there was nothing left for him to do but retire. This he did on 21 January, relinquishing power to Vice President Li "with the hope," said Chiang, "that the hostilities may be brought to an end and the peoples' sufferings relieved."[3]

[3] *Ibid.*, p. 292. It was at this time that Chiang, although out of office, readied what he regarded as "his" armies, navy, and air force for the retreat to Formosa.

CHAPTER XV

Negotiations and the
Amethyst Incident

FROM the beginning of February to 20 April 1949, when Communist forces crossed the Yangtze, a scene was enacted similar to that which had unfolded in early 1946. At that time Chiang, possessing the advantage of military superiority, had sought the cover of protracted negotiations while he massed his forces and prepared his attack. He would break off the talks at opportune moments, seize important bargaining counters, and then, in the devious Chinese way so dismaying to General Marshall, reopen negotiations with the Communists. Now it was Mao Tse-tung who had the military might. After the conquest of Manchuria and Peking he needed a few months in which to regroup his forces and prepare his decisive attack across the Yangtze. Consequently, he did not hesitate to undertake negotiations, deliberately foredoomed to failure, in which the concessions of his adversaries were to be met by his ever-increasing demands.

Shortly after the retirement of Chiang Kai-shek—who continued to direct the faithful from the wings—Acting President Li attempted to open negotiations with Mao, who on 14 January had issued his eight conditions for peace. These were:

1. Strict punishment of war criminals.
2. Abolition of the constitution.
3. Abolition of the Kuomintang legal system.
4. Reorganization of Nationalist troops according to democratic principles.
5. Confiscation of "bureaucratic" capital.
6. Reformation of the land system.
7. Abolition of "treasonous treaties."
8. Convocation of a Political Consultative Conference with non-participation of "reactionary elements," establishment of democratic coalition government, taking over all authority of the "Kuomintang reactionary government" and all its strata.[1]

Nationalist compliance with these eight demands would have been tantamount to unconditional surrender. Li rejected them on 31 January, without, however, breaking off the negotiations. He finally obtained the agreement of Yeh Chien-ying, the Chief of Staff of the Red Army and new Mayor of Peking, to the dispatch of an "unofficial" Nationalist mission to the Red capital at Shihkiachwang. This mission, with Shao Li-tzu, Dr. W. W. Yen, and Chang Shih-chao as members, arrived in Peking on 13 February. It was received by three generals, Yeh Chien-ying, Lin Piao, and Nieh Jung-chen, their political commissars Lo Jung-huan and Po I-po watchful at their sides. At Shihkiachwang the mission met with Mao and Chou En-lai. It returned empty-handed to Shanghai on 27 February, Mao having held fast to his eight points.

These negative results caused enormous difficulties for Acting President Li, who had to cope with the opposition of Dr. Sun Fo, as well as that of former members of the Kuomintang who had opposed Chiang Kai-shek. These refugees had now

[1] U.S. Department of State, *United States Relations with China, with Special Reference to the Period 1944–1949* (U.S. Government Printing Office, 1949), p. 293. *Tr.*

ended their long stay in Hong Kong and departed for the "liberated areas," whence on 25 February they addressed their congratulations to an all-conquering Mao. Among them were General Ts'ai T'ing-k'ai, the hero of Shanghai's valiant resistance against the Japanese in 1932; General Li Chi-shen, Chairman of the refugee RCKMT (the Revolutionary Committee of the Kuomintang); Mme. Feng Yü-hsiang, widow of the "Christian General";[2] Mme. Lu Hsün, widow of the "Chinese Gorki"; the writer Mao Tun; and Kuo Mo-jo, the poet and archaeologist. The presence of these anti-Kuomintang democrats was to prove useful to Mao Tse-tung, permitting him to create coalition governments which could use well-known personalities who, albeit non-Communists, were completely devoted to the party.

Moreover, in a spirit of broad conciliation, the Communists on 21 February effected an extremely clever reorganization of the Nationalist forces in the Peking area. Although Fu Tso-yi's headquarters was, of course, disbanded, his twenty-five ex-Nationalist divisions were transformed into twenty-five separate divisions within the People's Liberation Army. All officers, regardless of grade, who volunteered to serve in the Red Army were integrated without loss of rank or seniority. Those who preferred to leave the army were given three months' pay and authorized to take with them all their personal belongings; they were even permitted to depart with either one or two orderlies, the number depending upon the officer's rank. All this, of course, was nothing more than a propaganda gesture, aimed at the morale of the beleaguered Nationalist garrisons that still held out in North China.

The month of March brought new convulsions in Nationalist China, where the remnants of the expiring Kuomintang

---

[2] An opponent of Chiang Kai-shek, Feng was for some time a political refugee in the United States. On 4 September 1948 he met a mysterious end aboard the Russian ship *Pobeda*, which burned in the Black Sea while Feng was returning to China from the United States by way of the Soviet Union.

dissipated their dying energies in deplorable internal strife. Dr. Sun Fo, who had taken his Nationalist cabinet and part of the Legislative Yüan with him to Canton, was forced to resign, and was replaced as premier by General Ho Ying-ch'in. More than ever, it was now impossible to know who governed. Generals were practically their own masters in the provinces, and Chiang Kai-shek continued to give orders through the mouths of those who remained faithful to him. Everywhere, weariness and discontent continued to grow. Communist bands increased their strength in Kwangtung, Szechwan, and Yunnan. On 2 March the best warship in the Nationalist Navy, the cruiser *Chungking* (formerly H.M.S. *Aurora*), slipped out of Shanghai and went over to the Reds.[3]

Once again General Ho and Acting President Li sought negotiations with Mao, who was now reorganizing for the final assault and massing his forces along the north bank of the Yangtze. Since Mao wished to avoid the appearance of prolonging the war, the Central Committee of the CCP, meeting in plenary session at Shihkiachwang,[4] on 26 March decided that peace talks would be permitted to open at Peking on 1 April, with Mao's eight points as the basis of discussion. Arriving in Peking on 2 April, the envoys of the Kuomintang found themselves confronted by a stone wall. The Communists were now less willing than ever to make concessions: on the contrary, they set 12 April as the deadline for the acceptance of their conditions and declared that "come peace or come war," the Nanking government would have to accept the passage of Red troops across the Yangtze. The unhappy General Li turned in despair, and in vain, to the United

[3] The ship went to Chefoo, where it was sunk by the Nationalist Air Force on 20 March (according to the Communists, the *Chungking* was bombed and sunk off Hulutao. *Tr.*).

[4] It was during this session that the Chinese Communists, reversing their previous line, now proclaimed the primacy of the urban proletariat. In Mao's words: "The center of gravity of the Party's work has now shifted from the village to the city."

States; and one of his envoys to Peking, General Chang Chih-chung, who had always been on good terms with Chou En-lai, went over to the Reds!

On 15 April the Communists gave the Nationalist government five days to comply with the terms of their ultimatum. Still struggling feebly against the mortal danger which threatened it, the Nationalist government again appealed to the United States, and sought to bring an end to the divisive wrangling between Li Tsung-jen and Chiang Kai-shek. It was far too late. On 20 April Li rejected the Red ultimatum, but requested an armistice pending resumption of negotiations. The only reply to this request was the crossing of the Yangtze, on orders from Mao and Chu Teh, by the Red armies. On 23 April Li and Ho withdrew to Canton, and Chiang took wing for Formosa. The last act of the tragedy was at hand.

THE *Amethyst* INCIDENT

On 20 April 1949 the 1,480-ton British frigate *Amethyst*, commanded by Lieutenant Commander B. M. Skinner, started up the Yangtze for Nanking. Her mission was to relieve the destroyer *Consort*, bring supplies to the British Embassy, and assure, if need be, the protection of British subjects residing in the Nationalist capital. Upon reaching Chinkiang the frigate suddenly found itself under fire from Communist field batteries positioned along the north bank of the river. She joined battle, but soon, severely damaged, with seventeen dead, twenty wounded, and a mortally wounded captain, she ran aground on Rose Island, about seventy-five miles upstream from Shanghai. Admiral Madden[5] sent the cruiser *London* and the frigate *Black Swan* to her rescue. These ships too

[5] Vice Admiral A. C. G. Madden, second in command of the Far East Station. *Tr.*

were damaged and forced to withdraw, as was the *Consort,* which nonetheless succeeded in making its way downstream from Nanking to Shanghai. It was only with great difficulty that British seaplanes managed to come in alongside the *Amethyst,* which remained, however, in radio contact with Shanghai. For three months the frigate, which had been refloated, remained a prisoner of the Communists, who refused to let the ship weigh anchor so long as her new skipper, Lieutenant Commander J. S. Kerans, would not sign a document admitting British responsibility for the incident and the Communist claim that the ship had "criminally invaded Chinese territorial waters." On 30 July Kerans decided to attempt escape. Weighing anchor under the heavy fire of Communist batteries, and running another gauntlet of fire in passing the Kiangyin forts, the ship finally succeeded in rejoining the British fleet at the mouth of the Yangtze.

Although the frigate's exploit upheld the honor of the British Navy, it is nonetheless true that the *Amethyst* incident, considered in its entire context, constituted a heavy blow to white prestige in the Far East, and gained considerable "face" for the Communists. The Royal Navy enjoyed unequaled respect in China; for more than a century it had been viewed as invincible. In 1860 British ships had silenced the forts of Taku. In 1923 the mere arrival of a British naval squadron off Canton had sufficed to compel the withdrawal of Sun Yat-sen himself. Yet now the Reds had vanquished the invincible. The inhabitants of Shanghai looked on in amazement as the wounded were disembarked from British warships which had been ripped open by Chinese shells. Coming at a time when Chu Teh's armies were closing in on Shanghai, the psychological impact of the *Amethyst* Incident did more for a Communist victory than any strategic maneuver could possibly have done.

CHAPTER XVI ✧

The Communist Offensive
of 20 April

As final battle was joined, Nationalist dispositions, according to American reports, were the following: 350,000 men were in the Nanking-Shanghai area, 175,000 were at Sian, 120,000 in the Northeast, another 120,000 in the Hankow region, and 150,000 were scattered about in isolated garrisons. These figures do not include the 300,000 men of the "armies" that Chiang Kai-shek had already evacuated to Formosa.[1] The situation favored the Reds, all the more since Liu Po-ch'eng, promptly profiting from the conquest of the Peking area, had completely reorganized Communist lines of communication. He had restored to operation the railroads between Peking and Mukden, Kalgan and Shihkiachwang; more importantly, he had established the Peking-Tientsin railroad, with its major spurs of the Tsinpu (Tientsin to Pukow, near Nanking) and the Pinghan (Peking to Hankow), as the arteries of a rear base for logistical support of the Red armies in the field. For the first time in history, Chinese armies could count upon

---

[1] Chiang had also withdrawn "his" navy (some twenty-six gunboats), under Admiral Kuei Yung-ch'ing, and "his" air force, under General Chou Chih-jou, to Formosa

regular resupply of their needs in ammunition and other military stores.

The state of atrophy which prevailed on the Nationalist side stifled the adoption of any effective measures of defense. The admiral charged with responsibility for the defense of the Nanking-Shanghai sector was satisfied with scuttling a preponderance of the junks and sampans of the Yangtze. Nationalist divisions were stretched out over an average front of more than thirty miles. Confronting them, the forces of Ch'en I, which lay along the Yangtze from Nanking to Nantung, infiltrated the south bank of the river at will. Without difficulty or interference from the Nationalists, the armies of Liu Po-ch'eng had regrouped along the northern flank of the Tapieh range. And Lin Piao had been left free to concentrate his armies without opposition from the Nationalists, who once again remained frozen in a sterile and foredoomed defensive posture. The few organized forces remaining to the Nationalists were those of Pai Ch'ung-hsi, whose nine armies were deployed between Kiukiang and Ichang, and the armies on Formosa, which Chiang Kai-shek kept under his exclusive control.

The Communist push was launched on 20 April. On the left, his flank guarded by the sea, Ch'en I crossed the Yangtze without firing a shot, took Nanking on the 23rd, and pressed on toward the bay of Hangchow in a thrust designed to envelop and isolate Shanghai. In the center, Liu Po-ch'eng marched on Fukien, in the direction of Foochow, in order to cut off the retreat of the Nationalist armies. On the right, Lin Piao's Fourth Field Army[2] attacked Pai Ch'ung-hsi's forces

[2] In November 1948 the territorial designations of Chinese Communist armies were dropped, and Red forces were reorganized into four numbered "field armies" plus the North China Army Group, often unofficially called the "Fifth Field Army." It was Lin Piao's Fourth Field Army that was to be the major Chinese force committed in the Korean conflict. Tr.

THE FINAL OFFENSIVE
(APRIL — OCTOBER 1949)

• • • • FRONT LINE AS OF 20 APRIL
• • • • • • FRONT LINE AS OF 30 MAY
■ ■ ■ ■ FRONT LINE AS OF 15 JULY
▬ ▬ ▬ FRONT LINE AS OF 8 SEPTEMBER

0 ————————— 300

SCALE IN MILES

in the Hankow region. The Nationalists put up only a token resistance, even though T'ang En-po and Ch'en Ta-ching, the commanders in Shanghai, loudly proclaimed their resolve to resist to the end and make of the city "a second Stalingrad." Chiang Kai-shek dispatched several armies to reinforce the defenders, and came in person to deliver a speech in which he spoke of "total victory within three years." The defenses of the

222

city were prepared in the typical Nationalist manner, with hordes of coolies set to work upon an all-encompassing ditch and ten-foot palisade of no defensive value whatsoever.[3] Despite their numerical superiority, T'ang En-po's troops remained completely passive within their lines, thereby permitting the Reds to complete their investment of Shanghai without firing a shot.

Hangchow fell to the Communists on 3 May, and on the 7th they took Shaohing, on the road to Ningpo. While Lin Piao's forces in the west took the Wuhan cities, Shanghai by 16 May was completely surrounded. With the first bombardment, the heroic defenders quickly manifested their intention to surrender. The only troops to put up a momentary fight were the reinforcements that had been sent by Chiang Kai-shek; aided by air support dispatched from Formosa, they now sought only a safe evacuation from the mainland. On 25 May Ch'en I's troops, in perfect order, entered Shanghai, astounding the inhabitants of the great commercial metropolis with their discipline and decorum. Ch'en I, now mayor of Shanghai, provided for the security and supply of the city, whose fall had yielded the Communists more than 100,000 prisoners and two hundred guns. As for the Nationalists, the government and administration were moved to Canton, where the Ch'en brothers deluded themselves with dreams of a victorious resistance in the heart of the old Kuomintang stronghold. But Kwangtung and Kwangsi were already corroded by communism, and a force of more than sixty thousand Reds controlled a third of Kwangtung province.

At the end of May the Communists' lines of communication were cut by floods which lay waste the lower course of the Yangtze, and the Reds were thus forced to break off their of-

---

[3] Except to the enterprising officer who profited from the sale of wood for the construction of this medieval barrier.

fensive. They profited from this enforced pause by reorganizing their rear areas and consolidating their control over their new conquests, which in area exceeded that of all France.

Meanwhile, important events had occurred in other sectors since the launching of the Communist offensive on 20 April. On 24 April Taiyuan, the old capital of Shansi, fell after a siege which had lasted since the autumn of 1948. Marshal Yen Hsi-shan, the "model governor" and master of Shansi since as far back as 1911, had made of this province a virtually autonomous and highly prosperous state. More than six hundred miles of good roads had been constructed, as well as two rail lines. One of these, connecting with the Peking-Suiyuan line, ran the length of the province down the valley of the Fen from Tatung to Tungkwan; the other connected Taiyuan with Shihkiachwang, on the main Peking-Hankow line to the east. Yen had reforested the hills of Shansi with firs, and developed agriculture to a level at which the province enjoyed complete self-sufficiency. During the Sino-Japanese conflict, Shansi had almost completely escaped the horrors of war. And to exploit all of these advantages Marshal Yen had established a system of state socialism which, in his view, was far superior to Marxism.

When the Communists moved into Shansi, Yen grudgingly yielded them the field and pulled back into the towns, which fell, one after the other, to the Reds. Taiyuan, however, appeared to be impregnable. Behind its massive ramparts, thirty feet thick, were an excellent garrison and the biggest munitions plant in China, turning out rifles, machine guns, and ammunition. Only by starving it out could the city be taken, and Yen could have stockpiled large supplies of food and ammunition had he only seen fit to do so. Moreover, he had an excellent airfield for resupply by air. Yet he demanded of Chiang Kai-shek five thousand tons of rice per month, an amount sent to him right up to the moment when the Reds seized the airfield. The old marshal then vouchsafed, to an American journalist, that China's salvation would require "two hundred Flying Tigers and 100,000 Japanese mercenaries"; without these, he opined, defeat appeared certain.

Following the failure of a relief column from the south, feebly led by Chang Chih-chung, Yen quickly quitted Taiyuan. Leaving just before the capitulation of his capital to the Communists, he arrived at Canton just in time to succeed Ho Ying-ch'in, on 2 June, as premier of the Nationalist government. Immediately thereafter he went to Formosa to confer with Chiang, with whom he had always maintained good relations. The Nationalists were counting on the prodigious popularity of Yen, a diabetic old despot, to galvanize the last remaining forces of the Kuomintang.

On 20 May, after an offensive led by P'eng Te-huai, the city of Sian, capital of Shensi, surrendered to the Communists. Hu Tsung-nan, an old comrade of Chiang Kai-shek, beat a rapid retreat to the west, calling for help from Ma Pu-fang, the Moslem leader of Kansu who had defeated the Reds at Paoki in 1948. Ma hastened up with his cavalry and delivered a frontal attack upon P'eng's forces about seventy miles from Sian, while a force of 25,000 under his son, Ma Chi-yüan, took the Communists in the flank. P'eng, who had rashly ventured forth upon the "Great Northern Highway" (Sian-Chengtu) in order to invade Szechwan from the north, gave way before this unexpected assault and pulled back toward Sian, pursued by Ma and Hu Tsung-nan. The Nationalists hailed this victory with loud acclaim, and Chiang bestowed upon Ma Pu-fang the title of Commander in Chief in the Northwest, a post which had remained vacant since its treacherous abandonment by Chang Chih-chung. The Generalissimo also promised Ma parachute delivery of the weapons and ammunition so sorely needed by the Moslem leader.

The Nationalist success, however, proved to be short-lived. On Chu Teh's orders Nieh Jung-chen, with two armies, the Sixty-second and the Sixty-third, soon came to the aid of P'eng Te-huai. Moving by rail on the Lunghai line to Sian, Nieh's forces met Ma and his Moslems about thirty-five miles from the Shensi capital and dealt them a decisive defeat, facilitated by the fact that Chiang Kai-shek had failed to fulfill his promises of arms and ammunition. Exploiting their advantage, the Communists pressed on in pursuit of Ma's forces, at first along the sandy roads skirting the river Wei, then through the arid, 8000-foot mountains of Kansu. On 26 August, after a march of nearly three hundred miles, they made their triumphal entry into Lanchow, as Ma Pu-fang, the "Big Horse," sought refuge in Ningsia. The defeat of P'eng Te-huai was avenged; and Red domination of the Northwest, aided by prudent agrarian reforms and a policy of religious toleration toward the Moslems, was firmly established.

Meanwhile, on 2 June 1949 the Nationalists had lost Tsingtao, their last stronghold in Shantung, from which American naval forces had been withdrawn in February. On 20 June the Nationalist government declared a blockade of the entire coast from the mouth of the Liao, in Manchuria, down to that of the Min, at Foochow. The following day a British freighter, the *Anchises*, was bombed and damaged on the Hwangpu. Despite British protests the Nationalists remained obdurate, and European companies quickly concluded that the risk to their ships was not worth running. Here, at any rate, the Formosa-based air force of the Nationalists obtained undeniable results.

The Nationalists also maintained small garrisons on the islands off the China coast, enabling them to keep in touch with their remaining partisans on the mainland and supply them with arms and money. This insular strategy compelled the Communists to mount numerous landing operations, which went on up to the end of 1950.[4] On 20 August they attacked the Miao islands, in the Po Hai gulf off the north coast of Shantung, a base from which Nationalist ships were blockading Tientsin. As for the Nationalists, on 29 June their air force started a series of bombing raids over Shanghai and Nanking. Fearful of Communist antiaircraft fire, the high-flying planes could only claim a few civilians as victims, and the raids soon showed themselves to be ineffective.

In July of 1949 the first official Soviet military mission arrived in Peking. Headed by Colonel General Andrei Vassilievitch Zhdanov,[5] this mission included an adviser on strategy, Major General Klinmukaiev, and two training missions, one for the army, under Colonel Tikhanov, and the other for the air force, headed by Colonel Voroshilov. There were also a political adviser, N. Pokrishev, who rapidly became a very influential member of the group around Mao Tse-tung; Dr. Tojerkasov, an adviser charged with organizing party propaganda; and two economic advisers. The training mission set up schools for instruction of the Chinese Communists in the use of Soviet equipment. The Reds had made prisoners of more than fourteen hundred Nationalist aviation technicians at Shanghai, and a flying school was established immediately. But primary emphasis was placed upon the training of artillery specialists, in the interests of infantry support: Moscow

---

[4] Despite these operations the Nationalists still hold the islands of Quemoy and Matsu.

[5] Not to be confused with Marshal A. A. Zhdanov.

deemed the training of Chinese pilots to be an excessively protracted and costly process, and a useless task in view of the final victory which was now a certainty.

In truth, the situation of the Nationalists was a desperate one. When the Red offensive resumed, perfectly coordinated by Chu Teh, it was opposed by only a sporadic and uncoordinated resistance, easily broken by the Communists. Despite the levies hastily raised in the south, the Nationalists had only about 1,090,000 men (250,000 in Szechwan, another 250,000 in Kiangsi, 200,000 in Kwangtung, 200,000 in Formosa, and 100,000 troops evacuated from Shanghai). Facing them were 1,500,000 Communist troops, 730,000 of whom were massed in the center, in Hunan and Kiangsi.

In August, Lin Piao attacked Pai Ch'ung-hsi, his main effort thrusting southward along the Canton railway. Pai pulled back to Changsha. Fortunately for him the time-honored bandits of the Tapieh mountains, who made it their business always to oppose the predominant power (they had been Communists in 1930, anti-Japanese nationalists in 1940, and Communists again in 1945), now reverted to militant anti-communism and, posing as they did a formidable guerrilla threat to Lin Piao's rear area, delayed a Communist advance already slowed by floods. The attack on Changsha was marked by the successive treachery first of General Ch'eng Ch'ien, the city's Nationalist garrison commander, and then of his successor, General Ch'en Ming-ch'en, who went over to the Reds with some thirty thousand of his men. For the only faithful Nationalist general, Huang Chieh, there was no other course than to withdraw the remainder of the garrison, and Changsha fell to the Reds on 4 August. Continuing his advance, Lin Piao crossed the Lien river on 12 August and marched on Kwangtung, the cradle of the Kuomintang.

The Nationalists essayed a last and mighty effort. Chiang Kai-shek ordered General Liu An-chi, the Nationalist commander on Hainan, to send north the island's entire garrison of 150,000 men. These, when added to a force of fifty thousand from Formosa and the fifty thousand regulars of Yü Han-mou, the governor of Kwangtung, as well as the troops of Pai Ch'ung-hsi, could together constitute a strong army for the defense of Kwangtung. But once again the personal enmities of Nationalist generals came into play. Pai was a prominent native and former governor of Kwangsi, and Yü Han-mou had no desire to see him move into Kwangtung; he asked Pai to pull back toward the southwest, cover the Kwangsi capital at Kweilin, and keep well away from Canton.

Meanwhile, Liu Po-ch'eng had reached Kanchow, in southern Kiangsi, and Lin Piao had advanced beyond Hengyang, in Hunan, when Pai decided to give defensive battle. He inflicted a serious defeat upon Lin Piao and the thoroughly thrashed Twenty-ninth Red Army was forced to retreat as far north as Changsha. In the meantime, Chiang Kai-shek had laid plans for a clever maneuver designed to prevent Liu Po-ch'eng from rescuing his comrade. From Formosa an army under General Ch'en Ch'eng, Nationalist Commander in Chief in the Southeast, landed at Amoy with Foochow[6] as its objective. General Hu Lien, commanding at Swatow, was to move north and link up with Ch'en Ch'eng. Yü Han-mou, however, ordered Hu Lien to stay put and "cover Canton." Ch'en Ch'eng, who deemed his strength to be insufficient, moved north, was repulsed by Liu Po-ch'eng, and fell back to Amoy for re-embarkment. The Communists then assumed a temporarily defensive posture in the center, where the Hunan "front" stabilized

[6] Foochow had been taken by Liu Po-ch'eng's forces on 17 August.

along the line Taoyuan-Anhwa-Siangtan-Anjen. On their left, the Reds launched a vast envelopment of the Nationalists' right flank. In their rear, Ch'en I readied landing operations against the Chu Shan archipelago, off Ningpo, from which the Nationalist Navy was blockading Shanghai. At the end of August, as in July, floods brought a momentary halt to operations.

CHAPTER XVII ✧

The Last Act

At the beginning of July, Chiang Kai-shek again took up the conduct of Nationalist affairs. The Central Executive Committee of the Kuomintang was replaced by a Supreme Political Council,[1] with Chiang as its chairman. After once again proclaiming his resolve to fight on to the end, Chiang attempted to create an Asian anti-Communist front. On 10 July he left Formosa for a meeting at Baguio with Mr. Quirino, the President of the Philippines, who declared himself entirely in accord with Chiang on the necessity of facing up to the Red menace. On 7 August Chiang conferred with President Syngman Rhee at Chinhae, in South Korea, where the two men agreed on the idea of a conference of representatives of South Korea, Nationalist China, and the Philippines.

Nor had Mao Tse-tung, on his side, remained inactive. On 15 June 1949 he delivered a speech to the Preparatory Committee of the People's Political Consultative Conference at Peking in which he announced the impending establishment

[1] Also known as the Emergency Council. The Central Executive Committee of the KMT did not go out of existence with the creation of the Supreme, or Emergency, Council on 16 July 1949; but the latter became, "during the period of Communist rebellion," the "highest policy-making organ" of the KMT. See The China Handbook Editorial Board, *The China Handbook, 1950* (New York: Rockport Press, 1950), pp. 134, 239. *Tr.*

of a "democratic coalition government" and hailed the final victory:

> The people of the whole country supporting their own People's Liberation Army have won the war. This great People's War of Liberation, begun in July 1946, has now lasted three years. The war was launched by the Kuomintang reactionaries with the help they received from foreign imperialism. In unleashing this civil war against the people the Kuomintang reactionaries perfidiously and unscrupulously tore up the truce agreement and the resolutions of the Political Consultative Conference of January 1946. But in three short years they have been defeated by the heroic People's Liberation Army. Not long ago, after the Kuomintang reactionaries' peace plot was exposed, the People's Liberation Army bravely advanced and crossed the Yangtze River. Nanking, the capital of the Kuomintang reactionaries, is now in our hands. Shanghai, Hangchow, Nanchang, Wuhan and Sian have been liberated. At this very moment, the field armies of the People's Liberation Army are conducting a great march unprecedented in Chinese history into the southern and northwestern provinces. In three years the People's Liberation Army has wiped out a total of 5,590,000 of the reactionary Kuomintang troops. Now the remnants of the Kuomintang forces number only about 1,500,000, including regulars, irregulars and those in the military establishments and academies in the rear. It will still take some time to mop up these enemy remnants, but not long.[2]

Mao proclaimed China's resolve to be free and independent:

> China's affairs must be decided and run by the Chinese people themselves, and no further interference, not even the slightest, will be tolerated from any imperialist country...
> At the same time, we proclaim to the whole world that what we oppose is exclusively the imperialist system and its plots against the Chinese people. We are willing to discuss with any foreign government the establishment of diplomatic relations on the basis of the principles of equality, mutual benefit and mutual respect for terri-

[2] The English translation is from *Mao Tse-tung: Selected Works*, vol. V: *1945–1949* (New York: International Publishers, 1956), p. 406. Quoted by permission of International Publishers. *Tr.*

torial integrity and sovereignty, provided it is willing to sever relations with the Chinese reactionaries, stops conspiring with them or helping them and adopts an attitude of genuine, and not hypocritical, friendship towards People's China. The Chinese people wish to have friendly co-operation with the people of all countries and to resume and expand international trade in order to develop production and promote economic prosperity.[3]

On 1 July 1949, the twenty-eighth anniversary of the CCP, Mao published an article on doctrine which should have swept away all the illusions of those who thought him to be a democratic non-Communist, or merely a future Tito. In this article he clearly proclaimed his Marxist-Leninist faith:

The October Revolution helped the progressive elements of the world and of China to use the world outlook of the proletariat as the instrument for perceiving the destiny of the country, and for reconsidering their own problems. Travel the road of the Russians —this was the conclusion. . .

Under the leadership of the CCP, the Chinese people, after having driven away Japanese imperialism, fought the people's war of liberation for three years and gained a basic victory. Thus the civilization of the Western bourgeoisie, the bourgeois democracy, and the pattern of the bourgeois republic all went bankrupt in the minds of the Chinese people. Bourgeois democracy has given way to the people's democracy under the leadership of the proletariat, and the bourgeois republic has given way to the people's republic. A possibility has thus been created of reaching socialism and Communism through the people's republic, of attaining the elimination of classes and universal fraternity.[4]

In international affairs, Mao emphasized that China

[must] unite in a common struggle with those nations of the world who treat us on the basis of equality and with the people of all countries. This is to ally ourselves with the Soviet Union, to ally our-

[3] *Ibid.*, pp. 407–408. Quoted by permission of International Publishers. *Tr.*
[4] Quoted from the English translation of "On the People's Democratic Dictatorship" in Conrad Brandt, Benjamin Schwartz, and John K. Fairbank, *A Documentary History of Chinese Communism* (Cambridge, Mass.: Harvard University Press, 1952), pp. 451–452. *Tr.*

selves with all the New Democratic countries, and to ally ourselves with the proletariat and the broad masses of the people in other countries, to form an international united front. . . Internationally we belong to the anti-imperialist front headed by the U.S.S.R., and we can look for genuine friendly aid only from that front, and not from the imperialist front.[5]

He recognized the necessity of a "people's democratic dictatorship":

The right to vote is given only to the people and not to the reactionaries. These two aspects, namely, democracy among the people and dictatorship over the reactionaries, combine to form the people's democratic dictatorship. . ."Don't you want to eliminate state authority?" Yes, but we do not want it at present, we cannot want it at present. Why? Because imperialism still exists, the domestic reactionaries still exist, and classes in the country still exist. Our present task is to strengthen the apparatus of the people's state, which refers mainly to the people's army, people's police, and people's courts, for the defense of the country, and the protection of the people's interests; and with this as a condition, to enable China to advance steadily, under the leadership of the working class and the CP, from an agricultural to an industrial country, and from a New Democratic to a Socialist and Communist society, to eliminate classes and to realize the state of universal fraternity. The army, police, and courts of the state are instruments by which classes oppress classes. To the hostile classes the state apparatus is the instrument of oppression. It is violent, and not "benevolent."[6]

Finally, after affirming the leading role of the working class and its alliance with the peasantry, he went on to specify the three great lessons derived from the invaluable experience acquired by the CCP over the previous twenty-eight years:

A party with discipline, armed with the theories of Marx, Engels, Lenin, and Stalin, employing the method of self-criticism, and linked up closely with the masses; an army led by such a

[5] *Ibid.*, pp. 453, 456. *Tr.*
[6] *Ibid.*, pp. 456–457. *Tr.*

party; a united front of various revolutionary strata and groups led by such a party; these three are our main (lessons of) experience ... Our experience may be summarized and boiled down into one single thing, namely, the people's democratic dictatorship based on the alliance of workers and peasants led by the working class [through the CP]. This dictatorship must unite in concert with international revolutionary forces. This is our formula, our main experience, our main programme.[7]

Earlier, on 7 June 1949, the CCP had observed the twelfth anniversary of the outbreak of the Sino-Japanese War by publishing a manifesto which outlined specific party objectives. It called for a peace treaty with a democratized and demilitarized Japan; for the formation of a united Sino-Japanese front against the American occupation of Japan; and for the establishment of a firm Sino-Soviet alliance to shield the Far East against all aggressors. Finally, the CCP called for the ousting of all imperialists from China, appealed to the patriotic elements of the Kuomintang, and reaffirmed the determination of the People's Army to liberate Formosa and bring Chiang Kai-shek back alive.

THE FINAL OPERATIONS

After an intermission of one month, military operations were resumed in October, and the last act was on. Earlier, on 20 September, the Communists had announced the defection of the Nationalist governor of Suiyuan, and on the 25th the end of the struggle in Ningsia, where they had captured six Nationalist armies with all their officers. On the 29th it was Sinkiang's turn to succumb to the Communists. All of Northwest China was in Mao's hands.

Now, with the first days of October, the Fourth Field Army resumed its march on Canton. Chiang Kai-shek had spent all of September trying to stiffen the powers of re-

[7] *Ibid.*, pp. 460–461. *Tr.*

sistance in the provinces of the southwest. He had ordered Lu Han, the governor of Yunnan, to dissolve the provincial legislature, to close the university, to censor the press. All these efforts were in vain. In Kwangtung the advancing Red forces encountered, about thirty-five miles north of Canton, only feeble resistance. On 11 October Li Tsung-jen departed Canton for Chungking, while Yen Hsi-shan left the threatened city for Formosa. On 14 October the last Nationalist troops evacuated Canton, after destroying their depots, the airport, and the three-arched bridge over the River Pearl. On the 15th the Red forces entered the city and moved up to the Hong Kong border. Two days later they took Swatow, against no resistance, as well as Amoy, where the Nationalist rear guard fought with desperate fury to assure the evacuation of Chiang Kai-shek's last armies to Formosa. The capture of Swatow and Amoy gave the Communists complete control of the Chinese coast, but the Nationalists continued to occupy many small offshore islands from which, by blocking navigation, landing agents, and sheltering fugitives, they posed a real threat to the mainland. Thus, the coming months were to see numerous landing operations, mounted by the Communists in order to rid themselves of this crippling mortgage.

Having liquidated Nationalist resistance in Southeast China, the Communist armies turned west. Their pursuit of the last remnants of opposition turned into a veritable military promenade. In early November they overran Kweichow and Szechwan, taking Kweiyang on 13 November and Chungking on the 30th. The few remaining Nationalist "ministers," bolstered by the arrival of Chiang Kai-shek on the 14th, withdrew by air to Chengtu, whence they announced that the capital of the Nationalist government would henceforth be at Taipei, the capital of Formosa.

With December came the complete collapse of coordinated resistance against the Communists. On 11 December Lu Han proclaimed Yunnan's adherence to Peking, a defection imitated by the governor of Sikang on the 15th. The day before, Red forces had reached the frontier of French Indo-China at Mon Cay, sweeping before them some 25,000 Nationalist troops who were disarmed and interned by the French authorities. Finally, Chengtu fell on 27 December, a few hours after the last batch of Nationalist ministers made good their escape to Formosa.

It was all over. For the Nationalists nothing remained on the mainland except guerrilla activity, mostly in Sikang and Yunnan. For Mao Tse-tung there remained the "liberation" of Hainan, Tibet, and Formosa. The first two operations were to be far easier than the last.

The conquest of Hainan was rapidly accomplished. On 17 April 1950 some 110 motorized junks landed the 119th and 120th infantry divisions of Lin Piao's Fourth Field Army to the northwest of Limko, on the north coast of the island, while sixty more junks landed elements of the 121st and 125th infantry divisions to the west of Hoihow. The Nationalist garrison, more than 100,000 men under General Hsueh Yueh (the "Little Tiger"), was simultaneously hit from behind by Communist guerrillas, whose hold on the island's interior had never been loosened. Despite their numerical superiority, Hsueh Yueh's forces, obsessed by the thought of reaching Formosa's safe haven by an evacuation from the southern port of Yulin, were rapidly vanquished by the Reds. In four days the Communists gained complete control of the island, and the Nationalists lost an ideal base for their hypothetical return to the mainland of China.[8]

---

[8] Tibet, too, was later "liberated," without a shot fired, by the armies of Lin Piao, and a treaty signed in 1951 sealed the supremacy of Communist China over the "Roof of the World."

CHAPTER XVIII ❖

Organization of the New Chinese State

From 21 to 28 September 1949 there met at Peking a "Political Consultative Conference of the Chinese People."[1] The 662 members of this body represented not only the CCP, but such other anti-Kuomintang parties as the Democratic League, which sent 142 delegates;[2] regional democratic groups were represented by 102 delegates. There were also representatives of regional governments, of labor and peasant unions, of commerce and industry, of religious and cultural interests, of ethnic minorities, and of the overseas Chinese. All of these conference delegates had been designated by a Preparatory Committee whose own members, though not all Communists, had been picked by the party leaders.

The conference did some important work: election of the members of the central government; adoption of a "Common Programme"; designation of Peking as the official capital of

[1] According to Chinese Communist sources, the session lasted from 21 September to 1 October 1949. *Tr.*

[2] The *China Digest*, VII: 1 (Hong Kong, 5 October 1949), p. 10, lists a total of 142 delegates from fourteen political parties and groups. Of this total, sixteen delegates are listed as representing the CCP, while the Democratic League, also with sixteen delegates, combines with the other twelve non-CCP organizations for a sub-total of 126 delegates. *Tr.*

China;[3] adoption of the Gregorian calendar; adoption of a national anthem ("The March of the Volunteers"); and adoption of a national flag (red, with a five-pointed gold star, surrounded by four smaller stars, in the canton).

The Council of the central government was composed of a Chairman (Mao Tse-tung), and six Vice-Chairmen (three Communists: Chu Teh, Liu Shao-ch'i, Kao Kang, and three non-Communists: Mme. Sun Yat-sen,[4] Chang Lan, and General Li Chi-shen), and fifty-six members. Among the latter were a great number of Red military and political leaders (such as Ch'en I, Ho Lung, Liu Po-ch'eng, Lin Piao, Kuo Mo-jo, P'eng Te-huai, Chou En-lai, Li Li-san, Po I-po, and others), but there were also some turncoat ex-Nationalist generals (such as Fu Tso-yi, Ch'eng Ch'ien, and Chang Chih-chung); a Shanghai industrialist, Ch'en Shu-t'ung; a Chinese millionaire from Singapore, Tan Kah-kee; the widow of Feng Yü-hsiang, the "Christian General"; and minority-group representatives from Sinkiang and Inner Mongolia.

The "Common Programme" was in fact the constitution of the new state.[5] It first of all proclaimed the People's Republic of China to be "a people's democracy under a people's dictatorship, led by the working class and based upon the alliance of workers and peasants, rallying to it all the democratic classes and the nationalities of China." The Republic ✕

[3] Chiang Kai-shek, it will be recalled, had renamed the city Peiping, or "Northern Peace," in 1928. The Communists now, on 27 September 1949, changed their new capital's name back to Peking. See *ibid.*, p. 7. *Tr.*

[4] Soong Ch'ing-ling, the sister of Mme. Chiang Kai-shek.

[5] The conference also passed an "Organic Law," which together with the Common Programme was the basic law of Communist China until 1954, when the present constitution was promulgated. For an English translation of these two documents in Chinese Communist sources, see *China Digest*, Supplement to VII: 1 (Hong Kong, 5 October 1949) for the text of the Common Programme, and *ibid.*, VII: 2 (19 October 1949), pp. 7–10, for text of the Organic Law. The excerpts which follow are translated from the French rendering of the author. *Tr.*

was to be "firmly opposed to imperialism, feudalism, and bureaucratic capitalism." It was determined to "abolish the prerogatives of all imperialist nations in China; to confiscate bureaucratic capital; to transform the feudal system into a system of peasant proprietorship; to protect the economic interests and private property of the workers, peasants, and of the small and the national bourgeoisie; and finally, to transform the country from an agricultural into an industrialized nation." All the democratic rights to freedom of thought, speech, the press, assembly, association, correspondence, residence, movement, religion, and so forth, were guaranteed. Women, as well as ethnic minorities, were granted equality of rights. The Republic would of course severely punish all counterrevolutionary activities, all Koumintang war criminals, all reactionary elements, landlords and capitalists. These would be permitted to reform themselves, to become new men; failing such reform, they would be deprived of their political rights. Finally, the People's Republic of China resolutely placed itself on the side of the peace-loving nations, above all the U.S.S.R., to oppose all imperialistic aggression and defend world peace.

After this affirmation of basic principles, the Common Programme went on to delineate the organs of state. At the national level would be an All-China People's Congress, elected by universal suffrage; a Central People's Government Council would govern when the Congress was not in session; there would also be a People's Political Consultative Conference. At the regional level, governments would be elected by universal suffrage, and there would be local People's Political Consultative Conferences.[6]

[6] As authorized by resolutions of the National Committee of the People's Political Consultative Conference. *Tr.*

As the constitution itself indicated, this system assured complete centralization of power. For example, Article 15 of the Common Programme specified that the organs of state power, at all levels, were to be established on the basis of the principles of democratic centralism. These fundamental principles prescribed the responsibility and accountability of the Congress to the people, the responsibility of the central government Council to the Congress, and the submisson of Council and Congress alike to the principle of majority rule; but they called also for the submission of lower organs of state power to the decisions made at a higher level, and the submission of all local organs to the central government.

Articles 18 and 19 of the Common Programme can be viewed only as pious declarations of principle. Article 18 asserted that all organs of the state should act in a spirit of simple virtue and dedication to the people: corruption was to be severely suppressed; waste was forbidden; "bureaucratism," and the tendency of officials to isolate themselves from the masses, were to be combated. Article 19 called for the surveillance of governmental activity at all levels by watchdog tribunals, before which any organ or official of state could be haled by any citizen for any violation of law.

In Articles 20 through 25, the Common Programme went on to deal with questions of national defense. It envisaged a navy and an air force, which would join the existing army in subordination to a single unified command. At a "suitable time" conscription was to be introduced.

Questions of political economy were dealt with at length in fourteen articles (26 through 40) of the Common Programme. Here Mao developed his thesis on the necessity of a socialist economy, which in the interests of maintaining production would provisionally permit some forms of private enterprise. Agrarian reform was to be pursued with prudence, avoiding excessive "leftism." The position of the middle peasantry, unlike that of the rich peasants, was to be maintained. Reconstruction and economic development were to keep in step with the attainment of budgetary equilibrium and the circulation of a sound currency. As for foreign trade, complete control would be exerted by the state, which would also control currency circulation by means of state banks.

Articles 41 through 49 of the Common Programme proclaimed the need for development of education at all levels. Respect for all nationalities, and representation of minority groups in all organs of the state, were invoked in Articles 50 through 53. The program ended (Articles 54 through 60) by declaring that the foreign policy of the People's Republic of China would be conducted in the interests of national independence and the preservation of peace. Treaties concluded by the Kuomintang regime would be revised: though desiring commercial relations, on a basis of equality, with all countries, the new China would establish diplomatic relations only with those governments which repudiated the Kuomintang regime and adopted a friendly attitude toward the People's Republic.

On 1 October Mao Tse-tung officially promulgated the establishment of the People's Republic of China, and of a State Administration Council of fifteen members, headed by Chou En-lai. Thirty-seven Ministers were named. Chou En-lai combined the posts of Premier and Minister of Foreign Affairs, with Po I-po as Minister of Finance, Hsieh Chüeh-tsai as Minister of the Interior, and Li Li-san as Minister of Labor. Military affairs came under the jurisdiction of a People's Revolutionary Military Council headed by Mao Tse-tung, with Chu Teh remaining as Commander in Chief of the People's Liberation Army. Mme. Shih Liang became Minister of Justice, Mme. Feng Yü-hsiang[7] took over the Ministry of

[7] Also known as Li Te-ch'uan. Tr.

Public Health, and Fu Tso-yi, the ex-Nationalist general who had surrendered Peking to the Communists, was named "Minister of Water Conservation." Finally, Shen Chün-ju became Chief Justice of the superior court of justice, or Supreme People's Court.

The new government was promptly recognized on 2 October 1949 by the U.S.S.R., which broke diplomatic relations with the Kuomintang regime. The Russian example was followed on 3 October by Bulgaria and Roumania, on the 4th by Poland, Hungary, and Czechoslovakia, and by Yugoslavia on the 5th. The first non-Communist state to recognize Mao was Burma, on 9 December 1949. India followed suit on 30 December, Pakistan on 4 January 1950, Ceylon, Norway, and Great Britain on the 6th, Denmark and Israel on the 9th, Finland and Afghanistan on the 13th, and finally Sweden, on the 14th. Upon learning that London had recognized the Peking government, Mme. Chiang Kai-shek bitterly reproached a Britain that had "bartered the soul of a nation for a few pieces of silver," and predicted that "one day these pieces of silver will bear interest in British blood, sweat, and tears on the battleground of freedom."[8]

On 16 December 1949 Mao Tse-tung went to Moscow to sign with Stalin a treaty made public on 14 February 1950. This thirty-year treaty of "friendship, alliance, and mutual aid" was directed against the aggression of Japan, or of any other state allied, in any manner, to Japan. The two contracting parties further pledged themselves to press for the prompt conclusion of a peace treaty with Japan; one would never support the adversaries of the other; they would consult together on all important international problems; economic and cultural relations would be developed.

[8] From Mme. Chiang's radio address of 8 January 1950, as quoted in *The New York Times* (9 January 1950), p. 4. *Tr.*

The treaty was supplemented by two agreements. The first of these concerned the railroad running from Changchun to Port Arthur and Dairen. Immediately after the conclusion of a peace treaty with Japan, and in no case later than the end of 1952, Russia was to evacuate Port Arthur and turn the Changchun railroad over to China. In the event of aggression both powers would be entitled to joint use of Port Arthur. The question of Dairen was to be held in abeyance pending conclusion of the Japanese peace treaty, but it was clearly recognized that "administration of Dairen belongs entirely to China." By the second agreement, the U.S.S.R. extended to China a five-year loan, at 1 per cent interest, of an amount equivalent to $300 million. The loan was to help China pay for Soviet material aid in heavy industry, mining, railways, and so forth, and was to be repaid, within ten years, in "raw materials, tea, or American dollars."

These two agreements were followed by three notes exchanged between Vyshinsky and Chou En-lai. The first of these specified Soviet abrogation of the treaty of 14 August 1945 between the U.S.S.R. and the Nationalist government. The second stipulated recognition of the independence of Outer Mongolia by both parties. The third and final note called for the Soviets to turn over to China the Japanese property they had acquired in Manchuria, as well as the buildings of the old Russian military mission in Peking.

This treaty was extremely advantageous to China; it represented one more triumph for Mao Tse-tung, now the all-powerful master of one fifth of the entire population of the globe.

He had won the war; he had now to win the peace, and in this quest lies the key to the future. Foregoing here any prophecy of this future, one may still probe the past, to seek therein the roots of Mao's victory in the Civil War.

CONCLUSION

CONCLUSION

The Roots of Mao's Victory

It is always easy to explain events after the fact—even for
one who is always wrong in predicting the outcome of events
while they are actually occurring. In reading this account one
gains the impression that as early as 1946 the defeat of the
Nationalists was inevitable. Yet, right up to the end of 1948,
the best-informed and most impartial of observers—those
who best understood what lay beneath the surface of super-
ficial situation maps—hesitated to predict the complete victory of Mao Tse-tung. To Western observers Mao's solution
to the problems of China, with all that it implied for the future of the world, posed the prospect of a disaster which none
desired even to think about. They preferred to cling to the
most improbable of possibilities. Even after the Communist
victory at Suchow and the arrival of the Reds at the Yangtze,
many still hoped for a partition of China, as had once occurred
in the bygone days of the Sung dynasty.

At the outset, as has been shown, Mao's chances of success
were very slim. Clearly outclassed in numbers and matériel,
he dominated only a small territory; he had no money, no resources, no allies. Worst of all, the masters of Russian communism had abandoned him; they had recognized Chiang
Kai-shek, his mortal enemy, as the leader of China, and yielded

Manchuria to Nationalist sovereignty. Opposing Mao was a man to whom propaganda had given the stature of a giant, a prospective member of President Roosevelt's world-governing Big Four, the master of more than 350 million people, of war-hardened armies, of enormous stocks of modern military matériel, an ally assured of the total support of the great American republic, which in 1945 was the world's most powerful state. Between these two champions, who could have hesitated in his choice?

Four years later Chiang Kai-shek, the Chinese hero, was to find himself a vanquished refugee on the small island of Formosa, while his adversary set himself up in Peking as the master of 480 million human beings. What happened? What were the causes of an event which means so much in the history of humanity?

The profound lesson of the drama that was the Chinese Civil War is this: Even now, in this era of materialism and mechanization, spirit is always predominant, and it is morale that wins battles. Superiority in man power and matériel means little if men make no use of their weapons.

Here, in the Chinese Civil War, the adversaries were of the same race, of the same ancient civilization. How could the same man be a deplorably poor soldier under the Nationalists and then, after a few months of service with the Reds, become a veritable hero? How did hares so suddenly become lions? The answer is that the potential of man is enormous. He is as capable of heroism as of cowardice. But he will not become a hero unless he is inculcated with a faith, a belief, in a doctrine for which he will gladly give his life.

There is no such thing as a degenerate race or generation. The children of today possess the same innate qualities as did those of centuries past. The education of man—or, if one prefers, his "conditioning"—is everything. The cause of Mao's triumph lies in the fact that appealing as he did to ancient and deeply rooted reflexes, he gave a faith, a creed, to the peasants of China. Totalitarian doctrines are always based upon simple slogans, easy to exploit. Hitler chose, as the theme for Germany's external relations, abolition of the Treaty of Versailles; internally, the theme was the struggle against Jews and Communists. Mao had only to follow a beaten track. His external theme was the eternal theme of xenophobic nationalism, of the struggle against foreign imperialists, who themselves but barely emerged from barbarism, had "enslaved" the higher civilization that was China. As for internal themes, he cleverly appealed to the instincts of social justice and proprietorship which are so strong in the human heart. In proclaiming agrarian reform, in despoiling the landlords and lowering taxes, in giving landless farm hands plots to hold as their very own, Mao played the best of cards—to be cynically discarded once victory was won.

But beyond the achievement of these practical goals, it is undeniable that Mao knew how to make of his soldiers dedicated workers for "a powerful China, a respected China, where justice, truth, and peace would reign." He obtained this result by a sustained and patient effort of daily political education. In the everyday routine of the Red soldier, Marxist political indoctrination played a more important role than the manual of arms. Taken in hand by skillful political schoolmasters, the peasant-in-arms rapidly became a fanatic, an apostle of the new religion, ready to sacrifice his life for the better tomorrows. In this lies the essential reason for the victory of Mao Tse-tung. Victory, in a civil war, is almost always won by the side which knows how to gain the support of the people.

In order to win over the Chinese people, this Marxist leader chose the path of prudence. Although he had always

been an orthodox Marxist, a believer who would do no rend-
ing violence to the classic doctrine, Mao did not hesitate to
adopt a course of gradualism, so that the "first steps" would
reveal to the peasants only the advantages of the new regime,
and none of its fearsome flaws. This gradualistic policy was
clearly reflected in the typical sequence of developments which
followed upon the entry of the Red Army into a newly taken
village. Even in those provinces where there were few landlords and the pattern of land tenure was already one of small
holdings—as was often the case in Central China—there
were always rich peasants, as well as pro-Japanese collaborators.
And, always, there were miserably poor agricultural laborers
among the villagers. First the villagers would be deeply impressed by the perfectly correct behavior of the Red troops,
who far from giving themselves over to pillage, would ask
only to be of help to the peasants. Then the Communist
political leader would hold a meeting of all the villagers. He
would promptly pillory, to the plaudits of all, the pro-Japanese
bourgeois and the exploiting landowner. The lands of the con-
demned would then be distributed to the landless. The "poli-
truk"[1] would then announce that henceforth the people would
be able to elect their own administrators and participate
freely in public affairs. Since the officials of the Kuomintang
regime were often incompetent and corrupt, the enthusiasm
with which the population accepted the new representatives
of the People's Republic can be easily imagined.

Moreover, Mao Tse-tung very cleverly resisted "leftism" in
matters of agrarian reform, and so was always opposed to the
despoliation of the so-called "middle peasants." His reasoning
was based on the fact that the Communists had to have the
support of the majority of the population; only a minority,

[1] The Russian term for "political leader." *Tr.*

then, need be despoiled. This was successfully done. Without, of course, renouncing collectivization, the final goal of Marxism-Leninism, it was declared that this ultimate stage of the revolution would not be reached until the distant day of China's industrialization. For the moment the peasants were asked only to give their utmost support to the Red Army, which was liberating them from Kuomintang oppressors who were aided by American imperialists. It is easy to inflame a people against foreigners; in China this task was facilitated by the fact that the Nationalists used American aircraft, and that the bombs which fell on the civilian population were "Made in U.S.A."

The "Red Dragon" thus held important trumps: agrarian reform, xenophobia, the steadiness and discipline of the Red Army, the installation of honest officials, the careful avoidance of premature steps toward statism. But these trumps, without any doubt, would have been insufficient had Chiang Kai-shek been at the head of a strong political organization, and of a state which functioned in a normal manner. But such was not the case. Well before the end of the war against the Japanese, the Kuomintang was already completely rotten.

The drama in the revolution of 1927 was that, unlike all the other revolutions in Chinese history, it failed to conclude with a general clean-up of corrupt officials and local lords. The customary pattern of Chinese revolutions is well known. Thanks to an uprising caused by the incompetence and corruption of a regime which oppresses and starves the people, a new dynasty mounts the throne. The new emperor is a man of strong character, who in the unhesitating implementation of his plans for reform, cashiers corrupt officials and keeps careful watch over public order and the probity of his regime. But then he dies; and his son, already sinking into indolence, replaces him. After a few generations, the new aristocracy falls back into the old Chinese habits, and the tribulations of the people begin again. By nature long-suffering and patient, and brought up to respect their superiors, the people wait, sometimes for centuries, before rising once again. In this traditional cycle each revolution gave the people at least a temporary respite from oppression, if only of a decade or two. But Chiang Kai-shek, when he took power in 1927, was not strong enough to proceed with the necessary clean-up of corruption. On the contrary, Chiang, in order to secure acceptance of his authority, had to bargain with all the great war lords, the *tüchuns* who, like Chang Hsüeh-liang or Yen Hsi-shan, were the veritable proprietors of their provinces. Chinese administration, already corrupt and rotten under the Manchus, remained untouched by the revolution of 1927, and a long-suffering people received no relief.

A second result of Chiang's incomplete victory was that he was never able to put his own ideas into practice, not even in the bosom of his own party. The Kuomintang rapidly fossilized, and soon became a totalitarian instrument for the oppression of the people, rather than a faithful agent of the reforms desired by the dictator. Moreover, the most intelligent doctrinaires of the Kuomintang, the brothers Ch'en Li-fu and Ch'en Kuo-fu, were convinced Confucianists who denied the need for any change in the ancient structure of Chinese civilization. Their opposition to agrarian reform, on grounds of its absolute uselessness, was particularly pronounced. Perhaps they were right, from a philosophical and even economic point of view, China being in general a country of extremely fragmented landholdings. And yet, for all that there was still much that could have been done; at the very least, farm rents and usurious interest on loans could have been diminished. At any rate, by refusing to undertake reforms the Kuomintang deprived itself of a powerful means of influencing the people, who thus were thrown into the camp of the Communist enemy.

Apart from these general reasons, the Chinese Nationalist Party owed its impotence to its immobilism, and to a deplorable conception of the economic and military requisites of the Civil War.

In the first place, despite the enormous sums donated by the Americans, and the wretchedly poor pay of Nationalist soldiers and officials, the Kuomintang was never able to put its financial house in order. Basically, this was because of corruption. Among those around Chiang—himself completely honest— and throughout all echelons of the Kuomintang, everyone stole, everyone made deals. Members of the Soong family prudently invested tens of millions of dollars in America. From cabinet ministers right on down to the local party representatives in the small villages, everyone took such private bites out of public revenue that nothing remained for the coffers of the state. Apart from American subsidies, the sole remedy was the classic recourse to the printing press, a solution which led only to inflation and misery. Under such pressures the people sometimes grumbled; thus the considerable growth of the Kuomintang police. Such growth was initially justified by the struggle against collaborators; but the police rapidly became a powerful instrument of oppression, manipulated solely by the right wing of the party, the CC clique. In these conditions of growing misery, the people, who had manifested great qualities of patriotism and courage during the war against Japan, and had in general joyfully acclaimed the Kuomintang as well as the victory over Japan, became at first apathetic, and then resolutely hostile to the Kuomintang regime. In contrast, they soon favored the Reds, who appeared to the people as liberators: so did the Copts of Egypt, in their day, extend a cordial welcome to the Arabs.

The decline in the morale of the Chinese people, a direct consequence of the maladministration and corruption of the Kuomintang, had a direct impact upon the quality of the Nationalist Army. As pointed out at the beginning of this book, the Nationalist soldier, in the classic tradition of Chinese soldiery, was generally considered to be the scum of humanity. Except in several elite divisions, such a conception could not be changed, and morale remained low despite a multitude of promised reforms. No program of political education was launched, no valid mystique set forth: the soldier of Chiang Kai-shek knew not why he fought. Against the Japanese he could fight for his country and his people; but in this civil war a peasant soldier from Kwangtung had no idea why he should be fighting in Shansi and Manchuria. Poorly fed, poorly paid, poorly clothed, poorly cared for, poorly armed, often short of ammunition—even at decisive moments—unsustained by any faith in a cause, the Nationalist soldier was easy prey for the clever and impassioned propaganda of the Communists.

In turning to military matters of strategy and tactics, one can do no better than quote from the report of General Barr, who as chief of the group of Chiang's American military advisers from 1947 to the end of 1948, observed Nationalist troops and leaders at first hand. Writing early in 1949, General Barr reported as follows:

Many pages could be written covering the reasons for the failure of Nationalist strategy. I believe that the Government committed its first politico-military blunder when it concentrated its efforts after V-J Day on the purely military reoccupation of the former Japanese areas, giving little consideration to long-established regional sentiments or to creation of efficient local administrations which could attract wide popular support in the liberated areas. Moreover, the Nationalist Army was burdened with an unsound strategy which was conceived by a politically influenced and militarily inept high command. Instead of being content with consolidating North China, the Army was given the concurrent mission of seizing control of Manchuria, a task beyond its logistic capabilities. The Government, attempting to do too much with too little, found its armies scattered along thousands of miles of railroads, the possession of which was vital in view of the fact that these armies were supplied from bases in central China. In order to hold the railroads, it was also necessary to hold the large cities through which they passed. As time went on, the troops degenerated from field armies, capable of offensive combat, to garrison and lines of communication troops with an inevitable loss of offensive spirit. Communist military strength, popular support, and tactical skill were seriously underestimated from the start. It became increasingly difficult to maintain effective control over the large sections of predominantly Communist countryside through which the lines of communication passed. Lack of Nationalist forces qualified to take the field against the Communists enabled the latter to become increasingly strong. The Nationalists, with their limited resources, steadily lost ground against an opponent who not only shaped his strategy around available human and material resources, but also capitalized skillfully on the Government's strategic and tactical blunders and economic vulnerability.

Initially, the Communists were content to fight a type of guerrilla warfare, limiting their activities to raids on lines of communication and supply installations. The success of their operations, which were purely offensive, instilled in them the offensive attitude so necessary to success in war. On the other hand, the Nationalist strategy of defense of the areas they held, developed in them the "wall psychology"[2] which has been so disastrous to their armies. As the Communists grew stronger and more confident, they were able, by concentrations of superior strength, to surround, attack, and destroy Nationalist units in the field and Nationalist-held cities. It is typical of the Nationalists, in the defense of an

2 The "Maginot Line" syndrome.

area or a city, to dig in or retire within the city walls, and there to fight to the end, hoping for relief which never comes because it cannot be spared from elsewhere. The Chinese have resisted advice that, in the defense of an area or a city from attack by modern methods of warfare, it is necessary to take up positions away from the walls where fire and maneuver is possible. Further, they have been unable to be convinced of the necessity for withdrawing from cities and prepared areas when faced with overpowering opposition and certain isolation and defeat, while the opportunity still existed for them to do so. In some cases their reasons for failure to withdraw and save their forces were political, but in most cases they were convinced that by defensive action alone, they could, through attrition if nothing else, defeat the enemy. Because of this mistaken concept and because of their inability to realize that discretion is usually the better part of valor, large numbers of Nationalist troops were lost to the Government.

It must be understood that all through the structure and machinery of the Nationalist Government there are interlocking ties of interest peculiar to the Chinese—family, financial, political. No man, no matter how efficient, can hope for a position of authority on account of being the man best qualified for the job; he simply must have other backing. In too many cases, this backing was the support and loyalty of the Generalissimo for his old army comrades which kept them in positions of high responsibility regardless of their qualifications. A direct result of this practice is the unsound strategy and faulty tactics so obviously displayed in the fight against the Communists.

Cooperation among and coordination of effort between the Armed Forces leaves much to be desired. The Ground Forces, being the old and dominant arm, is the source from which the large majority of top military positions are filled. These officers, mostly old and loyal contemporaries of the Generalissimo, have little or no knowledge of the newer arms: the Air Force and the Navy. The Chinese Air Force, consisting of 8⅓ groups, is far in excess of what a country bereft of gold credits can support. Although it has among its personnel over five thousand United States-trained pilots, it accomplished little, other than air-lifting troops and operating its transports for personal gains. There was an ever-present reluctance to take a chance on losing equipment or personnel, which was clearly reflected in their constant refusal to operate at other than high altitudes. There was an ingrained resentment in the Chinese Air Force against killing Chinese Communists who had no air support. All of these factors are important and unfortunate because the Chinese Air Force, unopposed, could have rendered invaluable support in ground operations had its capabilities been properly employed. From a military viewpoint, the case of the Navy is not so important since its employment, right or wrong, could have had little effect on the final outcome; all operations were land-based. From an economic viewpoint, the Navy could have been of inestimable value in suppressing smugglers in Hong Kong-Canton waters had it been willing to suppress and not participate. It was completely relieved of this mission in March 1948, and reputedly millions of dollars in customs revenue continue to be lost to the Government.

It might be expected that the Communists, being Chinese themselves, would also suffer from these faulty Nationalist traits and characteristics, and to a certain extent they do, but they have wisely subordinated them and made their ideology of Communism almost a fetish. By means of total mobilization in the areas they control, propaganda, and the use of political commissars within their armed forces, they maintain loyalty to the established order. Their leaders are men of proven ability who invariably out-general the Nationalist commanders. The morale and fighting spirit of the troops is very high because they are winning.[3]

There is little to add to this analysis. At most, the additional observation must be made that the lessons of Western-type warfare, when learned by uncritical minds, have sometimes led to disastrous results. For example, even though the Reds had no air force, Nationalist units wasted endless time in confecting artful camouflage and digging innumerable shelters as protection against air attacks which obviously would never come. The emphasis which American instructors placed upon

[3] U.S. Department of State, *United States Relations with China, with Special Reference to the Period 1944–1949* (U.S. Government Printing Office, 1949), pp. 336–338. Tr.

the importance of digging-in was further exaggerated by the defense-minded Nationalists, who were convinced that a three-to-one superiority was a minimal prerequisite to engaging the enemy. At each temporary halt, tired men were set to digging trenches. With training such as this, Nationalist troops were incapable of standing up to enemy fire: with the first volley they would hit the dirt and lie there, face down, without reacting. Lastly, the lavish American standards for estimating required expenditures of ammunition induced Nationalist commanders to discover that there was never enough ammunition for attacks.

Confronting the Nationalists was a Red Army with high morale and a remarkable zest for the offense. Frequent bayonet assaults, carefully coordinated with guerrilla activity which sowed a feeling of insecurity in the Nationalist rear, soon vested Red troops with a pervasive aura of invincibility. And by 1949 this army had performed a feat which is unique in the military history of the world: the entire conquest of an enormous country at a rapid pace averaging six miles per day, an advance which swept from the fall of Mukden on 8 November 1948 to the capture of Canton on 15 October 1949. Some of the battles it fought, particularly the battles of Liaoning and Suchow, stand as genuine models of strategy and tactics which merit careful study by the officers of Western countries.

One may well conclude that the Chinese Red Army constitutes a remarkably effective ground combat force. Yet it must be noted that the successes of this army were almost always obtained with ease: never in the Civil War were the Communists confronted by truly resolute, well-armed, and well-led adversaries. In fighting against the Nationalists, the Red Army habitually committed itself only to sure things, to certain victories, in which its own losses would be extremely low. Its strong point was guerrilla tactics, which are excellent in one's own country, but of little use in an alien land. Thus, before the outbreak of the war in Korea, one could rightfully ask how well this army would perform against a Western opponent. The response of the Chinese Red Army in Korea demonstrated that its defensive capabilities are as remarkable as its capabilities for offensive action. When the day arrives that this army is supported by a modern air force, it will prove itself to be a truly formidable foe for even the best of adversaries.

The same may be said for China itself. When this immense agricultural country achieves an industrialization backed by the natural resources of Manchuria and Sinkiang, it will assume a leading role not only in Asia, but in the world. And the average Chinese, who is intelligent, adroit, patient, enduring, and fully capable of manipulating machines, is ruled by a man of eminent qualities who well knows how to exact obedience. It is true that China, for the moment,[4] is confronted by an immense task of reconstruction. But such was the case with Russia in 1918: this precedent proves that only twenty years suffice to industrialize a great agricultural nation—and the pace of history moves ever faster.

We must thus expect to see, a few years from now, the emergence of China as a very great power. For our descendants it will then be interesting to see whether racial instincts are stronger in man than the forces of ideology. In other words, will adherence to the same Communist faith suffice to silence, between a great U.S.S.R. and an enormous China, the antagonisms arising from the color of skin or the shape of eyes? Here is the secret of the future; and there can be no doubt that upon the answer to this question depends, in large measure, the fate of Western civilization and even, perhaps, of the human race.

[4] The author, it will be recalled, was writing in 1952. Tr.

Index

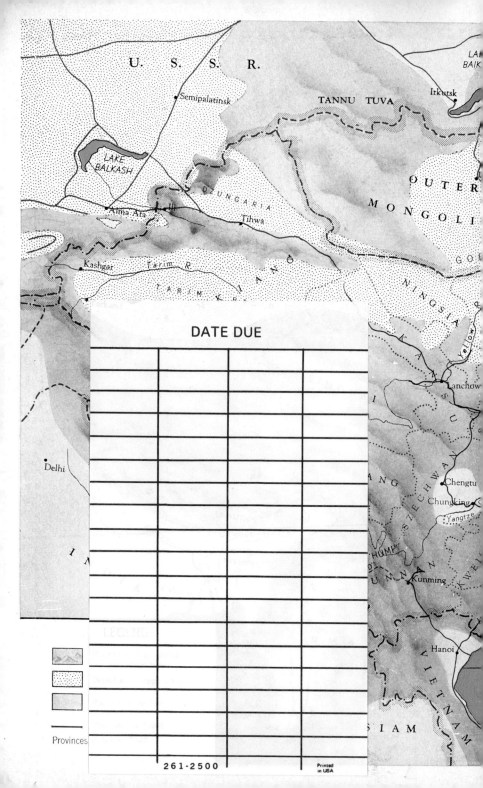